THE SUMMER OF 2020

RACE
RHETORIC
& MEDIA

Davis W. Houck, Series Editor

To: Ellen,
Thanks
for your
support.
Enjoy!

THE
SUMMER of
2020

GEORGE FLOYD
AND THE RESURGENCE
OF THE BLACK LIVES
MATTER MOVEMENT

ANDRE E. JOHNSON AND **AMANDA NELL EDGAR**

5/8/04

UNIVERSITY PRESS OF MISSISSIPPI / JACKSON

The University Press of Mississippi is the scholarly publishing agency of the Mississippi Institutions of Higher Learning: Alcorn State University, Delta State University, Jackson State University, Mississippi State University, Mississippi University for Women, Mississippi Valley State University, University of Mississippi, and University of Southern Mississippi.

www.upress.state.ms.us

The University Press of Mississippi is a member of the Association of University Presses.

∞

Library of Congress Cataloging-in-Publication Data

Names: Johnson, Andre E., author. | Edgar, Amanda Nell, 1981– author.
Title: The summer of 2020 : George Floyd and the resurgence of the Black Lives Matter movement / Andre E. Johnson and Amanda Nell Edgar.
Other titles: George Floyd and the resurgence of the Black Lives Matter movement | Race, rhetoric, and media series.
Description: Jackson : University Press of Mississippi, [2024] | Series: Race, rhetoric, and media series | Includes bibliographical references and index.
Identifiers: LCCN 2023051527 (print) | LCCN 2023051528 (ebook) | ISBN 9781496849748 (hardback) | ISBN 9781496849755 (trade paperback) | ISBN 9781496849762 (epub) | ISBN 9781496849779 (epub) | ISBN 9781496849786 (pdf) | ISBN 9781496849793 (pdf)
Subjects: LCSH: Black lives matter movement. | African Americans—Social conditions—21st century. | Racism—United States. | Racism in law enforcement—United States. | Racism against Black people—United States. | Social movements—United States—21st century. | Police brutality—United States. | United States—Race relations.
Classification: LCC E185.615 .J5875 2024 (print) | LCC E185.615 (ebook) | DDC 305.896/073—dc23/eng/20231114
LC record available at https://lccn.loc.gov/2023051527
LC ebook record available at https://lccn.loc.gov/2023051528

British Library Cataloging-in-Publication Data available

We dedicate this book to the many activists who stand in the rich tradition of protest, trying to make this country and the world a better place, and who continue to declare that Black Lives Matter.

CONTENTS

THE SUMMER OF 2020

ONE MORE LONG, HOT SUMMER

The first wave of Black Lives Matter was . . . a rallying cry, and then it wasn't as popularized in the press or maybe lost a little bit of momentum in the public eye, but then became aware of it again in this new energized form in May of this year.
—CERISE[1]

George Floyd's family and friends remembered him as gentle. A former tight end who stood at six feet, six inches tall, he frequently referred to himself as the "twin" of former NBA player Stephen Jackson. The two grew up playing together. But as an adult, Floyd was more interested in playing with his niece and young daughter, often hoisting them onto his towering shoulders. His niece eulogized him by recounting his spirituality. Describing her late uncle as an activist, she told a crowd that he "moved people with his words."

Breonna Taylor grew up a lot like Floyd's niece. Described as "the light to [her] family," she had a bubbly personality that she used to uplift her family and friends, including an aunt who described Taylor as a "mini-me." Above all, her family remembers her as someone who uplifted and celebrated their every victory, no matter how small. An emergency room technician, she had a caring heart and was known for checking in with friends for no other reason than to express her love and support. She balanced her work aspirations with her personal life and had a bright future ahead of her, full of margaritas, new shoes, and girly hairstyles.

Ahmaud Arbery was close to his auntie as well. In a summer 2020 interview, she recalled seeing him run down the road near his grandmother's house. She pulled over to ask if he wanted a ride, and he joked that he would beat her to the house. A sprinter, he loved to run. He also loved his family. Describing him as "humble" and lovable, his family remembers him as a generous, caring person. "If he had a dollar in his pocket and you needed a dollar," his father said, "he would've given it to you."

Arbery was murdered by white supremacists on February 23, 2020. Breonna Taylor died at the hands of seven police officers who broke into her boyfriend's apartment in the middle of the night on March 13, 2020. And George Floyd was killed on the street by white police officer Derek Chauvin on May 25, 2020. Chauvin knelt on his neck for nine minutes and twenty-nine seconds, even as bystanders—and Floyd himself—begged him to stop. Between Arbery's murder and Floyd's—a short three-month span—the *Washington Post* police shooting database lists sixty-two additional Black men and women killed by police across the United States.[2]

Sixty-two nieces, nephews, aunties, and uncles. Sixty-two human lives. Gone in just three months.

And that number doesn't include victims like Arbery, a Black man who, like Trayvon Martin before him, was killed not by police, but by white vigilantes emboldened by the state's disregard for Black lives. As we read through the list of names in the *Washington Post* database, we recognized many from the news. Others were unfamiliar, their lives disregarded by both the police and the mainstream news cycle.

Very few were made as visible as Arbery's, Taylor's, and Floyd's.

Black Lives Matter targets the invisibility of so many Black people murdered by police. And in the summer of 2020, millions of people took to the streets in the names of white supremacy's victims. The protests began in Minneapolis, Floyd's adopted hometown, where he'd moved to carve out a new life for himself. Within twenty-four hours, uprisings had spread to Los Angeles and Memphis. St. Louis quickly followed, with Atlanta and New York adding to the ballooning number of protesters. In fact, some estimates placed the number of US-based protesters at twenty-six million people, a figure that makes 2020's summer BLM protests the largest in history. Polls conducted around this time found that two-thirds of Americans supported the movement, a surprising finding in a time with unprecedented levels of political polarization—and more than half of these supporters responded to poll workers noting *strong* support for BLM.[3]

Perhaps even more awe-inspiring was the response of major US media companies. As Summer Harlow writes, the *Kansas City Star* and other similarly sized outlets published apologies for previous coverage that contributed to racial injustices.[4] *USA Today* and *Axios* actively participated in uprisings, with the former publication running a major BLM ad and the latter encouraging its reporters to participate in the uprisings.[5] Across the country, protests pushed corporations, politicians, and individual friends and family to take a stand on issues of racial injustice, overpolicing, and white supremacist violence, and books like *How to Be an Antiracist* and *White Fragility* sold in record numbers.[6] This unprecedented wave of protest energy was well-covered in local, national, and global media coverage. But most news outlets failed to consider the personal perspectives, motivations, and commitments of the individuals on the streets. Without a sense of *why* so many came together in support of BLM, organizers and scholars lose crucial—and ephemeral—information about what drove the massive rally to support justice for Floyd, Taylor, Arbery, and so many other victims of senseless, targeted violence.

With the hope of amplifying the perspectives of BLM participants, *The Summer of 2020* argues that the movement for Black lives grew larger and, therefore, more complex during the surge of interest following George Floyd's public murder. Social movements are often portrayed as monolithic, guided by a principal organizer or leader. However, as we argue in this book, movements like BLM—and, from our perspective, historical movements as well—are better understood as ambivalent collectives. Participants gather around a particular cause, and, while that cause reshapes their identities and commitments, their identities and commitments simultaneously impact the movement's meanings, goals, and actions. As we argue in this book, the surge of interest in BLM meant that discussions of racial injustice were omnipresent in many social circles during the summer of 2020. This led many previously inactive people to join the movement, including those with no prior political involvement and those whose participation had been limited to other, tangentially related causes. For new activists especially, BLM participation itself—in addition to Floyd's murder—profoundly changed the way they understood their place in the world. Their presence, in turn, impacted the viewpoints of existing activists.

At the same time, the influx of new participants meant that the movement was pushed in ways that reflected the various commitments of these new participants. Sometimes this was quite literal, as when disability activists pushed for more accessible mechanisms of participation. In other cases, central tenets of racial justice organizing that had been implied, if not crystalized, were challenged by the fresh perspectives of newly activated supporters. Some of these apparently new ideas weren't particularly new at all. For instance, participants questioned the role of the media in spreading messages of racial justice. As we argued in our previous book, this concern is as old as the mass media, and it was certainly on the minds of midcentury civil rights organizers. In other cases, though, BLM faced challenges nearly unprecedented in recorded movement history. The combination of a global pandemic and a fascist government exceeded anything experienced by several previous generations of organizers.

By demonstrating these ideas through our participants' words, we further argue that the ephemerality of historical moments demands methodological adaptability. Even at the time of writing, just under two years after we concluded interviews, the communication surrounding BLM has changed significantly. The only way to capture specific moments in social movement history is to speak to people at that moment, recording and considering their ideas in the context in which they were shared. In the following pages, we present a thematic analysis of BLM participants across the country. Yet, as scholars of rhetoric, public address, and media, we remain invested in the history of social movement criticism from a rhetorical perspective. To that end, we situate this work within the context of traditional social movement rhetoric.

A New Page in an Old Book

Traditionally, the study of rhetoric has been concerned with establishing good order, civility, decorum, and persuasion. However, with the apparent breakdown of order and decorum during the turmoil of the 1960s, several rhetoric scholars began to examine the idea of confrontation in the study of rhetoric. One of the first studies was Robert L. Scott and Donald K. Smith's "Rhetoric of Confrontation."[7] In their essay, they argued that scholars needed a "broader base for rhetorical theory" for the times in which they lived. They called for rhetoric scholars to "read the rhetoric of confrontation, seek understanding of its presuppositions, tactics, and purposes, and seek placement of its claim against a just accounting of the presuppositions and claims of our tradition."[8] The following years would bring exponential growth in the field now known as social movement studies, as rhetorical scholars scrambled to understand the power of civil rights, Black Power, feminist, Chicano, Young Lords, Stonewall commemorations, and other movements.

Much of this early work focused on categorizing social movements. Following Robert S. Cathcart's generative essay, "Movements: Confrontation as Rhetorical Form," rhetorical critics labeled social movement rhetoric as either managerial or confrontational. The former includes those "which by their form uphold and re-enforce the established order or system," a format that is by its nature institutionally conservative.[9] Confrontational rhetoric, however, aims to upend the system, exposing its harm. Seeing movements as "ritual conflict," Cathcart defines confrontation as the "symbolic display acted out when one is in the throes of agony."[10] Arguing that confrontation contains the rhetoric of "corrosion" and "impiety," Cathcart asserts that the "dramatic enactment of this rhetoric reveals persons who have become so alienated that they reject the mystery and cease to identify with the prevailing hierarchy."[11] He further asserts that "through confrontation, the seekers of change (the victims) experience a conversion wherein they recognize their own guilt, transcend the faulty order, and acquire a new perspective." Confrontation is not, as Cathcart reminds us, "an act of violence per se; nor is it a method of warfare. Rather it is a symbolic enactment which dramatizes the complete alienation of the confronter."[12] By refusing to replicate systems of oppression, confrontational rhetoric makes visible the forms of repression, retaliation, and persecution that typically go unnoticed. Confrontational rhetoric rips back the curtain to reveal the mechanics of violent systems, forcing those who control the cogs to admit their complicity or join the movement in the fight for change.

Cathcart's essay was published in 1978, forty-two years before the unprecedented uprisings of the summer of 2020. And yet, his observations provide a foundation for understanding the contemporary Black Lives Matter movement. BLM carries through many of the strategies of its midcentury predecessor while simultaneously adapting those strategies for a new era. Comparing BLM to the Black Power movement, with specific attention to popular culture commentary on racial justice, Thomas O. Haakenson writes, "#BlackLivesMatter does not demand a separate and new kind of 'black life' per se. Rather, it is the name given to a movement that seeks to make the injustices perpetrated against black bodies and black lives visible, to make the already ongoing systemic violence against people of color—and black people in particular—unequivocally seen."[13] Haakenson's emphasis on visibility is key to understanding the connection between midcentury organizing and the summer of 2020. By forcing visibility—of discourses, networked connections, systemic injustices, and allegiances—BLM organizers followed their predecessors in pressuring various stakeholders to take a stand, one way or another.

This is perhaps most obvious in the case of established powers. By making visible the systems that disproportionately allocate power to particular stakeholders, confrontational rhetoric forces the institutional power to respond to the confrontation, whether directly or through their failure to engage. Either response fans the flames of polarization, driving the movement's visibility and funneling support toward the movement (even as it necessarily fosters resentment from others). Invariably, some of those who choose to stand with protesters will be "legitimizers," or people who hold positions of power in governments, judiciaries, chambers of commerce, churches, and other high-visibility positions.[14] By forcing establishments to respond to confrontation, social movements provide political cover for these opinion leaders to appear alongside protesters, which, in turn, allows more ordinary people to join the movement. Understanding BLM and other racial justice movements from the perspective of leaders and actions, the movement often uses confrontational rhetoric to define "its identity, its substance, and its form" because, according to Cathcart, "no movement for radical change can be taken seriously without acts of confrontation."[15]

Yet, while confrontational rhetoric has remained a constant from the civil rights era to the movement for Black lives, the contours of confrontation have changed markedly as the context, culture, and environment of protests have evolved over time. Calling attention to the "ideological approaches to protests," Morrison and Trimble write,

For the "true believers" in civil rights, the approach will always be a nonviolent campaign that is well planned and calculated. For members of the "Black Lives Matter" movement, the approach to protest will also be non-violent, but more of an "in your face"; that is, direct action orientation that may take the form of more "edgy" tactics like outburst, slogans ("hands up, don't shoot!"), interruptions, and so on, coupled with the use of social media to agitate the opposition and bring attention to their cause.[16]

This "in your face" style of protest appears to be uniquely millennial, evolving alongside the wealth of communication technologies that assist today's movement. Alicia Garza, a founder of BLM, argues that the movement, marked by Ferguson's explosive solidarity, represented an end to respectability politics.[17] Black protests, she writes, traditionally play to white sentiments that demand nonviolence and an adherence to police commands. Garza argues that, by following that rhetoric, Black people can only protest racism in ways that white society approves of.[18]

Garza's comments imply that civil rights organizers centered a respectability frame, and that the divergence from such a frame represents the primary difference between twentieth-century and twenty-first-century activism. However, in our book *The Struggle Over Black Lives Matter and All Lives Matter*, we argue that this ideological divide is not as pronounced as many would believe. Misunderstandings of Black Lives Matter stem from the "misremembering of history." We suggest that the "idea that BLM was 'not your grandparents' movement,' for example, highlights the ways civil rights organizing has been systematically misremembered."[19] In short, what BLM activists did in the summer of 2020 in cities such as Portland, Kenosha, Minneapolis, Los Angeles, Washington, DC, Memphis, and a host of other places was to connect history to the present and to fulfill Martin Luther King Jr.'s call to bear witness to injustice or to communicate a truth that was sometimes hard to communicate.[20]

Since BLM, as a movement, is not predicated upon the legitimization of any one leader or institution, the way they legitimize themselves is through the "use of confrontation and the spotlight of established platforms to state their case."[21] In other words, the BLM movement truly is a movement by the people. BLM represents a growing social movement grounded both in traditional social movement methods and contemporary online organizing. Since its origin in 2013, BLM has grounded itself in the "experiences of Black people who actively resist de-humanization."[22] As we assert in our first book, "while definitions may vary by regional and local goals, BLM's national online platform defines the movement in terms of both policy and ideals, striving to highlight and dismantle anti-Black racism and white supremacy and the ways these systems target Black lives."[23] At the core of the movement is a strong affirmation: Black life deserves to be recognized not only for its resilience, strength, and contribution to society, but, as has always been the case for middle- and upper-class white life, simply for its humanity.

Studying Black Lives Matter

In her book, BLM cofounder Garza drew a firm line between the online momentum of movements like BLM and the existence of those movements. She wrote,

> You cannot start a movement from a hashtag. . . . Movements do not have official moments where they start and end, and there is never just one person who initiates them. Movements are much more like waves than they are like light switches. . . . We inherit movements. We recommit to them over and over and over again . . . because they are essential to our survival.[24]

And yet, the online presence of BLM has arguably been the primary site of study for contemporary social movement scholars.

This research focus is understandable, given the masses of online commenters who take to various platforms following every widely publicized police killing. As Sarah J. Jackson reminds us, while the "Black Lives Matter movement can be traced to the legacy of the larger Black freedom movement," it also finds its home in the work of Black millennial groups.[25] This work leads BLM to respond to injustices with "discourse and tactics both familiar and unfamiliar to members of the old guard."[26]

However, for many outside the movement, BLM's meaning seemed hazy or, at least, ambivalent. Armond Towns succinctly describes the purpose and goals of BLM, describing three connected discourses that define the movement.[27] First, he notes, BLM defines Black lives mattering as a situation in which white people are held accountable for murdering Black people.[28] Julius Bailey and David J. Leonard support Towns's contention, arguing that BLM is "first and foremost a challenge to the affront of racial violence and prejudiced policing."[29] It is also a "challenge to white privilege and supremacy, and it seeks to disrupt the status quo by forcing America to unflinchingly examine the ways in which state-sponsored agents treat Black Americans as, at best, second-class citizens."[30] Channeling support into preexisting movements toward police reform and prison abolition, among others, this particular interpretation of BLM's message is perhaps the best known.

But this is only one factor in understanding the meaning of the movement. A second discourse Towns describes involves the critique of how Black lives have *not* mattered historically, at least to those in power.[31] In this definition, BLM calls for attention to the ways Western governments have historically oppressed and persecuted Black citizens. Bailey and Leonard, too, support this approach, arguing that a primary intervention of BLM discourses is to highlight the historical nature of police violence. In doing so, protesters call out how systems ostensibly designed to "protect and serve" have, in truth, always been driven by violence against Black people. This message aims to challenge the "very foundations upon which

Americans claim their democracy is built: that we are all created equal, that all are equally entitled to life, liberty, and the pursuit of happiness."[32] While many of the new participants in the summer of 2020 were undoubtedly familiar with BLM's message against police violence, this historical grounding grew even more prominent as BLM gained momentum, calling for institutions from education to journalism to corporations to reflect on the US history of racism and commit to change.

Forcing others to reveal their allegiances is a key demonstration of confrontational rhetoric. Framing the issue of BLM scholarship in the context of public relations, Julie O'Neil, Ashley E. English, and Jacqueline Lambiase spoke with twenty-five Fort Worth residents to understand how residents understood responses to the police killing of Atatiana Jefferson, a Black woman who was murdered in her home while playing video games with her nephew Zion.[33] Their participants spoke to the prevalence of pseudolistening from government officials, who seemed more invested in pretending to care than creating real change.[34] Less than a year after Jefferson's murder, the massive response to Floyd's death put a spotlight on political "thoughts and prayers" responses: with the eyes of twenty-six million protesters on them, politicians, officials, and corporate leaders simply could not ignore the pressure to take a stance. The isolation of the early months of COVID-19 meant that ordinary people, too, saw more pressure to take a stand.[35] As Pollyanna Ruiz notes, the egregious nature of George Floyd's murder crossed communication boundaries, bringing people out of their homes and into the conversation. The video of Derek Chauvin kneeling on Floyd's neck transformed the already strained communication during COVID-19 "in such a way as to foreground solidarity—rather than care—as a political practice and explored the way in which this reconfigured the relationship between neighbors, especially those in predominately white communities."[36] In other words, conversations about Floyd—at least in the UK, where Ruiz explored the topic—revealed the political nature of many community members where political leanings had not been previously clear.[37]

Media outlets were also pressured by BLM's confrontational rhetoric. Often collectively referred to as "the media," stakeholders ranging from individual journalists to massive news corporations were targeted based on a history of racist media coverage from MLK to BLM. As a 2017 content analysis of mainstream journalistic media notes, the majority of BLM protest coverage employed a negative frame, emphasizing violence and criminality, and racializing movement participants.[38] BLM's confrontational rhetoric illuminated this tradition, demanding that mainstream journalism outlets respond to the summer's uprisings, and not just by continuing to feign objectivity. This wasn't new to 2020, nor was it new to BLM. But since the 2014 Ferguson protests, movement-affiliated thought leaders had been honing their strategies for pressuring mainstream outlets. In the Ferguson protests, many on-the-ground protesters shared stories on Twitter. These stories, and the people who shared them, often explicitly called on major news outlets like CNN to show up to cover the uprising.[39] This strategy was effective and resulted in over a year of coverage of BLM that no doubt set the stage for the massive, global uprisings in the summer of 2020, reframing racial justice protests as urgent, necessary, and just.

Their tactics worked. An interview-based study conducted during the summer of 2020 revealed that journalists overwhelmingly believed that the phrase "Black Lives Matter" was neither subjective nor inappropriate for media use, and most felt an urgent need to take a stance against police killing of Black people.[40] The study's results weren't monolithic: Harlow, the study's author, notes that a few "older, [w]hite journalists" disagreed. But, through social media pressure, the traditional pillar of ostensible objectivity in the face of injustice toppled.

BLM's confrontational style did more than simply push traditional institutions to address long-standing issues; it also allowed participants to find support and solidarity in others within the group. This is, of course, in no way new to today's protesters. But the use of social media to forge new connections is a keystone to understanding contemporary protest movements and thus has been one of the most studied aspects of BLM. Specifically, Marcia Mundt, Karen Ross, and Charla M. Burnett write that the strong connections formed between BLM supporters on social media platforms allowed the movement to "scale up" by leveraging preexisting relationships to draw in new group members, many of whom were involved in other political causes.[41] This offers potential for coalition-building while strengthening BLM participants' sense of being part for a larger group—a clear means of motivating participants to take action in a variety of ways. Yet, as Garza writes, while BLM's social media deployment was particularly effective, networked resistance is neither new nor particularly technologically dependent.[42] In discussing the importance of organization, she points to a common trait of humanity: we are all connected to one another at some point and we all rely on one another to survive.[43]

This networked component of BLM, and humanity in general, requires participants to consistently engage in disruptive communication by moving seamlessly between platforms and formats. In the case of social protest, this practice flows seamlessly from platforms like Twitter—arguably the most active location for Black discourse during the summer of 2020—into the physical location of the streets. In fact, this has always been a feature of BLM, as demonstrated by the use of hashtags to alert potential protesters and watchdogs to developments on the ground from Ferguson to Minneapolis and beyond. The transplatform approach of BLM took on new meanings in the summer of 2020 as a global pandemic isolated people from one another. Ruiz notes that the combination of Floyd's murder and pandemic isolation created a new form of community engagement.[44] Specifically, posts of solidarity on social media were replicated in the physical world through the form of placards, posters, and signs. The increase in yard signs and window posters pressured neighbors to make their stance visible, creating small-scale political cover for those who might otherwise have held back from the movement—and it forced those in opposition to BLM to reveal that stance, too.[45] In other words, the increased visibility of racial justice allegiances in the physical world visualized the end of color-blind politics, a key factor in previous BLM backlashes.[46]

BLM was certainly not immune to backlash. Opportunities for news organizations to reach people outside their predetermined target demographic are much more limited than they were in previous generations. In a study exploring which news consumers chose to engage with stories about violence against Black people, Lanier Frush Holt and Dustin Carnahan note that, in a largely negative news ecosystem, most people were more interested in reading negative news stories about people in their own race.[47] They argue that this could, theoretically, make it more difficult for BLM to reach white supporters.[48] Still, in the midst of mass protests, over a third of Republicans replied positively to polling questions about BLM. This number is, of course, significantly less than the 92 percent of Democrats who supported the movement.[49] And yet, at a time when avowed anti-BLM Donald Trump maintained millions of supporters, the number is striking. Furthermore, at least one quantitative study of implicit attitudes and racial bias before, during, and after the peak of 2016's BLM uprisings points to the impact of BLM on those who might typically reject its claims. A study conducted by Jeremy Sawyer and Anup Gampa considered white people's implicit and explicit pro-white attitudes, measured by the Harvard Implicit Attitudes Test and a single question about participant preference for either white or Black Americans, respectively.[50] The longitudinal study found that, while Black participants' attitudes did not change, white participants pro-white attitudes lessened significantly during the period of intense BLM discourse.[51]

This was, perhaps, helped along by the circumstances of the summer of 2020. Not only did economic suppression caused by the pandemic lead to increased wealth gaps—a core platform issue for the movement for Black lives—but, as one research team argued, the isolation and stress of the early pandemic led to an increased willingness to participate in uprising just as work-from-home arrangements for many professional-class white people in particular made protest a more attractive prospect.[52] In 2014 and 2015, Black Lives Matter protests broke out more frequently in areas with an established history of police murder.[53] Protests were also more likely in cities that tended to lean Democratic in presidential elections.[54] A later study, conducted in 2018 but not published until 2020, drew similar conclusions, noting that BLM support is highest in areas where police are perceived to be more discriminatory, although, as this study notes, older white men are more likely to oppose the movement regardless of location.[55]

These studies highlight an important point that is often overlooked in large-scale studies of movements like BLM: while quantitative data is useful in understanding the scale of particular movements, it cannot reveal the specific motivations of participants. If, as we argue, "a movement is its people," then it must be studied as such.[56] The reasons people attend protests are always speculative—unless we ask.

Capturing the Moments of a Movement

Since this book aims to capture BLM's meaning in a moment of rapidly increasing support, we base our arguments on our participants' perspectives. This is not to discount the work of text-based rhetorical and media critics or the increasing number of quantitative studies on BLM published in the past several years, but rather to honor the viewpoints of movement participants during a historic moment in racial justice organizing. With this in mind, we approach this project from a rhetorical field methods perspective. Our reason is three-fold.

First, in the inevitable and necessary process of summarizing historical moments once they have passed, these moments' specificity is often lost. Internal contradictions and nuances within and between movement participants shift out of focus when we speak about historical movements as a whole. This project was designed to capture nuance and internal conflict which will be instrumental in a more accurate retelling of this period.

Second, between the murders of Michael Brown and George Floyd, public discourse about BLM shifted, intensified, and spread. This evolving conversation was captured from outside perspectives of journalists and pundits, but less often through a systematic analysis of participants conducted to find out what happened inside the movement. By capturing that conversation, this project aims to crystallize BLM's impact in the pivotal moment of the summer of 2020.

Finally, most social movement studies focus on particular leaders, with much of the literature on racial justice organizing centering on Martin Luther King Jr. While we support and have contributed to this work, we also wish more scholarship captured the perspectives of civil rights participants in the moment, in a way that oral history projects conducted decades after the fact simply cannot achieve.[57] Therefore, this project approaches BLM through the thoughts and feelings of the people, capturing a perspective before it can be lost to time.

While, ideally, we might have spoken with participants in person, the global COVID-19 pandemic made this impossible. We made the best of this situation by embracing a national participant sample facilitated by the increased awareness and availability of Zoom during this time period. Beginning in late September 2020, we recruited participants through word-of-mouth and social media ads. These methods allowed us to recruit a total of forty-six participants. All participants were US residents ages eighteen and older who had participated in BLM, either through social media or in-person activities. While we did not filter participants by criteria beyond residence, age, and self-reported participation, we observed that participants represented a range of involvement and experience levels and were dispersed across demographic categories as well. Specifically, participants ranged in age from twenty-one to eight-four, with an average age of forty-two. Twenty participants were African American or

Black and one was Afro-Latina. One participant each was Asian and Middle Eastern. The remainder described themselves as white, Anglo, or Caucasian, with the exception of one participant who declined to complete the demographic questionnaire. Twenty-eight participants described their gender as female or woman. One participant each described themselves as trans female, genderqueer/femme leaning, and nonbinary, and with the exception of the participant who declined the questionnaire, the remaining participants described themselves as male or man. Finally, participants reported a variety of employment types, including attorney, pastor, disabled person, teacher, sales associate, manager, unemployed person, and caregiver.

We interviewed participants in sixteen sessions between October 6 and November 1, 2020, with an average of three participants per group. Using a semistructured interview approach, group leaders—including the authors and two research assistants—guided participants through prompts designed to center participants' motivations, interpretations, and investments. The questions were designed to align with rhetorical field methods and media reception studies, and thus followed three central tenets: (1) the idea that people who engage with particular messages like those of BLM are aware of and able to discuss their influence,[58] (2) the understanding that different audiences interpret messages differently depending on their social location,[59] and (3) the idea that interpretations of messages help audiences to collectively form responses to new and uncertain information.[60]

The interviews generated a total of nineteen hours and seventeen minutes of audio which was professionally transcribed and coded using the constant comparative method, identifying new codes as they emerged and comparing them to previously identified themes.[61] This process of analysis results in thematically organized data, which we report in the chapters that follow. While we've structured the following chapters thematically, it should be noted that these themes emerged in conversation with one another. We aimed for organic, natural conversations with our participants, which meant that their conversations wandered across and between the themes we later identified. In other words, the themes that comprise the following chapters aren't discrete—rather, they speak with and against one another as individual participants articulate their experiences of BLM. Thus, while the chapters that follow are organized to facilitate ease of communication, we encourage readers to consider how themes of activism, protest, violence, intersectionality, faith, politics, and media work both individually and in concert within protesters' lived experiences of the summer of 2020.

Marching Forward

Centering our participants' perspectives, we move through this book according to the themes that organically emerged from our interviews.

In chapter 1, we recount how George Floyd's murder catalyzed new participants in the BLM movement. Prior to the horrific incident, many believed that the movement for Black lives was fading in relevance. But Floyd's murder reenergized a collective of people who saw their own concerns and situations reflected in systems of police violence, disregard for basic human rights, and general anti-Blackness. Yet, while Floyd's murder drew new participants to BLM, many adherents struggled to articulate the systemic issues at the heart of the movement, making the movement's messages more important than ever.

Chapter 2 considers the particularly threatening environment of 2020 for protesters around the nation—and across the world. In the midst of a global pandemic, unprecedented levels of police hostility to protesters, and active threats from white supremacist organizations, demonstrators had much to fear. Their persistence in the face of these threats, we argue, demonstrates the depth of the BLM calling for movement participants. While news organizations spouted misleading stories of violent protesters, our participants shared stories of love, care, and community, recounting the gratitude they felt for the opportunity to gather seeking justice. But the dedication to one another grated against their fear for the safety of themselves, their family, their friends, and their communities.

Chapter 3 considers the concept of intersectionality. While Crenshaw's term had been in use for over thirty years during the summer of 2020, it found a resurgence alongside the deaths of George Floyd, Ahmaud Arbery, and, particularly, Breonna Taylor. Movement participants understood the urgency of intersectionality and, relatedly, cross-movement coalition-building, and they framed their investment as a personal issue. In this way, our participants used intersectionality as a way to join the personal with the communal. While, at times, participants struggled to clearly articulate how intersectionality might look in practice—and certainly, some participants shared harrowing stories of anti-trans rhetoric, ableist policies, and other problematic, anti-intersectional actions—many actively connected BLM with existing movements focused on poverty, disability, housing, trans rights, and feminism.

In chapter 4, we extend the concept of BLM's intersectionality to the movement's egalitarian faith practices. In contrast to some previous conceptions of racial justice movements, BLM was viewed as a space that welcomed both people of faith and those agnostic to any religion or spiritual practice. The movement's openness to various faith traditions, including atheism, made it a welcoming space for participants to explore the meanings of Blackness, a particularly important component for Black participants who used the movement to better understand their own personal identities. The exploration of faith within BLM also allowed those whose faiths were holding them back to cut ties with toxic and harmful traditions.

Exploring the connection between electoral politics and social movements like BLM, chapter 5 argues that BLM positively impacted participants' relationship to voting. Many movement participants who came to BLM ambivalent about elections became more motivated as a result of their participation. Since BLM drew both political and apolitical participants, the conversations at movement events and social media gathering spaces motivated many to consider their role in US politics. Specifically, those who were already involved in politics—from canvassers to voters to get-out-the-vote activists—often shared information and inspiration, moving others to prioritize voting. By connecting electoral politics to BLM, politically experienced activists used a topic of shared interest—racial justice—to bring new voters to the polls.

Chapter 6 considers the ambivalent relationship of BLM to the media landscape. While many seasoned activists saw platforms like Facebook and Twitter as potentially harmful, particularly when it came to sharing videos of Black death, they also understood that social media could galvanize new members to their cause. Similar issues exist in considerations of more traditional media formats like print and broadcast journalism, where movement participants often brought a cynical perspective to media coverage of racial justice. Across media platforms, participants approached their reading, viewing, and listening habits with skepticism and care, neither unthoughtfully believing what they saw nor rejecting messages out of hand. This points to the potential for media to reform in a way that advances BLM's messages and causes—but reminds us that this potential requires reform.

Finally, we conclude by summarizing this book's arguments. This final chapter asks readers to consider the evolution of BLM since Floyd's murder. An eternal and essential component of movement activism, we ask readers to celebrate the wins that have occurred since the summer of 2020. At the same time, we call for justice for the many Black men, women, and children who have died at the hands of the state in the short years since Floyd's murder.

This book is both historical documentation—an oral history in situ—and a call for further action. As you continue into the next chapters, we hope you will keep an open mind and an open heart, allowing the perspectives, experiences, and our participants' messages to propel you forward in the name of long overdue social change.

Chapter 1

"I SAW THE VIDEO"

George Floyd and the Meaning of Black Lives Matter

On May 21, 2020, the *Economist* published an article titled "Whatever Happened to Black Lives Matter."[1] Had "BLM lost its way?" the article asked. The publication's editors claimed that, when measured by Google searches, interest in Black Lives Matter had significantly declined. Arguing that BLM had not been able to "stir a national debate" surrounding the COVID-19 deaths among African Americans, which were 2.6 times more common than among white Americans, the article called BLM's "unusual structure" a "hindrance." The group's leadership by "disparate individuals, rather than a single charismatic figure in the mold of Martin Luther King," they argued, made the movement significantly less appealing to potential participants.[2] Activist and rapper Tef Poe agreed, attributing BLM's decline to leadership. The movement's primary spokespeople, he argued, were "too liberal, coastal, and removed from places like Ferguson."[3]

While Tef Poe's analysis places a heavy emphasis on physical location, many activists cited in the article defaulted to an analysis that placed BLM support in the online sphere. The movement's once robust social media presence, it argued, had been overrun by Russian bots who aimed to use the movement as leverage in the impending US presidential election. Tufts University professor Eitan Hersh agreed, arguing that liberal and progressive movements often "fizzle soon after they draw attention to a particular problem," Hersh suggested that online activism rarely impacts "the real world." Movements like BLM, to his mind, were primarily populated with "political hobbyists, those Americans who post avidly online about social matters—like racial equity—but do nothing practical to follow up offline."

Underlying many of these arguments—particularly as they were collected within the *Economist* article—was a sense of fatigue exacerbated by the combination of a high-stakes presidential election and the COVID-19 pandemic, then a relatively new phenomenon. Cofounder of the BLM's Los Angeles chapter Melina Abdullah, for instance, believed that "interest had drifted" following Trump's 2016 election, as leftist activists scrambled to address a number of competing causes, including Bernie Sanders's presidential campaign. By Abdullah's estimation, the "general public [was] a bit exhausted."[4] However, Abdullah was quick to qualify her comment. "Black people don't have the privilege of feeling exhausted by a campaign for civil rights," she noted, pointing out that the loss of racial justice engagement seemed most prevalent among the "white, well-educated and liberal-minded." Put simply, BLM was no longer a "new and sexy thing."[5]

Four days after the *Economist* published its article, former police officer and now-convicted murderer Derek Chauvin killed George Floyd. Seventeen-year-old Darnella Frazier captured the murder on her cell phone. By uploading the video to her social media accounts, she showed the world how ruthless, inhumane, and demonic this killing was. Police placed Floyd in handcuffs and forced him face-first on the ground. Then, for what we now know was nine minutes and twenty-nine seconds, Chauvin put his knee on the man's neck, ignoring his pleas that he could not breathe. Floyd died calling for his momma. Soon after, mass protests erupted, with people chanting "Black Lives Matter," not only in Minneapolis, but worldwide.

In this chapter, we outline how Floyd's murder (re)shaped BLM's meaning. We first overview the rhetoric surrounding Floyd's murder, highlighting the rhetorical (re)shaping of narratives concerning BLM. Drawing from this lens, we discuss how participants understood not only BLM generally, but also their place within the movement after Floyd's murder. While some participants previously had little or no understanding of BLM, Floyd's murder aroused them to reassess what little they knew. They discovered—or reaffirmed—that the movement spoke to many of their situations and concerns, even as it struggled to help them articulate those expressions to a broader audience.

BLM, Policing, and the Murder of George Floyd

When the video of Floyd's murder started circulating on a never-ending social media loop, Minneapolis officials were horrified. Mayor Jacob Frey became emotional when speaking of Floyd's murder at a press conference. "For the better part of the night," he announced, "I've been trying to find the words to describe what happened, and all I keep coming back to is that he should not have died." Andrea Jenkins, Minneapolis City Council vice president, included the deaths of Ahmaud Arbery and Breonna Taylor in her comments about Floyd's murder. In an interview with a local station, she said,

> My heart is breaking for the tragic loss of life last night near Thirty-eighth and Chicago. Our community continues to be traumatized again, and again and again. We must demand answers. Now not only do we have to be concerned about our physical health, but our emotional health is continuously being damaged by watching all of these videos of Black people being murdered while jogging, Black women being murdered in their beds, Black men being murdered like animals on the streets of Minneapolis. This is unacceptable and this must end.[6]

Neighboring St. Paul mayor Melvin Carter shared the Minneapolis politicians' concern. On Twitter, he wrote, "the video of a Minneapolis police officer killing a defenseless, handcuffed man is one of the most vile and heartbreaking images I've ever seen."[7]

As the video spread, professional athletes and coaches joined in the conversation. Stephen Curry posted on Instagram,

> If this image doesn't disturb you and piss you off, then idk. I've seen a lot of people speak up and try to articulate how fed up and angry they are. All good and well but it's the same same same reality we live in. George Floyd. George Floyd. George has a family. George didn't deserve to die. George pleaded for help and was just straight up ignored, which speaks loud and clear that his black life didn't matter. George was murdered. George wasn't human to that cop that slowly and purposefully took his life away.[8]

LeBron James posted on his Instagram account a picture of Chauvin on Floyd's neck alongside a picture of Colin Kaepernick kneeling and asked, "Do you understand now!!??!!?? Or is it still blurred to you?? #StayWoke" Golden State Warrior coach Steve Kerr tweeted, "this is murder. Disgusting. Seriously, what the hell is wrong with US????" and Utah Jazz center Rudy Gobert criticized Chauvin's fellow officers, arguing, "if you let your coworker do that to another human being without trying to stop him or talk to him out of it, you are as guilty as he is."[9]

Across the country, thought leaders, journalists, politicians, and others shared and commented on Floyd's atrocious murder.[10] The posts were similar in many ways to viral responses following the deaths of Mike Brown, Eric Garner, and so many others. But unlike past incidents, Floyd's murder brought new participants to the conversation: police officers. Miami police chief Jorge Colina declared that no US police department offered training that condoned Chauvin's "deeply disturbing" tactic.[11] Posting on Twitter, the police chief of Austin, Texas, Brian Manley, pointed out that Floyd had told officers he couldn't breathe, but they ignored his pleas. "As law enforcement professionals," he declared, "we must do better in service to our communities."[12] Dallas police chief Renee Hall also condemned the actions that led to Floyd's murder. Besides backing up Colina's claim—that police training does not include the type of force that killed Floyd—Hall argued that the murder was "not indicative of who we are in law enforcement. There was no empathy in what we saw, and it is disheartening."[13] Police organizations across the country came forward to denounce Chauvin's actions, an unprecedented occurrence, even in an era when so many Black deaths have been brought to the fore of public consciousness.[14]

Even the Major Cities Chiefs Association (MCCA)[15] went so far as to issue a press release condemning the death of Floyd while also praising the actions of Minneapolis Police Chief Medaria Arradondo:

> The death of Mr. Floyd is deeply disturbing and should be of concern to all Americans. The officers' actions are inconsistent with the training and protocols of our profession and MCCA commends Minneapolis Police Chief Medaria Arradondo for his swift and decisive action to terminate the employment of the officers involved. MCCA members have worked tirelessly to build trust between law enforcement and the communities they serve. What occurred in Minneapolis is a sobering reminder of how quickly bad policing can undermine that trust. The law enforcement community must do better and hold ourselves to a higher standard. We extend our deepest condolences to the Floyd family and will lift them up in prayer during this difficult time.[16]

For once, the optimistic among us hoped that powerful police organizations might be forced to reckon with the fact that, while Chauvin's tactics were unusual, the outcome was not.

But, contrary to these statements, the MPD had been busy crafting another narrative—hoping to turn public support toward themselves, at least prior to the release of Frazier's video, spokesperson

John Elder sent a brief statement to the press. The subject line read, "Man Dies After Medical Incident During Police Interaction."[17] According to the initial report, a "suspected money forger" had "physically resisted" arrest:

> Two officers arrived and located the suspect, a male believed to be in his 40s, in his car. He was ordered to step from his car. After he got out, he physically resisted officers. Officers were able to get the suspect into handcuffs and noted he appeared to be suffering medical distress. Officers called for an ambulance. He was transported to Hennepin County Medical Center by ambulance where he died a short time later.[18]

The report made no mention that the physical distress resulted from the weight of Chauvin's knee on Floyd's neck for nearly ten minutes. Nor did the report mention that Floyd repeatedly begged for relief, clearly telling officers that he could not breathe. The report even ignored the bystander who tried to reason with officers, pointing out that Floyd was suffering—dying—under Chauvin's weight while three other officers stood by and did nothing.

Frazier's video far eclipsed the MPD's efforts to obfuscate the true cause of Floyd's death. And, as an added result, the video brought droves of new supporters to BLM. Christy,[19] for example, had heard of the movement before but didn't connect with its message until she saw the video of Floyd's murder. She described being "a wreck that whole day, and that's when I started researching more and looking into it more." For Christy, and many other white people, the cold cruelty of Chauvin's murderous actions went beyond anything they had imagined. The video of Floyd's murder, uploaded during the lockdown period of COVID when workplace and activity distractions were limited for many, refused to be ignored. As a major cultural touchpoint, it demanded the attention of people who had otherwise avoided watching videos of Black men and women being murdered or beaten. Elaine,[20] a white woman like Christy, hadn't watched these videos before, and she was shocked by what she saw. When she finished watching the video, she realized, "I watched someone be murdered, okay, on my iPad on YouTube. I watched someone being murdered with absolute impunity, with absolutely no expression on [the murderer's] face. I watched this murderer kill this man. And that should never have been able to happen. That should never have been able to happen." The glaring cruelty of Chauvin's act motivated many of our participants and, we suspect, people around the world. While Floyd's death was one of so many Black people murdered by police and other white supremacists, the video's clarity—and Chauvin's unapologetic disregard for Floyd's life—pushed many over the brink and drew them into the streets.

The video was shocking even for those familiar with BLM's cause. Even Malcolm,[21] a seasoned BLM supporter, found himself questioning what he'd seen. Frazier's footage simply seemed, for many, too horrifying to be true. He knew that police violence against Black people was a problem, but he didn't believe police could do something so heinous:

> I remember watching it the first time I saw it. And at that point in time, I saw it, it was like over a million and a half views. I'm like, "This is live? This is real?" And someone said, "Yeah, that just happened in Minnesota." I was like, "No, there's no way a cop acted like that." And just to give you a little bit about my background, I'm an air force veteran, I have friends that were, that are cops still, they're police officers even here locally now. And I was like, "There's no friggin' way this happened. No."
>
> I mean to this day, I have a friend of mine who I play fantasy football with, and I remember he was the first person I reached out to. I was like, "Can I ask you a question?"
>
> He's like, "Absolutely."
>
> I was like, "What happened?"
>
> And that was all I asked, and he knew exactly what I was talking about. And he was like, "Well . . . that's departmental training."

> And I'm asking my questions as a Black man. I was like, I need to
> be scared, like really. I was like, I mean, this is going on.

Disbelief in a police officer killing a man in such as way should not
come as a surprise. Since the 1960s, most Americans have expressed
confidence in and support of the police.[22] A Gallup survey just two
months after Floyd's murder showed that 81 percent of Americans—
including 61 percent of African Americans—wanted police presence to remain the same in their neighborhoods. While it's easy to
assume that this perspective always comes from a place of privilege, the poll also asked how often respondents saw police in their
neighborhood. A full two-thirds of Black participants who "often
see police in their neighborhoods" wanted to either maintain or
increase police presence.[23]

And yet, for many, the extreme violence and disregard captured
on Frazier's video was more than they could bear. State-sponsored
violence is, and has always been, a key rallying cry for BLM and
the movements that preceded it. In fact, police violence—and the
national anti-Black violence generally—produced the initial and
secondary peaks in BLM support. Trayvon Martin was not killed
by police, but Zimmerman was undeniably propelled to action by
his status within Neighborhood Watch, which defines itself as "the
portal for training to assist law enforcement agencies" in a variety
of ways.[24] Therefore, it is unsurprising, although no less important,
that many BLM participants connected the meaning of the movement with the concrete policy issue of police violence.

The Catalyst of Violence

Police brutality and misconduct allegations have been at the forefront of the Black Lives Matter movement from its inception. Indeed,
as Silver et al. noted, "calls for police reform and Americans' mixed
reactions to them have become a staple of U.S. public discourse, with

the Black Lives Matter (BLM) movement often serving as a public lightning rod for such discussions."[25] As they and many others note, a central thread of BLM's message involves police violence, a frequent occurrence that factors heavily into Black oppression, particularly for poor and working-class African Americans. The movement has long called for active steps to address police bias, including disbanding or defunding law enforcement agencies across the country. So, perhaps unsurprisingly, calls to end racist police violence—even beyond Floyd's murder—provided a primary way of understanding BLM's meaning among our participants.

For instance, many respondents told us that they first heard, learned, or eventually became involved with the movement from protests against law enforcement killings of unarmed Black people. Both Akira[26] and Jennifer[27] named "police brutality" as a primary issue for the movement, the former noting that BLM stands against "systematic oppression" and the latter identifying the organization's goal as ending "any racially-motivated violence towards Black people." Hunter[28] told us that the first time he got involved in a protest or social movement was when "police murdered Darrius Stewart" in Memphis, Tennessee. Another respondent, Bright Eyes,[29] told us that the continued "instances where Black people were killed, incarcerated, or beaten by police" made her take notice of Black Lives Matter and its central role in protesting against police brutality.

For some participants, such as Stephanie,[30] Black Lives Matter means that "police should police all races the same." Cerise[31] teased out the nuance on this stance, identifying how movement brings a systemic analysis to the particular instances of police violence and other issues of bias in law enforcement and incarceration. As Natalie[32] noted, BLM is about "police accountability" and the "dichotomy between how police treat white individuals and how they treat Black individuals." She continued, "my understanding of it is that it really started with policing and a focus on police reform towards Black individuals and has grown to include some more things, societally and politically." Perhaps unsurprisingly, these participants identified that the central argument of BLM related to anti-Black racism in policing, a connection that made sense in the context of Floyd's then-recent murder.

Many BLM supporters not only mentioned but demonstrated the systemic analysis at the heart of the movement. Connecting BLM to issues of lynching, brutality, and general mistreatment, Malcolm[33] traced contemporary movement activism to the long history of anti-Black racism across the country. This analysis was salient to Malcolm,[34] who described his process of digging into history to make sense of contemporary issues. He explained,

> I started doing like long-term type research, like run-ins with police and being police, being a Black man, the history of policing in America. And then learning that it kind of was this thing that grew out of the slave patrols. Like when slaves would break away and went free in the South, they had these patrols that pretty much ran them down that became, eventually, the modern-day police departments and police academies and things of that nature.

Virginia,[35] a white woman who, at eighty-four years old, was the oldest of our participants, also drew connections between contemporary activism and slave patrols. Connecting Floyd's death to history, she noted that, during the "days of slavery," Black people "were not considered a whole person," continuing to say, "it's sad to say that after this many years, we still haven't gotten over that." Malcolm's and Virginia's comments are particularly revealing in that they not only explain their understanding of the connection between historical and contemporary police violence but they also underscore the practice of reading, research, and systemic analysis among many of BLM's participants.

While this practice didn't always connect back to the history of policing per se, as in Malcolm's comment, it often drew lines between Floyd's murder and police—and police-inspired—murders. Macy's[36] comment is illustrative in this respect. Pointing out that BLM highlights the deaths of Black people who are lost at the hands of police systems or by people who "idolize police systems," she remarked, "Trayvon Martin wasn't murdered by technically a police officer, but it was someone who idolized that. And then you have other situations like Arbery down in South Georgia, where they weren't technically police, but they idolized police systems. And so, I think the big thing is that it's highlighting those deaths, because otherwise, people just don't talk about it." While Macy's comment initially mapped the connections between Floyd's death and two nonpolice murders, she nonetheless defined BLM as primarily focused on police violence, an understandably common theme among the people we spoke with. Calls to "defund the police" rose alongside summer 2020 movement messaging, and Macy, as well as others, elided the meaning of BLM with defunding efforts. Demonstrating a clear awareness of the compounding issues of anti-Black police violence, qualified immunity, and mass incarceration, she continued, "you have people who have disciplinary record after disciplinary record still on police forces . . . and there [are] organizations who are trying to move toward defunding police and abolition of prisons movements as well."

While these conversations long predate Floyd's death, the degree to which they dominated mainstream conversation was unprecedented. White people, in particular, had not joined in calls for police reform—at least not en masse—during any period prior to that summer. As new white movement participants joined in the fight to assert that Black lives matter, many, like Elaine,[37] expressed frustration with her peers' lack of understanding. She explained her position, animatedly, by noting,

I've seen them say stuff like, "Well, when you get pulled over by the cops, if you don't do exactly what they say then you get what's coming to you."

Well, no, that is actually not the case, okay? I try to explain to them, you know what, "Look, if you get pulled over by a cop,

what do you say? 'Oh, dammit, what the hell did I do? I got to get a
ticket?' Have you ever thought I might die right now? I might die in
the next ten minutes. You've never thought that. Every single Black
person who has an encounter with the police thinks that."

   And it's true, and that is horrible. And they don't realize it
because they can't see outside of their own perspective. And they
can't see that police are approaching people and dealing with people
and interacting with people in very, very different ways based purely
on their race.

It would be easy to respond cynically to Elaine's comment. After
all, her Black peers have been frustrated by the same lack of understanding for centuries. But Elaine's, Macy's, and even Malcolm's
explanations offer tangible evidence of the effectiveness of movement education. Each of them articulated clear, topical explanations
for the dire urgency of the police violence problem. Without the
persistent engagement of BLM participants, online and off, these
reactions would not have been possible.

Pedagogical Activism

The summer of 2020 saw not only an outpouring of activist energy
on the streets but it also saw a push for BLM supporters to inform
and educate those around them. Beyond the many "syllabi" that circulated through online spheres, books like *White Fragility, How to
Be an Antiracist,* and *Me and White Supremacy* saw their sales jump
by 2000 percent collectively.[38] The idea of a BLM syllabus wasn't
entirely new; Frank Leon Roberts's "Black Lives Matter Syllabus"
and others have circulated the web since at least the mid-2010s.[39]
As Florini argues, this push for education isn't an anomaly but a
feature of BLM's online presence, which has always served "as an
incubator for the discourses that the movement propelled onto
the national stage."[40] This consistent pattern was amplified in the

months following Floyd's murder, bringing new followers into the fold and arming them with information.

Often the educational role of activism involved urging participants to think or discover more on their own. While one participant who called herself Bright Eyes[41] explicitly noted that she'd first learned of the movement through social media, she pushed herself to follow new developments, quickly noticing a pattern. "We've had so many instances where Black people were killed, incarcerated, or beaten by police," she told us. "And so, each time we had one of those instances, Black Lives Matter became a central focus point in terms of protests." Jerrica,[42] too, discovered BLM through media (television, in her case), but didn't understand the movement until she engaged with social media postings. She saw the phrase several times before realizing she needed to do her "own research." Careful to qualify that she wasn't "one of those All Lives Matter people, not at all," she told us that she wanted to "understand where the movement was coming from." She found that information online. These cases and others demonstrate the potential for synergy between traditional media outlets, social media postings, and active movement participants. By combining to drive new supporters to seek more information, BLM builds a networked pipeline of support, welcoming people into the community.

Bright Eyes's and Jerrica's comments were indicative of many participants, in that most were brought to BLM through police and vigilante murders. But by the summer of 2020, BLM protests had spread to some degree of saturation across the country. This meant that some participants first learned of the movement not from violence or death per se, but rather from activism itself. For example, while unable to remember the first time she heard of BLM, Amy[43] remembered the moment she realized BLM was indeed a movement:

I would say that I can't really pinpoint a moment that I really learned about Black Lives Matter as far as the movement that it is today. But I do remember the first moment that I realized that it was

a movement or was growing to be a quote/unquote thing. That was
when Senator Bernie Sanders was speaking. This was during one
of his rallies when he was running for president. I remember there
were some individuals, and I remember one woman in particular
that I think she had a sign, or she stood in front of him. So that's
kind of the moment that's stuck in my head.

Similarly, Akira[44] recognized the movement when she was a high
school student. Although she struggled to articulate whether the
protest she saw "was sanctioned by Black Lives Matter," a techni-
cality we would argue is difficult to discern, she heard about the
movement when local activists protested "in Memphis . . . and shut
down the bridge."[45] While some could not recall precisely the first
time they heard about BLM, most remembered moments where
BLM made an impression. In contrast to our earlier research, in
which BLM was a relatively new phenomenon, participants' ability to trace their own experiences with the movement notes how
far BLM has come.

For many participants, repeatedly seeing activists in the streets
was the spark that connected them to the movement. This was true
for Desiree,[46] who reported following BLM beginning with the death
of Mike Brown and the Ferguson uprising. Since those uprisings
were her introduction to the movement, she didn't yet know much
about BLM. She recalls "see[ing] images of people kind of in the
streets and things like that." Understandably, she couldn't then have
named the group since, "that kind of labeling, at least for me in my
recollection, came after that." But, because she was both politically
predisposed to support BLM and curious about the scenes broadcast
from Ferguson, she explored the movement more deeply, eventually
becoming an active participant.

But many current BLM supporters who first learned of the movement years earlier did not initially see themselves as a good fit. For
example, Brian's[47] story was similar to Desiree's with one marked
difference: he had previously identified as a conservative. He recalled

seeing protests on television, but it was not until he enrolled in a progressive seminary program that he understood what the movement was about. At first, he opposed the movement. This perspective wasn't common among our participants, but many expressed ideas that imply a sense that they didn't initially belong. After grappling with the meaning of BLM, Elaine,[48] a white disabled woman, "decided that Black Lives Matter is not a Black issue. . . . It's an American issue." She expressed her commitment to fighting against the "deeply ingrained systemic racism in this country," and explained that she had been looking for a way to help—she just hadn't figured out how to join the community until Floyd's murder: "I wanted to be part of it because I'm a firm believer in that saying that the only thing that is required for evil to triumph is for good men to do nothing. And I didn't want to do nothing. I just didn't know what to do. And here is the movement that can give me something to do." Some felt hesitant about whether non-Black people were welcome in BLM. In those cases, it often helped to see others who looked like them sharing the movement's messages on social media. An Asian participant who called herself Salted Plum[49] offers a rich example of how movement messaging can help cross this barrier:

> I came across somebody who had created a sign and it was called Asian Americans for Black Lives Matter. I thought, "This is so cool!" So, I put it on, which I hardly ever go on Facebook, but I posted it on my Facebook page. There was some criticism, not of me, but of the origin of the sign itself. Of course, there's criticism of everything, but I thought it was relatively minor. I just felt really strongly like I want to get one of these signs for the yard, you know? I just thought, "Yeah, this is important."

In each of these cases, activist education was much simpler than teaching a course or even recommending books; it was simply about showing others, through everyday actions and speech, what it means to fight for Black lives. These actions and others invited new participants into the movement, and they also gave existing supporters an opportunity to reflect on the movement's meaning.

Meanings of BLM

While, as the *New York Times* reported, many protesters joined the movement in the summer of 2020, BLM itself was far from new. Founded in 2013 by Alicia Garza, Opal Tometi, and Patrisse Khan-Cullors after the acquittal of George Zimmerman in the killing of Trayvon Martin, and becoming more pronounced during the events in Ferguson, BLM began as a movement to resist Black dehumanization.[50] The movement quickly became so widespread that no one leader could encapsulate the movement's meanings. As branches spread across the nation, movement goals adapted to the specific needs of individual communities. These needs, at times, focused on culture and ideals. Other moments demanded a policy-oriented perspective. But, in all cases, the organization challenged anti-Black racism as a system of violence and control. As a unifying principle, the organization confronted police brutality and misconduct, consistently affirming "Black folks' humanity, [their] contributions to this society, and [their] resilience in the face of deadly oppression."[51] And yet, while police violence remained a salient aspect of BLM, the issue of policing invited broad analyses of the philosophical meaning of the community driven by the phrase "Black Lives Matter."

That phrase, while containing nuanced differences at various times and in various locations, had been relatively consistent since the movement's birth. And yet, as evidenced by reports from the *New York Times* and other outlets across the country, Floyd's death sparked an unprecedented level of energy adding new adherents to a seasoned movement. When we asked participants when they first heard about BLM, the response affirmed the *Times* contention that about half of protesters had never attended a rally: while many of our protesters were new to BLM, many had been supporting the movement since its inception.[52] Cerise[53] told us that she first heard about Black Lives Matter "with the passing of Trayvon Martin and the protests [against] George Zimmerman's acquittal and then Ferguson a little later." Jennifer[54] also heard about Black Lives Matter in the wake of Trayvon Martin's death, noting that Martin's death urged her and other pastors to incorporate movement participation into their theology. For most longer-term participants, the movement's meaning was personal. Jennifer cited her father's background as an activist, Cerise highlighted the effects of anti-Black racism on her family, and Katlyn,[55] a white participant, described being moved to participate by her best friend and roommate, a Black woman. As they watched the Zimmerman acquittal unfold, she explained, she both felt the injustice herself and "[saw] her experience with it." That sense of personal connection, she shared, was "what made the larger impact for me."

While a sense of inclusion in a community played a significant role in bringing participants into the movement, others were motivated by the predominantly white, conservative tendency to deny the issue of racial bias in policing. A man tried to explain to Cheryl[56] that Eric Garner's death "was just an anomaly—it wasn't going to happen anymore." From that point on, she told us, she championed the movement even more fiercely than she had before:

> And I just felt really compelled to say that that was indeed incorrect, and I do think . . . I honestly believe that because he had taken such an approach . . . after that, I was riled up. I was committed to making sure that people understood that Black lives do matter, and that the protests don't stop. And so that's what I did: just started following them on social media, and then, wherever I could become engaged, I was, and whenever I could use the pulpit to talk about Black Lives Matter, I did. And when I could talk about it amongst family and friends, that's what I've done. That's what I did next, what I've done.

Cheryl's remarks provide a key reminder of the importance of community. For her, BLM served both as a respite from those who deny

the reality of anti-Black police racism and as a resource for information. BLM's online presence provided a place for her to find information which she then shared with others in her circle.

A common thread among participants was that, while friends,
family, and their broader communities brought them into the movement, they still had to uncover what BLM meant to them. As we
expected, many articulated similar hopeful messages as the participants in our previous book.[57] These interpretations framed BLM as
a "liberation movement," to borrow Hannah's[58] phrasing. While this
statement may seem overly simple, it reflected a meaningful intervention for many of the people we spoke to. Akira,[59] for instance,
found the existence of BLM to be personally validating. Describing
how important it was for her to feel that "there's an organization
out there that cares," she told us that "it makes me feel like there's
somebody out there that's fighting for everybody, for equality for
Black people. And when I hear it, it makes me just feel like I'm not
alone." This uplifting timbre echoed through Autumn's[60] response,
too. Noting that the movement was "constantly moving forward to
advocate change—much-needed change," she shared a powerful
metaphor: for her, BLM was a "bridge of hope," linking her with the
possibility of a better future for her and those she loved.

While some articulated their hope for the changes BLM could
make, others focused on the movement's goal of dismantling white
supremacy. Carlton,[61] for instance, when asked about BLM's meaning, told us, "It's right there in the name that Black lives do, in fact,
matter. And the fact that it has to be said is one of the more troubling
pieces." Gayle[62] went even further in noting the problem of having
to remind others that Black lives matter.

> Black Lives Matter means that there is a problem in a society where
> people who are of that society have to speak out to let you know that
> they are as important as anybody else in society. In this case, it hap-
> pens to be Black people, people of African descent, here in the United
> States of America. Black lives matter because we are children of God,

we are children of this world, we are children of this nation, and we are not less important than anybody else who is existing in this space.

This interpretation reframed the idea of movement "awareness" by refocusing not on a particular instance of police violence but on the patterns of violence across the country. Calling BLM a "magnifying glass" that amplifies the problem of white supremacy, Jerry[63] noted that the movement drew "attention to privilege—I'll just say Caucasian Americans." He continued to explain that the movement's apparently simple name reflected an effort "to get you all to see this is our reality." For Jerry and many others, the issues BLM draws into mainstream conversation highlight a pattern of disregard that should have been addressed long ago.

As Malcolm and Virginia discussed above, many BLM participants connected the movement's meaning back to history, an outcome that may have been connected to major media projects like Nikole Hannah-Jones's the 1619 Project and other interventions designed to trace the history of Black subjugation in the US. Echoing the comments of Carlton, Gayle, and Jerry, Mr. Kirchfield[64] responded that, for him, BLM means "an emphasis of understanding that Black people matter, and that in this country, historically that has not been the case by the majority of the dominant race." Elaborating on this contention, Salted Plum[65] added a call to "people who aren't Black." She described seeing "a lot of bad history to overcome." Cerise encapsulated the primary concern for those who referenced history by noting that BLM "sheds light on how people of color, particularly African Americans' lives, are undervalued, and you can see that in our criminal justice system and in the lack of regard and the disparities of how African Americans are prosecuted." These responses reflect how the movement is both simple and complex. For a phenomenon that simply asks the country to recognize that, in Green's[66] words, "we exist too. And that we are not less than because we are Black," BLM is a simple phrase whose meaning overflows, transforming into different ideas for different people.

At its most basic, the phrase "Black Lives Matter" demands recognition of Black humanity. This was reflected in an affirmative exchange between Christy[67] and Maria.[68] Noting that BLM's meaning lies in treating "people who are Black like they're human beings," Christy shared that this considerably basic definition "really pretty much sums it up for me. They're just not treated like they're human." Maria agreed, noting, "it's the statement of, 'We matter' . . . it's not an elevation; it's not . . . we are, like you said, [Christy], we are human." This concept is rooted in "love and acceptance of everyone," Katlyn noted. But for Katlyn, the phrase took on an even deeper meaning. As a teacher, she shared she sees the urgent need for the movement every day in her classroom. As she shared,

> I think Black Lives Matter is really just looking for the kids in my classroom, in my school that doesn't get equal opportunities, don't get a voice, don't get to see themselves and places and just kind of holding them up and trying to give them as many opportunities as possible. And then on the flip side of that, teaching my white students to not grow up in the same way that I did, to give them more information, to teach them about parts of history that aren't taught correctly, to have them start questioning things, critically looking at things.

Katlyn's[69] definition articulates the educational aspect of BLM, particularly salient in the summer of 2020, that mimics the African proverb, "each one, teach one." However, where the phrase originated as an urgent call for enslaved Black people to spread skills in reading and writing, BLM takes up this mantle in properly teaching the history and ethics at the heart of the movement's call for justice.

While, as Carlton and others point out above, "Black lives matter" should not be a necessary phrase, it became, once again, a powerfully meaningful rallying cry in the summer of 2020. Its most basic meaning, Amy[70] argues, calls for recognizing the "humanity, personhood, and divinity" of Black people. Clarifying that divinity, in her definition, simply means "divine as far as something that is special," she also noted that BLM, as a statement, revealed how "deep and wide the evil, the malevolence, the violence against Blackness in and of itself." She went on to offer a fuller definition that clearly encapsulates the meanings of the movement as a whole:

> And so I think in saying "Black Lives Matter," it's also speaking to all that can mean, right? And so for me, particularly as a Black woman, I hear it and for me already I'm like, "Yeah, I do matter." Because I feel the humanity, the divinity, the personhood, the dignity within myself. But I understand that many people, unless I present myself in a particular way, and even then, will not allow me to matter. So I think that Black Lives Matter—there's really no one way. There's a wrong way to define it. I definitely don't think that there's a right way to define it . . . but I think that'll be my answer for now . . . dignity, personhood, divinity.

Conclusion

In 2015, a Kaiser Family Foundation/CNN poll revealed that a majority of America (65 percent) did not support (49 percent) or had not heard (16 percent) of Black Lives Matter, while 35 percent of Americans identified as supporters.[71] An ABC News poll conducted just a month after Floyd's murder revealed a marked change in both national awareness and support. With 63 percent of Americans supporting BLM—a near-total flip from those who rejected the movement just five years prior—a record 69 percent of the country agreed that "Black people and other minorities are denied equal treatment in the criminal justice system."[72] The *New York Times* even ran a headline that read, "Black Lives Matter May Be the Largest Movement in U.S. History."[73] According to the *New York Times*, by July 2020, more than 40 percent of US counties had hosted a protest.[74] Ninety-five percent of those counties are majority white. And, as the organization's reporting noted, a majority of protesters had seen video evidence of police violence against either Black people, protesters, or both. Fully half of those who protested had never attended a demonstration before, but they were moved, even despite antiprotest violence, to take a stand.[75]

Before Floyd's murder, some perceived Black Lives Matter as irrelevant. Even strong movement proponents questioned whether BLM had lost its way. However, that quickly changed on May 25, 2020, when Darnella Frazier captured a video on her cell phone of former police officer Derek Chauvin murdering George Floyd. When the video went viral, many were horrified at what they saw. Even police departments issued statements that repudiated how then-officer Chauvin acted. However, the subsequent protests that would revive Black Lives Matter to make it the largest movement in US history almost did not happen. The initial police report issued by the Minneapolis police department was at odds with Frazier's video. When news of this came to light, not only did the department fire the officers involved, but it also led to calls for police reform and accountability. These were BLM's founding themes, and they placed the movement at the protests' forefront.

While there have been reasons offered as to why this case sparked this unprecedented level of activism, one that our participants helped us to understand was the simple fact that this was a case of violent police brutality that we all watched, and it was something that BLM activists had spoken about since its inception. It was how some participants first heard about BLM, how they shaped their understanding of the movement, and how they first got involved. In short, participants in our focus groups saw this as an issue that highlighted the importance of BLM—an importance that some forgot, and some did not know of, until Floyd's murder.

This importance also bears out in the many *mea culpas* heard after Floyd's murder. From former New Orleans Saints quarterback Drew Brees[76] to NFL commissioner Roger Goodell[77] to colleges and university administrators,[78] to US Soccer,[79] and others,[80] many claimed after Floyd's murder, they began to "understand." For most of the members in our focus groups, however, it did not take Floyd dying for the world to see for them to understand. For them, BLM, as one respondent said, is "treating Black people like there are human beings." They didn't need to see Floyd dying in the street with a knee on his neck to understand that.

Chapter 2

"FACE THE FEAR AND DO IT ANYWAY"

Protesting in the Face of Compounding Threats

In June 2020, James Bennet resigned from his position as editor of the *New York Times* editorial page in the midst of a staff revolt. At a moment when unprecedented numbers of US Americans were taking to the streets to protest Floyd's murder and anti-Black police brutality generally, Bennet ran an opinion piece by Arkansas senator Tom Cotton titled "Send in the Troops."[1] In it, Cotton suggested that the hundreds of protests around the country should be actively suppressed through military intervention—in essence, that the US military should be unleashed upon the nation's own people. Although the protests were very much in line with the long history of dissent in the US, Cotton called them an "orgy of violence [excused by elites] in the spirit of radical chic." The protests explicitly called for action in the face of senseless murder, and yet Cotton argued that they "not only will destroy the livelihoods of law-abiding citizens but will also take more innocent lives." And, despite his party's failure to act following the *actual* insurrection at the US capital only six months later, Cotton urged lawmakers to use the Insurrection Act to launch "an overwhelming show of force" upon millions of peaceful protesters across the country.[2]

Cotton's op-ed unleashed a firestorm on social media and in the *New York Times* newsroom, but perhaps the most telling response was in the polls. Just a few days after Cotton's op-ed was released, the *Washington Post* published an opinion piece arguing that the US population in general was opposed to violent antiprotest rhetoric like Cotton's.[3] According to a Monmouth poll cited in the article and released the same day as Cotton's writing, most US Americans believed that protesters were justified in some regard: 54 percent of people polled believed that protesters' actions, including the burning of a police precinct, were at least partially justified.[4] While public opinion polling is an important component in understanding summer 2020 protests, particularly in a context with such vile sentiments as Trump's and Giuliani's, they tell us little about the experience of actually protesting in the wake of George Floyd's murder. The regular dangers of demonstrations—from backlash violence to police and military interventions—were amplified by a deadly, highly contagious virus. And yet, the murders of Breonna Taylor, Ahmaud Arbery, and George Floyd, all within a three-month period, demanded a response.

In this chapter, we explore the experiences of protesters during the protests of 2020. In particular, we asked participants how they coped with the threats of a particularly hostile police force, the increased visibility and government encouragement of white supremacist violence, and the COVID-19 pandemic. Activists described feelings of ambivalence that positioned the dangers of protesting in opposition to the dangers of *not* protesting. In other words, they noted that the harrowing forces of governmental power and explicit, violent white supremacy demanded that some risks be taken. Still, those particularly susceptible to COVID-19 participated in alternative protests, with adaptations and accommodations for those with chronic illness, underlying conditions, and/or disabilities setting new accessibility expectations. In the end, the experiences of protesters—who joined together in community to uplift one another and the ideals of justice—looked very different from the experiences described in mainstream and right-wing media.

Protesting under Fire

As deplorable as Cotton's op-ed was, it was in no way isolated. Much of the media covered the demonstrations as violent, destructive riots. Such framing is common in mediated discussions of protests, and of racial justice in general, but reports of protest coverage were particularly telling in the summer of 2020. Drexton Clemons, a protester in New York City, told FiveThirtyEight that reporters tended to show up in the evening, "as if to capture some of the brutality that the police are doing onto the protesters, as well as the rioting or looting."[5] Unfortunately, this meant that those who were absent from the protest site had a skewed understanding of the events. Clemons told the website that "they're missing hours and hours and hours of people peacefully protesting . . . but it almost seems as if they don't care about that particular narrative."[6] Clemons was right to say that most protests were peaceful and uneventful. In fact, a September 2020 report by the Armed Conflict Location & Event Data Project (ACLED) found that 93 percent of BLM protests were peaceful—and this analysis likely *overestimated* violence from protesters, as the study included things like "fighting back against police" within their "violent demonstration" category.[7] When self-defense—a supposed civil right within Stand Your Ground states—is removed, just fewer than 7 percent of protests would count as violent.

The framing of protests as either peaceful or violent is important not because protests must be nonviolent to be respectable. Rather, the way that violence is attached to these protests—which are, at heart, about countering violence against Black people—impacts how the message can be spread and received. From its origin, Black Lives Matter was concerned about issues of violence and death. As we discussed in chapter 1, BLM activists across the country unapologetically supported a variety of issues related to anti-Black violence and the unjust killing of Black people by state actors. These issues include not only police brutality, our participants' most common point of identification, but also issues of healthcare, housing, reproductive

rights, and poverty, all issues of inequality that determine the pos-
sibilities of Black survival. And yet many right-wing and even ostensibly centrist pundits, journalists, and politicians project this threat
of violence onto protesters themselves. In their "Black Lives Matter
Memoir," Patrice Khan-Cullors and asha bandele recall a petition
that circulated in the earlier days of the movement, urging the White
House to label BLM a terrorist organization. Highlighting the irony,
Kahn-Cullors and bandele described themselves, the proposed terrorist leaders, as "we, who in response to the killing of that child,
said Black Lives Matter."[8] The very violence the movement seeks
to counter is dismissed as less consequential than the unfounded
fears of white people living in cities where protesters have taken to
the streets.

In an additional turn of events—one that is certainly not new
to Black Lives Matter—BLM protesters face not only the violence
that instigated any given protest, but also the threat of violence *at*
protests. A primary form of violence during the protests of summer
2020 came from police presence. Contrary to Cotton's deplorable
claim that demonstrations should be met with *more* state violence,
protesters encountered such an intensely militarized police force
that multiple agencies reported a failure by the state to protect its
citizens; Amnesty International's report on the issue was aptly titled,
"The World is Watching: Mass Violations by US Police of Black Lives
Matter Protesters' Rights."[9] In this report, researchers noted nineteen inappropriate instances of police using batons and so-called
nonlethal projectiles as well as a whopping 110 cases in which tear
gas or pepper spray were used as a first resort to dispersing groups
of peaceful protesters.[10] Together, these numbers represent an average of twelve human rights violations *per day* at the hands of police
during the peak of summer 2020 protests. And while this rate of
police violence against protesters was slightly higher than normal, a
database assembled in September 2020 included reports of over one
thousand incidents of unlawful police violence against protesters in
the months following Floyd's murder.[11] Put succinctly, as Amnesty's

Ernest Coverson does, "the unnecessary and sometimes excessive use of force by police against protesters exhibits the very systemic racism and impunity they had taken to the streets to protest."[12]

Protesting in the summer of 2020 not only carried a risk of police or white supremacist violence; protesters also faced the threat of COVID-19, a disease that was not yet well-understood during the peak of the season's activism. Here, too, media perspectives often defaulted to blaming protesters for a violence beyond their agency. Just as in the case of police violence and BLM protests, the threat was, in many ways, parallel to BLM's central claims: that systemic racism flows through all of American life, creating disparate outcomes in terms of poverty, healthcare access, educational opportunities, safe work spaces, and life expectancy. In fact, according to the CDC, all of the above listed aspects of general racial discrimination had a direct impact on COVID-19 outcomes.[13] Black US Americans were twice as likely to die from COVID-19 as their white peers and three times as likely to be hospitalized.[14] The tenacity of protesters to raise their voices is thus an act of heroism in the face of disproportionate threat. Many Black protesters were well aware of their increased risk of contracting, spreading, and dying from COVID, relative to their white peers. And while total protection from this threat was largely out of participants' hands, given lackluster regional and national efforts to contain the virus, BLM protesters largely wore masks and practiced social distancing.[15] In other words, the fact that the threat was real urged more, not less, precautionary action.

Despite risking their lives to bring awareness to a key and consistent issue of inequity in the US, protesters were consistently blamed for violence and destruction, most of which was either exaggerated or fabricated entirely. Descriptions framed protesters as inherently violent as a way to justify the types of massive police and military response called for in Cotton's op-ed. Stoking the flames of white supremacist violence, then-president Donald Trump referred to protesters as "vandals" and "terrorists," before tweeting a message that was quickly censored by the platform for its glorification of violence, not to mention its racist origins: "When the looting starts, the shooting starts."[16] As with so many issues of the time—particularly those involving Trump—public opinion was starkly split on both the protests and police response. While a striking three-quarters of US Americans were supportive of the protests, 50 percent of those polled believed that police responses to protests were reasonable and correct. And a follow-up poll conducted by ABC News found that slightly more than half of respondents agreed with Cotton and hoped that military force would be exerted on protesters. While polling showed that most US Americans believed that property damage was being done by either outside agitators or non-BLM opportunists, it quickly became common for right-wing commenters, including Trump, to refer to all protesters as "thugs."[17]

Certainly, this rhetorical pattern is no newer than protests themselves. Kellie Carter Jackson notes that violence against Black people who have called for an end to anti-Black violence is as old as the US.[18] The murder of Crispus Attucks, she writes, is widely understood as the initial act of violence in the Boston Massacre. But while Attucks is often remembered simply as a patriot, in reality his act of patriotism came in protesting the British occupation of the city. As a result of his objection, Attucks was murdered by British soldiers, and the act of his murder was justified by then-president John Adams, who argued that Attucks was a "terrifying" Black man. Adams argued that the soldiers were justified in murdering him, because they feared for their lives.[19] Aside from the clear parallel to continued police justifications for killing Black people, Jackson's account of this incident reminds us that protests have always been suppressed through rhetoric that paints uprisings as violence, both distracting from the violence these protests respond to *and* warning other would-be protesters of the danger of joining the movement. Still, in the centuries following Attucks's murder, protesters have continued to show up to bear witness to unjust murder at the hands of the state. In the face of violent threats, such striking tenacity speaks to the degree of injustice witnessed by generations of Black US Americans as well as Indigenous, Latinx, Asian, and other people of color.

What It Means to Protest

This history drives the motives of many contemporary BLM activists, drawing them out into communion not only with other protesters of the time, but with those who came before. Writing about the fiftieth anniversary of the Selma march in 2015, Morrison and Trimble note that Black protest marches are "a commemorative enactment of the past, a way of addressing issues of the present, and a movement toward the future."[20] Echoing their statement, Green[21] told us that she feels a sense of ancestral connection in the communal act of bearing witness. In a statement that bears quoting at length, she said,

> For me, I would say, at least the motivation to go was, I don't know, more of like just knowing that my ancestors protested, they fought, they marched, they boycotted. And I don't know, just feeling like we're still doing this today. Like we're still having to do this, but it was, like I said, that kind of intergenerational connection, knowing that I'm fighting for the same things that my ancestors fought for, just basic rights, the feeling was humbling . . . there's fear, but in it also is very empowering because . . . you just feel like a change will come. You know that you're fighting for something. And I just keep hearing, if you don't stand for something, you'll fall for anything. And so you're just out there and you're standing for something. And regardless of what may come from it, you've been out there, you've done your part, you've been in unity with everyone else and you all are all there and fighting for the same thing.

The connection of history and community in Green's[22] response was echoed by Malcolm.[23] As someone with training in security and martial arts, he told us he felt compelled to take his skills to contribute to the march. More than that, though, he also wanted to be "a part of history." His motivation came "from not wanting to have watched history pass me by because I don't know what occurrence can happen and what my role will be. . . . If I use my body and my voice as part of the numbers, [then] I would be strengthening the movement. And as far as the feeling goes, I think that the solitary is a great feeling." Just as Morrison and Trimble said, these Black participants felt drawn to the movement as a way of connecting with history and looking forward to a better future.

Perhaps the most moving account of historical memory of protest violence came from Cole.[24] He shared with his father that he was getting involved in the local BLM chapter, primarily doing organizing work through social media and other communication channels. In a conversation that stuck out to him as particularly enlightening, his father said, "I've told you for so long [to] stay out of it. Keep your head down, work hard, grind." Cole contextualized his father's statement by noting that his father is "an eighty-four-year-old Black man who grew up in the rural South." During the conversation he heard "his [father's] voice crack" as he told him, "All right, just don't do the protesting thing because one, you're my son. Two, you're all I got. And three, you beat cancer, and I'm not losing you to some cop who doesn't know how to restrain themselves." Conversations like this one speak to the lingering memories of protest violence and the ways they can stifle protest activity across generations.

Morrison and Trimble's excellent work analyzes the Selma commemoration. As they point out, that march was a state-sanctioned event that offered protection and safety for participants. Protests of summer 2020, on the other hand, often saw animosity from police, with threats of violence that looked more like the original march to Selma than the commemorative event. These memories of violence, whether stretching back to the civil rights movement or just to Ferguson, hovered in the back of activists' minds during protests. Malcolm,[25] for example, told us that he "thought about, am I willing to die for this?" He realized that staying home wouldn't save him from violence, since he could "survive this [protest] and then go for a jog and [get] murdered." In thinking through this tragic dilemma, he "thought about my foremothers and fathers and forefolks who stood up, and were bitten by dogs, and sprayed by water hoses, and smacked by batons, and thrown in jail and starved." In this way, Malcolm channeled his ancestors in thinking through his approach to today's protests, and the violence of the state toward civil rights protesters weighed on his mind.

Many Black participants told us they struggled to cope with the trauma of seeing so many Black people being beaten, gunned down, and otherwise killed by police and other white supremacists, a key theme of chapter 6. Our white participants, on the other hand, did not have to deal with this threat in their everyday lives, and so felt it acutely in preparation for protests. Bonnie[26] articulated this as a clear distinction, noting that

> I had to learn to face the fear and do it anyway. I started volunteer-ing to be a marshal and learned how to find a role model to show me how to be willing to put more out there. . . . I've learned a lot from trying to become a better activist. [The scariest part was] . . . watching my friends be threatened with running police cars and throwing themselves down in front of it. That upset me.

The "education in itself," as Bonnie called the experience of increasing her protest activity, was a harrowing but necessary experience for white BLM participants, many of whom were new to protesting in general.

As more and more white people joined the hundreds of protests around the country, cultural commenters increasingly urged white movement participants to follow the direction of experienced Black leaders. Like Bonnie, Katlyn[27] shared that she had to grapple with her own limitations and impulses in order to make herself a better ally. She told us she heard people urging, "If you're going to a protest as a white person, you need to be in the front of the line, you need to be there to be able to be arrested over a person of color because you're going to be able to get out and not have any consequences from it." The conversations Katlyn described were prevalent on social media platforms like Twitter, and they responded in many cases to reports of so-called white "allies" who were more invested in looting and destroying property than they were in actually standing with and for their fellow Black activists.[28] Katlyn went on to say that the responsibility to put her body on the line "was also something personally I wrestled with too, was like, I feel like I would want to be that person [who stood between police and Black protesters], but then if it came to that decision, would I actually do it?" These conversations were crucial as the movement ballooned in numbers over a relatively short time period. And while fear is a powerful motivator, moving us to action or often inaction, in this case, the fear of violence at protests was poignant. As Balquiss[29] noted, "It's not going to stop me because . . . this fear is what a lot of people deal with in their daily lives. This is just a taste."

Among the people we spoke with, there was an intense awareness of the probability that police would show up ready for a confrontation. In a May 2020 article for the BBC, Clifford Stott noted that police violence was the result of the very relationships that drove the protests in the first place. He noted that the healthier the relationship between a community and its police force, the less likely for a violent outbreak, a fact no doubt reinforced by the fact that whiter, wealthier communities tend to have better relationships with police. Additionally, however, police response to the demonstrations can quickly turn antagonistic.[30] Cheryl[31] contextualized this point by saying, "When you show up in riot gear, and with AK-47s, when you show up with rubber bullets, when you show up with batons, you intend to do violence. It doesn't matter what I'm coming with, because if I'm only coming with rocks, if I'm only coming with a placard, if I'm only coming with my voice, what can I do to you?"

The tendency for police to show up to demonstrations already primed for conflict increased as protests spread across the US. This was evidenced, in part, by the Fayetteville, Arkansas, police behavior at an early protest for George Floyd. Maria[32] told us, "Literally people got to the square and [police] shot tear gas. It was almost immediately. Like riot gear, tear gas." In Maria's case and many others, there was no time for protesters to create a violent atmosphere, even if they had wanted to—police immediately instigated demonstrations of force.[33] Gayle[34] described this as "crazy." Phrasing her bewilderment as though she were addressing police, she continued, "Either you're scared or you just want to show off for your boys or whatever." This violence, exactly the type Cotton called for in his op-ed, is horrendous, but it is also the same type of openly displayed state violence that helped to bring the civil rights movement to its tipping point. A *New York Times* article printed in May 1963, fifty-eight years nearly to the day when George Floyd was publicly murdered, noted that the graphic imagery of "a young Negro sent sprawling by a jet of water, of a Negro woman pinioned to the sidewalk with a cop's knee at her throat, of police dogs lunging at fleeing Negroes" caused "millions of people—North and South, black and white [to feel] the fangs of segregation and, at least in spirit, [join] the protest movement."[35] While public opinion may not have swayed as firmly as it did following the violent police spectacle of mid-1960s Birmingham, the imagery and accounts of how protesters experience violence remains an important piece of the historical record, firmly demonstrating the protesters' point.

The theme of violence is inescapable in the BLM setting. Of course, this is not to say that BLM is itself violent. Rather, as an organization founded to cry out for justice in the face of unspeakable violence, BLM necessarily incorporates violence into its messaging. Resistance to continued systemic violence is a consistent thread in the stories activists tell about their arrival to the movement. And an awareness of the probability of violent responses to protests weighs heavy on these activist's minds. Like clockwork, the state meets these protesters with more violence, assuring that the cycle continues. An experienced organizer, Hunter[36] shared a story that aptly concludes this section in its concentration of violence, fear, pain, and the physicality of bearing witness in a moment of national uprising:

> That's something [that] stands out to me, I've got a lot of situations, I get arrested often for my participation and actions and marches or whatever. But towards the beginning of the George Floyd protests, there was one downtown, and we were marching—nonviolently . . . and came face to face [with police]. I mean, with a mob of riot-shielded, billy club-clad officers with gas masks who were impeding our march. And some of the Black leaders sent allies to the front. So I got on the front line facing off against these paramilitary police officers. They're in simply because we were marching. Nobody had done anything. And so it gets pretty heated and we tried to push past the police officers and my shoulder was in a riot shield. And this officer lifts his billy club to crack me on my head. And my natural instinct was—I reached up and snatched that billy club out the officer's hand, and backed off the situation. And within seconds, they launched five to ten rounds of tear gas at us, and the situation just erupted into chaos. Men and women were on the ground crying. It was just an intense, heated moment. And it really exposed the underbelly of the police.

To be clear, the volatile and dangerous situation Hunter described is precisely what Tom Cotton was calling for. Cotton justified his call, in part, by claiming historical precedent for calling in US troops to fight US citizens exercising their right to assemble. On that count, Cotton is right; throughout history, when activists protest against state violence, they are nearly always met with more state violence. While this moment in history may not have seen the type of public pushback on police and military intervention at protests that the civil rights movement did, activists certainly saw this connection, and, in many ways, it drove them to push harder.

Social Movements, Social Distancing

When Cotton penned his op-ed, his party had not yet acknowl-edged the real threat of the coronavirus. During the summer of 2020, Republican leaders and voters alike resisted even the small-est of precautions, including masks and social distancing, creating a tense ideological divide between liberals, who mostly approached social interaction with a sense of caution, and Republicans who did not. As a result, while Cotton's op-ed criticized protesters for a sup-posed "dissen[t] into lawlessness," many liberals criticized the sum-mer's demonstrations for bringing people together.[37] For those who would have otherwise braved the threat of police or white suprema-cist violence, the risk of COVID required different and uncertain calculations of risk. Martin,[38] for example, emphasized that "when it's time, it's time. And the situation doesn't wait for you . . . even a pandemic doesn't wait if it's time." And yet, for Martin, the threat of COVID-19 caused him to "recalculate[] participation in some sorts of events." He shared that he chose not to attend some events that he normally would have, particularly those events that are more abstract in their focus and that are likely to be well-attended in his community. On the other hand, he said, "there was a Black man who was attacked by five white folks, and they attempted to lynch him down by the lake on July 4. And so in response to that, we had a number of large rallies. And so for that sort of thing, obviously you can't be like, 'Well, the pandemic, what can we do?'" Martin's careful consideration of which events were significant and which were not is telling of the calculated choices that were required of pandemic protesters.

Eric[39] agreed with Martin's assessment that some circumstances demand action regardless of context. He said, "Opportunities of a lifetime have to be seized within the lifetime of that opportunity, right? So there are certain times when things happen, and the motivation is . . . that you have to react or you have to respond, no matter what the risks." Still, like the vast majority of activists in our focus groups, Eric was clear that safety precautions were taken by the organizers of the events he attended: "People wore masks and we social distanced when we had to." In the summer of 2020, scientists had speculated that outdoor gatherings might be safe, particularly with masks, but social distancing was still prudent, given that little was known about the virus at that early point in the pandemic.[40] Regina's[41] organizing work also involved careful protests, including masks and regular COVID tests, but as she pointed out, "what the establishment wants is for us not to protest so they can move on with these legislations." Regina and many others recognized the risks, both of protesting and of *not* protesting and thereby allowing harmful legislation to be passed without dissent.

Despite the criticisms that BLM protests were not COVID-safe— leveraged by the same populations who refused to admit that the disease was a serious issue and who, to Regina's point, had the most to gain by protesters staying home—the activists we spoke with demonstrated an abundance of caution.[42] Martin[43] noted that protesters should "go out and you do what you can to remain safe." Jennifer,[44] too, said that she "was very careful, very safe, everything. Covered, lots of hand sanitizer. And you would think, in a moment of protest, you wouldn't be concerned about that kind of thing. But we were. We had on our masks. We were very careful about touching, and even when we think about voices carrying and lots of shouting, we were as careful as we could be." Alan[45] told us that "organizers were screaming at participants who were not wear-ing masks . . . you weren't allowed to be there if you didn't have the mask on . . . and people brought tons of extra masks, and they wanted to make sure everybody was healthy before you did any-thing else." Again and again, we heard from protesters who attended rallies where organizers took on not only the typical logistical tasks of organizing but also the role of COVID safety officers. Desiree[46] had taken on this role herself as she organized a small daily dem-onstration. She noted,

We obviously meet in public, so open-air, distance. We have done things, like when there's been another group that was presenting at the same time that wasn't a fan of ours, we've actually put little Xes and tape marks down to keep social distance. Maybe [by the] second week we have hand sanitizer, we have extra masks. We have like a supply bag basically that I bring to the protests every day with that kind of stuff, just to keep people safe.

After the fact, most research into the spread of COVID-19 at protests revealed that protest events were not "superspreader" events.[47] In fact, some research demonstrated that the massive outdoor gatherings deterred others from riskier behaviors, like indoor dining or shopping, and thus, the protests actually reduced spread during that time period.[48] But for those at high risk of complications or death from COVID-19, the uncertainty of whether protests were safe was a major factor in their decision on whether to attend. As Kim[49] noted, "I would have loved to see more people out, but there was a fear of people to come out and to protest. Which was interesting, because even with the additional support there [of organizers encouraging masks and distancing], there was a genuine fear of actually coming out. And I saw that in the community." The sheer number of people who attended protest events following George Floyd's murder was impressive by any measure. Every state in the US saw some protest activity, and polls indicate that up to twenty-five million people may have participated in a rally or march.[50] Even more remarkable, those people gathered under threat of police agitation, counter protester violence, and a global pandemic. On this note, we agree with Martin's[51] assessment: "In some ways, it's all the more powerful because people are not just out there, giving this support—they're out there, literally risking their lives in a pandemic to show support."

For many protesters and would-be protesters, the decision on whether or not to attend rallies and marches depended upon their comfort with leaving the house in general. Cerise[52] told us that she "was not going out for any protest, but also," she only left her house for groceries and doctor's appointments. "That's pretty much it," she said, explaining that COVID posed a disproportionate risk for her, given an underlying health condition. Similarly, Virginia[53] noted that "my husband has a heart condition and we're in the 'very high risk' group. So we just don't go out anywhere unless it's the doctor." Often activists sent proxies to attend marches, or held protesters in their thoughts when they were unable to attend. Brian,[54] for example, told us that he was disappointed that his health did not allow him to attend rallies, but that his son said, "Don't worry about it. I'll go down, and you'll be there in spirit . . . we'll walk together in spirit." Brian's comment speaks to the feelings of ambivalence and regret that many protesters felt about COVID. Cerise, too, marched by proxy through her home event's live-streaming component, explaining that she would typically have attended.

Cerise's use of technology to participate even when she was unable to physically attend raised an important point. Organizers in her city thought ahead enough to realize that a live-stream option would be valuable to those who were unable to attend. This type of contingency was important during COVID, but crucially, it was not a new idea: disability advocates had been urging protest leaders to facilitate participation options for those unable to march for quite some time.[55] Participants like Virginia[56] recalled participating in earlier protests in which "I had a wheelchair . . . having somebody push me and the whole deal," but as disability advocates point out, this type of accommodation is not always available, particularly when marches draw larger crowds or when marches and rallies change course midstream. In other words, these types of accommodations require planning and forethought to recognize the intersection of BLM and disability advocacy, an issue that became more visible to currently able-bodied people during the pandemic.[57]

Given that these types of options were in no way widespread during the summer of 2020, many BLM activists looked for other ways to participate in movement actions. For Cole,[58] this meant coordinating march logistics. He shared that, in his city, the organizers set up "ten different places to drop off supplies." Movement supporters reached out to him through Facebook to ask how they could help, and he recounted responding, "we need twenty bottles of water, we need umbrellas, we need backpacks . . . antacid tablets, if you can pick some of those up. Things like that." Participating in this way demonstrated to him that, "protesting is also so flexible and amendable—just so fluid." His organizing group even worked to create a sense of community that might have felt lost to some during the quarantine phase of the pandemic. He told us that his leadership group coordinated "sign-making parties on Zoom. Which was like you literally open up a Zoom room and like you'd have all these screens and videos of people making signs. And that was really stinking rad, was just the creativity that folks made in these protests with their signage and stuff."

Across the country from Cole, Bonnie[59] used her skills and knowledge as a retired registered nurse to help others prepare for protests. While she also participated in protests on the day of, helping to identify symptoms of dehydration, heat stroke, and heat exhaustion, she also worked online before events to educate new protesters on what they would need to bring. Responding to another activist's comments about the importance of educating participants about the demands of physical protest actions, Bonnie said,

> You need to bring snacks for people who have diabetes next to you who are about to pass out because they didn't eat dinner before the alarm bells went off and they ran out the door with a jacket. You need to bring water for them. You need to have a little electrolyte packets in your pocket so that if they're dehydrated or getting sick because they didn't eat, you have something to put into them to keep them going until they get to a place where they can fix that problem. These are important details.

By thinking ahead and using her previous experience with demonstrations and rallies, Bonnie was able to participate safely in marches before they happened.

For organizers like Cole and Bonnie, Zoom and social media were helpful, allowing them to connect with the slew of new protesters who were eager to join the movement. Other protesters found nondigital ways to participate safely during COVID. Expressing some concern about the pandemic as well as her own struggle with visibility in the months leading up to a campaign for state legislature, Natalie[60] told us that she "posted up at the jail . . . with a wad full of cash, and I just started bailing out the people who had been arrested . . . it was a way that I felt like that was an actual thing that I could do, get those people out of jail so that they could go back out the next night and demonstrate again." Natalie's decision to leverage economic power against the unjust system of cash bail speaks to the surge in awareness about the many ways people can participate in movement activities beyond marches. Just as a number of articles circulated speaking to the need to bail protesters out of jail, others spoke to nationally coordinated boycotts. Cerise participated in one of these, recalling that she did "some internal digging into how can I translate [protesting] into some sustained action in my own part and call other people in the action too." Scrolling online one day, she came across a call for "Blackout day," a day when BLM supporters refrained from spending money. For Cerise, this was about "realiz[ing] the power you have."

In many areas of life beyond protests, the COVID-19 pandemic pointed out a variety of health issues. These ranged from the obvious racial disparities in healthcare to the general lack of public accessibility for people with disabilities. As these issues converged around the murders of George Floyd, Breonna Taylor, and Ahmaud Arbery, seasoned activists struggled to define what public dissent might look like in the midst of a raging pandemic. The protests of 2020 were unusual in a variety of ways. Not only were protesters facing a contagious and deadly virus, in many cities and towns across the US, movement leaders were also struggling to facilitate public action among a larger group of participants than ever before.[61] Despite these challenges, BLM activists found ways to make sense of the movement, even expanding accessibility in ways that they hoped would have a lasting impact on the movement in the future.

Conclusion

In accounts that ranged from Malcolm's and Green's sense of connection with their ancestors to Bonnie's and Cole's sense of care for their fellow protesters, our participants described an experience of protesting centered on community. From these narratives, it is clear that BLM efforts, at least for the people who shared with us, were rooted in love. And yet, those who participated in protest actions found themselves faced with a form of mediated gaslighting. A popular term following Trump's election, gaslighting is a form of psychological manipulation in which an abuser repeatedly denies the truth of the victim's lived experience. In this case, pundits and reporters focused on the very small percentage of protests with destructive elements, forcing movement participants to repeatedly defend their perception of the events they attended.

Overwhelmingly, protesters saw a distinction between the demonstrations they attended and the destruction they saw on television and social media. This does not mean that these protesters were willing to be abused by police without standing up for themselves. Nor does it mean that they uniformly rejected acts of rage against police stations or capitalist institutions in their communities. But, as Stephanie[62] aptly stated, it does mean that the vast majority of BLM participants were interested in peaceful but firm demonstrations against unnecessary, violent, and deadly police force across the country: "A protest and a riot are totally different. They are totally different. A protest is where you come together to get common ground. A riot is when we're going out and looting, tearing up stuff, breaking into stuff, hurting people. There is a difference."

Key to Stephanie's statement is her emphasis on common ground. Particularly in this moment of mass quarantine, the sense of uniting to stand for justice is powerful. It speaks to the long and proud history of social movements and reiterates the coalitional stance taken by the leading voices in political organizing and social movement rhetoric. As Karma Chávez and Cindy Griffin write, "A coalitional agency implies that our ability to affect social change, to empower others and ourselves necessitates seeing people, history and culture as inextricably bound to one another."[63] In this spirit, BLM has been a movement for community. It is perhaps the most intersectional, coalition-based movement in the history of social movements, and the stories participants shared illustrate the ways that ideal unfolded in protests and demonstrations, even in the middle of a global pandemic. In her bestselling memoir *The Purpose of Power*, BLM founder and movement leader Alicia Garza argued that "movements are the story of how we come together when we've come apart."[64] In this way, the gathering of groups against anti-Black violence—protests, as well as rallies, demonstrations, organizing meetings, and other community-building activities—is the heart of BLM.

In this chapter, we shared protesters' stories of demonstrations sparked by the murder of Floyd and others. In the midst of a global pandemic, millions of people gathered to call out for justice. Participants saw the call to gather as a deep calling that drew them out into community with others, even as they experienced threats of violence from the very state actors they were there to protest. In addition, protesters described their fear of contracting a deadly disease, and many shared their organizations' concrete actions toward accessibility and safety. Together, these stories paint a picture of love and care, and they speak to the nature of social justice organizing. For BLM, at least, these gatherings were never about creating violence. Instead, they were about drawing attention to a culture of anti-Black violence and calling for an end to the state sanctioned destruction of Black lives.

Chapter 3

"WHAT'S MORE IMPORTANT IS THE BIGGER PICTURE"

Intersectionality as a Personal Investment

According to Google trends, Black Lives Matter searches peaked in June 2020.[1] During that month, the number of searches for the phrase more than tripled the previous record.[2] Alongside this record interest in BLM, discussions about intersectionality surged. Coined in 1989 by Kimberlé Crenshaw, the term "intersectionality" describes how various systems of oppression intersect.[3] People whose identities subject them to multiple forms of discrimination rarely experience them as distinct. Rather, these various oppressions interlock into a force that cannot be explained in terms of any singular oppression, but only by considering their intersection. Or, as Patricia Hill Collins and Sirma Bilge write, "in a given society at a given time, power relations of race, class, and gender, for example, are not discrete and mutually exclusive entities, but rather build on each other and work together."[4] During the weeks following George Floyd's murder, many organizations scrambled to release a statement on their commitment to diversity, and many of these institutions intentionally included a statement of intersectionality. For example, GLAAD (the Gay and

Lesbian Alliance Against Defamation), blogged that "there can be no Pride if it is not intersectional."[5] And UN Women, the United Nations group that focuses on gender discrimination, wrote that "intersectional feminism . . . matters right now."[6]

Yet, while summer 2020 brought mainstream interest in intersectionality, the theory itself is not new. Even before the term was coined in 1989, and certainly in the years since, social movements have often been critiqued based on their failure to account for the particular, personal experiences within ostensibly, but not actually, homogenous groups. LGBTQ and women's groups, in particular, have often been rightly called out for failing to attend to issues of race, just as some civil rights groups were critiqued for a lack of investment in gender politics. Stokley Carmichael's infamous (and perhaps decontextualized) joke about "the only position for women in the movement [being] prone" offers one specific example. Likewise, ACT UP's racist decision to segment Black and Latinx organizers into a special interest group was harmful to the group's adhesion, and feminist leaders have frequently created rifts by focusing solely on issues experienced by white middle- and upper-class women at the exclusion of others. The history of every movement contains examples such as these, where, to quote Crenshaw, "ignoring difference within groups contributes to tension among groups."[7]

When failures like these come to light, movements can either ignore them at their own peril or identify spaces for necessary growth and improvement. In other words, movements are actively harmed when leaders and other members project their own positionalities onto the full group, rather than attending to the intersecting oppressions that shape unique personal experiences. The most successful social movements approach this task by considering how groups are made stronger by diversity while simultaneously recognizing that any group of people is likely to face moments of disagreement, differences in perspective, and discrimination. Karma R. Chávez and Cindy L. Griffin write that social movements must recognize the ways that "people, history and culture [are] inextricably bound to one another."[8] As Chávez points out elsewhere, this truth is far from utopian; it can mean, she notes, borrowing Judith Butler's phrasing, that "we're undone by each other."[9] This paradox—in which coalition-building processes create intragroup rifts that must be healed through more coalition-building—is a foundational observation of intersectionality. The solution of "placing those who currently are marginalized in the center" requires attention to the personal stories and self-reflections of BLM members, so as to tease out the intersectional oppressions that might be hidden or camouflaged, but that are central to achieving true liberation.

This chapter considers the role of the personal as an extension of intersectionality in the contemporary Black Lives Matter movement. By exploring how the concept of intersectionality became a rallying cry for the movement during the summer of 2020, we argue that BLM participants were not only aware of the need for coalitional politics but many actively invested in increased access and inclusivity. Crenshaw's concept is often framed as a systemic intervention. Yet, as she and others have done in their writing, BLM participants often discussed intersectionality in terms of personal examples of both pain and self-reflection. In this way, the protesters of 2020 elevated the role of the personal, combining a focus on intersectionality with the imperative to position themselves and others within broader social systems. Still, talking about personal experiences doesn't always facilitate intersectional analysis. The cultural focus on personal growth and self-care can also deflect from coalition-building and movement solidarity. Perhaps recognizing this dynamic, many critiqued their BLM organizations for falling short of true intersectionality while simultaneously applauding those groups' efforts. This model, we suggest, demonstrates the strength of the BLM movement and movement participants' commitment to building a truly intersectional, inclusive activist vision.

A Traveling, Trending Theory

In 2017, Jennifer C. Nash wrote, "These are anxious times for intersectionality and its practitioners."[10] While Nash's work focuses primarily on the scholarly approach to intersectionality, especially in Women's Studies departments, her observation extends to public discussions of the concept as well. In the years since 2017, intersectionality had become a central concept for social movement organizing. It had also become a boogeyman of conservative politics. In a 2019 segment, for instance, Tucker Carlson called intersectionality a "never-ending car crash" in which Democrats were supposedly vacillating between whether "sexual politics [are] more important than race politics" or vice versa.[11] Carlson's bad faith argument aside, his segment reveals the way intersectionality can be used for purposes far adrift from the concept's intent or even activist parlance; in fact, Carlson's very syntax positions "sexual [gender] politics" as oppositional to "race politics," rather than considering how the two intersect. At the other end of the spectrum, Nash rightly points out that many scholars elide the term "intersectionality" with Black feminism. In her analysis, scholarship often seeks out "Black woman as the quintessential location of complexity and marginality," in a way that considers the intersecting oppressions of racism and sexism but that avoids the political project of liberation from which the concept emerged in the first place.[12]

At the heart of these conversations is the flexibility of the term and concept of intersectionality. The term and concept, Sara Salem persuasively writes, might best be considered a "traveling theory." Following Edward Said's use of the phrase, Salem writes that "as theories travel, they not only lose their radical edges, but also may fulfill a more radical potential."[13] The propensity for the meaning of intersectionality to shift and change depending on its historical and cultural context allows for a variety of readings. Intersectionality, in other words, is vague enough to be infinitely useful, but this ambiguity also leaves the term vulnerable to misunderstanding or intentional, malicious misinterpretation.

Nash calls on scholars to resist a "corrective impulse" toward intersectionality, in which the history of the term is constantly excavated to defend it from critique.[14] And yet, it is worthwhile to consider how the term is used in public parlance, particularly as part of the larger "culture wars" of the early twenty-first century.

Much of the discussion surrounding intersectionality over the past several years focuses on the historicization of the term. In venues as various as academic conferences and Facebook affinity groups, people scrambled to assign a historical origin. While it was Crenshaw who coined the term in 1989, Vivian M. May points out that Black feminists from Sojourner Truth to Ida B. Wells to Anna Julia Cooper had long practiced the "matrix thinking" at the concept's core.[15] The practice of thinking intersectionally—that is, considering how various systems of oppression interlock and bolster one another—has always been baked into Black feminist activism. Collins and Bilge rightly critique academic commentary for framing intersectionality as "discovered by academics."[16] Positioning the concept within the academy clouds its potential as praxis, Collins writes elsewhere.[17] As phrases like "intersecting power relations" morph into buzzwords, they shift away from tools for social change and become "placeholder term[s] with minimal political impact."[18]

Instead, Collins and others argue that our focus should remain on the concept's practical applications. This approach allows the concept of intersectionality to remain flexible so that it can serve the various situations in which it is necessary. It can fulfill a range of needs from finding ways to make protests more accessible for disabled participants to shifting legal strategies to more accurately serve Black women victims of violence.[19] These approaches align with Crenshaw's work, in which she calls intersectionality "a provisional concept."[20] While her scholarship focuses on the intersection of racism and sexism, she highlights the concept's adaptability to situations including economic exploitation, discrimination on the basis of sexual orientation, agism, and colorism, among other issues.[21] It allows for activists and practitioners to recognize that the issues that Black women face will be very different than those that white women face. Queer Black women will experience different barriers than straight Black women, and disabled queer Black women, poor Black women, Black transwomen, and others each experience unique challenges and bring a variety of insights to activist work.

Understood in this way, intersectionality exceeds its use as an academic term. It is a way of making sense of particular lived experiences, especially those of Black women and other women of color who are in coalition with Black women activists. And it is also a way of thinking through movement agendas to ensure that the central focus of any particular movement or action is designed with intersections of oppression in mind. Amber Johnson calls this "political intersectionality." Unlike "structural intersectionality," or the analysis of how social systems and structures harm people based on intersecting oppressive forces, "political intersectionality" refers to the development of movement strategies with intersectionality in mind.[22] Thus, while intersectionality is perhaps most hotly contested within the halls of academia, its true power lies in enabling social change for those who have been "marginalized in the margins":

> Frontline social actors within bureaucracies as well as those working in grassroots organizations often look to intersectionality to help solve thorny social problems such as homelessness, health disparities, mass incarceration, educational disparities and ever-present violence. Social workers, teachers, lawyers, nurses and similar practitioners engage intersectionality to help solve social problems. For front line political actors, the power hierarchies that create social inequalities and their concomitant social problems seem evident. Within bureaucratic contexts, social actors who claim intersectionality seek guidance for how it might inform their problem-solving strategies. Blacks, women, Latinos/as, indigenous people, women, undocumented people and other similarly subordinated groups who are most affected by social problems often see intersectionality as essential for their political projects.[23]

As Collins and others note, intersectionality is far from an abstract theoretical buzzword. It is simply a term that most accurately describes the work that activists, and particularly Black women and other women of color activists, have been doing for centuries.

Even with an eye toward intersectionality, though, social movements sometimes get it wrong. The solution-based approach of political intersectionality can, and often does, unintentionally recreate many of society's unequal power structures. Writing about Black Lives Matter, in particular, Johnson notes that, while protests calling for justice for murdered Black people were common in 2016 and 2017, the largest of these rallies centered Black cismen and ciswomen. During those same years, Johnson notes, fifty-two trans and nonbinary Black people were killed: "Their names did not go viral, there was very little physical support outside of small private crowdsourcing, and vigils were more popular than protests for these victims, who were all Black, but not cisgender."[24] As they point out, these shortcomings aren't necessarily shortcomings of intersectionality, although they are perhaps an effect of the term's framing around cisgender Black women. Still, they write, the most useful way to understand how intersectionality frames movement communication is through its ability to map "the multiple and overlapping ways in which bodies not only perform as political entities through discourse but endure the systematic attempts to maintain power through representation, politics, and institutions."[25] This mechanism of thinking will always reveal movement shortcomings; its true value is in the way it offers a structure for finding and enacting solutions.

The Importance of Intersectionality

The summer of 2020 saw an increased and vocal focus on intersectionality, particularly within social movements. The term had circulated the year before as a pejorative buzzword on Fox News and other right-leaning cable news networks, a trend that may have paradoxically brought the term into larger circulation. But perhaps even more, several recent social movements had come under criticism for excluding possible participants by failing to think intersectionally. As Johnson points out, the 2017 Women's March on Washington, in particular, was widely criticized for being exclusive to many transwomen and nonbinary femmes by placing the genital-referencing "pussy hat" at the center of the march's branding efforts. Public conversations like these led the *Washington Post* to call intersectionality a term "used by social activists as both a rallying cry for more expansive progressive movements and a chastisement for their limitations."[26] A generous read might interpret this quandary as the natural outgrowth of people's messiness—every individual participant and organizer brings different experiences and priorities to the table, and they are all fallible and imperfect to varying degrees. Others attribute failures in intersectionality to a more cynical read, where intersectionality seems to be used as a buzzword to generate social cache without much investment in the praxis implied by the concept.

Despite this cynicism, the BLM supporters we spoke to had a clear sense of how intersectionality could and should play out within the BLM movement. Articulating his understanding of how various axes of oppression complicate coalitional politics, Peter[27] described his experiences with intersectionally minded activism. He had "been to rallies that were started by and focused on Black trans women, and they started out by saying, 'none of us are free until Black trans women are free,' because they were starting to get to the root of, 'They're queer, they're trans, they're women, and they're Black.'" Peter's focus on Black trans women speaks to an apt metaphor in one of Crenshaw's germinal essays on intersectionality: the basement metaphor. In this metaphor, Crenshaw describes a basement full of people, all standing on one another's shoulders. Those who face only one axis of oppression—such as middle- or upper-class white women or Black men—are at the top of the pile and able to reach the basement's ceiling. Those who are multiply marginalized, on the other hand, are so far away from the ceiling hatch that they cannot even be seen by those looking down into the basement. Peter's description of considering Black transwomen at the center of the movement is a clear application of Crenshaw's original thinking, particularly her remark that "placing those who currently are marginalized in the center is the most effective way to resist efforts to compartmentalize experiences and undermine potential collective action."[28] In fact, Peter extends Crenshaw's analysis noting that, "we've got to really start [with Black transwomen] to start untangling classism, sexism, racism, queerphobia."

And yet, Peter had a sense that others might be hesitant about adopting an unwavering focus on intersectional oppression. While he felt clear that "there's a lot of room to navigate all of that intersectionality within Black Lives Matter," he felt others might believe that this was an overly myopic focus in a context of the "emergency state of, 'Hey, there's rampant police violence. It's an election year. No one knows what's going to happen.'" In another focus group, Natalie,[29] a white transfemale, saw BLM's intersectionality somewhat ambivalently as well. She shared her sense that BLM hadn't always welcomed queer activists, noting that "Black Trans Lives Matter is very much a 2020 thing." As a seasoned activist with years of political and organizing experience, she felt that BLM was "definitely starting to get better, but as far as including LGBT people—and especially T[ransgender] people—in the BLM movement, that is something that is a relatively new phenomenon for the movement and for society as a whole." Finally, Desiree[30] had also seen an increased focus on the intersection of queerness and Blackness through protest signs. At the daily protests she helped organize, she had seen "multiple signs about Black trans lives mattering. We've had students come with rainbow flags, and just all different kinds of visual demonstrations that they're coming at it from sort of particular angles, if you will, or seeing the confluence of their angles and identities." She elaborated that not all of the movement participants she interacted with were able to think intersectionally about Black Lives Matter, nor were they all interested in doing so. These participants demonstrated ease in articulating the meanings of political intersectionality, and yet, they felt ambivalent about their fellow activists' ability and willingness to think about multiple marginalization.

While BLM was founded by queer Black women, BLM is a national movement made up of individual people. Like all movements, then, BLM is not without its inner conflicts, whether those result from the intersection of racial, sexual, and gender identities or from other key intersections of identity and oppression. Regina[31] noted that intersectionality "has entered into the conversation," but she felt that "there's more work to be done." For Regina, this was largely related to issues of how respectability politics are often filtered through a lens of class. She had often seen

> this judgment [about] how you're supposed to say stuff, how you're supposed to do stuff. And so instead of [saying], "You didn't come at me the right way, so now we're not going to have the conversation," we've got to stop that. Because what's more important is the bigger picture, and it is the intersectionality, not because I said these words which differ from how you would have said it, or I came at you a different way than maybe you would have. I do believe that sometimes that intersectionality for some people they think it's a weakness because they're like, "Well, if I work with this one [axis, such as racism] and if I combine these [as with the intersectionality of racism and sexism], then it's taking away from the bigger picture." Which is not true. . . . Let's talk about the fact of getting people to understand how we can come together so that these various pieces can come together so that we can move forward and "not one step back," as Poor People's Campaign says.[32]

Responding to Regina's commitment on coalitional politics, Jo[33] added an additional intersection to the conversation. After "second[ing] everything Regina said," she noted that, "we're not considering intersectionalities enough. Especially when it comes to disabled persons . . . what I have told my people is, 'Just look around you. Who is at the table with you?'" This eye toward inclusion does more than point out the shortcomings of Black Lives Matter; it also highlights an ethic of care for a stronger movement and a more inclusive future. All of these participants clearly point to the ways that inclusion is a holistic commitment. From Natalie's connection between "the movement and . . . society as a whole" to Jo's definition of "the table" as including boardrooms and workplaces, these participants were focused on stretching the ideals of uplifting others across all areas of their lives.

Part of this shift in focus, at least according to many online commenters and some participants, may be a result of generational shifts. Gen Z, a term referring to those born after 1995, are often discussed as being more attuned to social issues thanks to their adolescent and teen access to websites like Tumblr, long known as hubs for identity politics-based messaging and art, and the remarkably progressive *Teen Vogue*. These young adults, the *New York Times* writes, are "the postmillennial group of Americans for whom words like 'intersectionality' feel as natural as applying filters to photos on Instagram."[34] In the wake of summer's protests, many argued that Gen Z not only contributed to the massive uptick in movement participants, but that they also worked at the forefront of efforts to make protests more inclusive. Speaking precisely to this issue, Ashley[35] noted that her interest in pushing for more inclusivity through BLM was related to her observations about where the Women's March had gotten things wrong. The Women's March was widely criticized for being primarily populated by white middle- and upper-class able-bodied cisgender women. Ashley found this, "really interesting as far as trying to call in [and bring] intersectionality into it." This stuck out for Ashley, not only as something to focus on moving forward but in terms of her perception of where this critique came from. "I've seen a lot of people in my generation speak about that [intersectionality]," she said, "but I do think that is something that needs to continue to grow."

Autumn[36] also felt that Gen Z—her generation—was driving much of the growth in BLM, both in terms of intersectional inclusion and in the energy of the movement in general. Speaking to her personal connection to the movement, she shared that "when Michael Brown got killed, because we were the same age . . . I was like, 'Oh, wow.'" This drove her to think about the way that "this generation needs to put [energy] into this and set things in place and advocate for a change." Autumn's response focused on intersectionality through her discussion of "women, Black women, in every aspect of who we are. I keep seeing that they keep posting that Black women are the least protected in the world." Ashley's and Autumn's perspectives on Gen Z's participation in BLM, and the way that this particular generation is invested in inclusivity through intersectionality, speaks to broader statistical trends. A summer 2020 Yubo poll found that 88 percent of Gen Z-ers supported Black Lives Matter.[37] This rate is strikingly higher than the already respectable 67 percent of supporters across the country at that moment in time.[38] And, as many college faculty have noted, Gen Z tends to bring a stronger understanding of race to the table from the beginning of their studies, including key movement terms like "intersectionality." The fact that their participation in the movement is driven by a desire to make protests more inclusive should not come as a surprise.

As tempting as it may be to think of shifts in acceptance and inclusion as influencing the movement from the outside, keeping an eye toward intersectionality is very much an intentional movement strategy. In her memoir, BLM cofounder Alicia Garza writes that "community organizing is often romanticized. . . . It is often the work of building relationships among people who may believe they have nothing in common so that together they can achieve a common goal."[39] This was clear to Ashley,[40] who recognized that "the leaders of the Black Lives movement have spoken a lot about intersectionality and have spoken a lot about how they want to branch that out." The coalitional focus of Black Lives Matter is not a matter of chance. The orientation of the movement as a larger coalition-building strategy is a central lesson from the civil rights movement that has been carried through by contemporary organizers. As Regina's reference to Martin Luther King Jr.'s "Poor People's Campaign" highlights, the idea of aligning one movement's mission with other intersecting movements is not just a matter of individual inclusion. It is a step toward a more powerful political bloc. While Black Lives Matter may not have reached saturation in terms of activism across intersections, the strength of the movement speaks to a large number of members' efforts to contribute to the coalition-building at the center of political and social change.

Self-Care as Intersectional Imperative

A widely shared article on the importance of self-care for Black women began with an Audre Lorde quote: "Caring for myself is not self-indulgence. It is self-preservation, and that is an act of political warfare." In the rest of the article, Evette Dionne encouraged Black women to focus on the ways they had "spent generations in servitude to others," making a focus on the self a radical, political act.[41] While Dionne's article surfaced several years before George Floyd's murder, her sentiment remained prominent that summer. Garza echoes this sentiment in her memoir, praising the evolution of self-care from something that is "indulgent" to a crucial component for movement longevity.[42] The narrative that organizers should always be humbled at the opportunity to be burned out and exhausted, she writes, was particularly harmful for Black women, and she was glad to see it ushered out by new trends in activist thinking. Moreover, for Garza, self-care is always intertwined with movement goals. She asks, "What is self-care without the care of the community? . . . Self-awareness and tools for dealing with trauma and grief and loss are one part of the battle; the other part is healing the systems that create inequality and feed on trauma like a parasite."[43] This perspective on self-care is therefore an excellent example of how intersectionality can link the personal with the social. While caring for the self may appear to be a way of breaking off from the social and into the personal, it is instead a way of coping with the effects of the social in a way that will allow the participant to return to the movement stronger than before.

This powerful message speaks to intentionally positioning the self within the community, and it was something we heard over and over. A seasoned and well-established activist, Regina[44] told us that she had resisted seeking out care for the trauma she had experienced both beyond and within her activism work. She said, "I finally admitted that I had to go to therapy in order to have the capacity to work with so many other people." In Regina's description, the link between caring for the self and caring for others became clear. Self-care in the form of therapy allowed her to better advocate for herself and others, something she did on a daily basis well beyond the summer of 2020. She went on to say that she had also found it useful to learn, "how to talk about it like we're talking here [in the group interview], and learning to talk about it and engage with other people on these subjects has been critical because that helps me work through this and know that we may have different perspectives on something, but we're not alone in this. Because when you stay to yourself you feel like, 'I'm the only one going through this. Nobody else understands it.'" Regina's use of the term "learning" to describe her self-care practices is telling. In her self-care journey, she realized that she needed support and help to process her experiences as an activist. But she also realized through this process that others need this support as well. Her self-care practices therefore led her to arrange a variety of spaces in which she could help to support others in similar journeys by offering a listening ear and an empathetic presence.

Crucially, even the self-care Regina did for herself was facilitated by another person, in her case, a therapist. This situation points out another important way self-care was centered in the summer of 2020. Just like Regina, some participants described finding ways of creating safety for others as a way of making self-care available for those who might need it. Macy[45] shared that she had taken on a slightly different form of activism than the typical protest. As a supervisor at her work, she found it important to "creat[e] spaces where [people can] be able to be themselves and to have joy and just relax." This move, she told us, allowed her to provide spaces for self-care for those who needed them, even in the workplace. She continued by saying that "people get sometimes so focused on the trauma piece of it, that they don't realize they can help enable and encourage and create spaces for joy and healing and just existing." In this way, activism and self-care are linked in that Macy used her position of power and privilege to make room for the healing processes others might need.

As a white, queer, femme member of BLM, Zoe[46] experienced her own intersectional oppressions, but was careful to practice self-care that included a focus on her racial privilege. She thoughtfully shared that she had "doubled down on my self-care, so that I could double down on my activism." For Zoe, this meant staying consistent with medications and getting treatment for sleep issues, so that "I could have energy to sustain moving forward." She was cognizant, as were most of the white protesters we spoke with, that "as a white woman, I'm not experiencing that oppression every day and so making it an everyday practice to think about what I could be doing and what I'm doing, and is it harmful. And just taking care of myself but also taking care of myself for the goal of being able to sustain action." The idea of caring for one's mental health as an extension of movement activism was prevalent during the summer of 2020. Online spaces saw an influx in the circulation of Audre Lorde's statement on self-care, as protesters across the country embraced serious investments in caring for their own mental health, thereby positioning themselves in terms of both the personal and the social.

White People for Black Lives

The summer of 2020 marked a record level of white participation in movements for Black liberation. In fact, a study conducted by the

Pew Research Center in June 2020 concluded that nearly half of the summer's protesters were white.[47] Beyond protesters, social media feeds were packed with white people who were trying, with varying degrees of success, to contribute to the movement by sharing articles, protest and rally information, reading lists, and statements of support. Often, the exuberance of new white participants created problems for movement organizers, as when the "social media Blackout" day, a campaign of dubious origins, led many white people to flood social media with Black squares hashtagged #BlackLivesMatter. While most of these posters were likely well-intentioned, the use of the hashtag to promote Black squares disrupted its utility as an important communication channel for activists at a time when demonstrators depended upon fast, effective communication in the face of an increasingly violent police response. This example and others highlight the propensity for movement participation to fall flat when conceptualized through a lens of diversity rather than relationally. In other words, activism is hampered by a focus on individual identities at the expense of coalitions.

Ambivalent conversations surrounding "allyship" underscored the ambivalence of this conversation. Many seasoned protesters worried that the "ally" label would be claimed by white people as a reassurance that they aren't racist. As Johanna C. Luttrell argues, this entry point can block coalition-building by recentering white identity at the expense of genuine empathy.[48] But others felt optimistic about the number of white people who attended summer demonstrations, recognizing that some white support for Black liberation movements was not entirely new. Bright Eyes,[49] for example, noted that, "we see a lot of—just like we did in the '60s with the SCLC and all these groups—we see a lot of white people who are coming out and saying . . . , 'Look, this is wrong, and we stand with you in solidarity.'" She believed that this white support was positive, noting that "I don't see anything wrong with that . . . I think we have to applaud them" for protesting when they are likely to face some scrutiny from their white friends and family.

Bright Eyes is correct in saying that white support has always existed. However, her very positive outlook on white participation is not entirely historical. When busloads of white college students began arriving in Mississippi in the mid-1960s, SNCC organizers worried that they would not be committed to listening and following. They worried, as do many Black organizers today, that white people would try to take leadership roles from young Black activists or that white participants would not be committed enough to the movement to withstand the coming backlash.[50] As Brooklyn organizer Benjamin O'Keefe told NPR in a summer 2020 article about white participation in protests, many organizers recognized that "we exist in a white supremacy culture in which even people who want to do good do not necessarily want to be led by a Black person."[51] This ambivalence defined Malcolm's[52] perspective. In a joking tone, he told us that the rise in movement participation was a result of "the pandemic and folks was bored." He went on to say that, "for the liberal white folks . . . I don't know. Maybe, finally, enough was enough . . . I have mixed feelings about it. I think that only time will tell what the true intentions of those folks were." Even this cynical take was tempered by Malcolm's contention that white protesters' "presence may be necessary if it's purposeful."

While Malcolm and other Black organizers had good reason to be cautious about the influx of white protesters, many of the white people we spoke with articulated a commitment to self-reflexivity. Both seasoned activists and those new to BLM noted that it was important to them to consider their positionality or the ways their race, gender, class, and other factors made them more or less vulnerable than others in society. Yet, as Jesse Singal wrote in a sweeping piece for *The Cut*, in the years since BLM began its advocacy, rifts have emerged between those who would like to focus on changing the hearts and minds of white people and those who are more focused on concrete policy reform. Ideally, both would change, but in practical terms, many activists have debated which should come first and, thus, which should draw the clearest focus.[53] While our

Black participants tended to be more focused on issues of policy and self-preservation, our white participants often shared about their self-reflexive work. Particularly for more seasoned white activists like Hunter,[54] the imperative to interrogate their own white privilege was in constant conversation with the fight for antiracist policies:

> One of the main things that I do is, first off trying to re-educate myself out of racism, right. That's a continuous thing that I will have to do for the rest of my life. But I've organized teams of white marshals, to help be a barrier at some of these protests between Black people, right? I spend a lot of my time educating white people on these issues and sharing that information and educating them about institutional or systemic racism. I continuously show up to these events, I document these events, I participate. You hear, there's an ally and there's an accomplice. Yeah. And I do try to be an accomplice. I'm not on the periphery. I am boots on the ground, following the Black leaders of the city.

Hunter's statement makes clear that he is interested in both white personal reflection *and* policy change. He not only begins by focusing on his own lifelong self-reflection as he "tr[ies] to re-educate myself out of racism," but he also invests in helping other white people to do the same. At the same time, he understands that protests are about systemic and institutional issues, and that self-reflection will not keep Black people from being murdered in the streets, at protests or elsewhere. While journalists tend to frame these two aspects of activism as a dichotomy, Hunter wove them together, as did many white BLM supporters during the summer of 2020.

Hunter was not the only white participant who realized that self-reflection needed to be a driving factor in other public demonstrations. While his comment reflects some insecurity and, perhaps, defensiveness, Dave's[55] statement is illustrative. When asked to define BLM, he referenced his "demographic," which we take to mean his whiteness, and replied,

I'm not comfortable responding to that question, because I don't think that . . . I have a right to interpret that phrase. I think that phrase shouldn't mean anything particular to me. I think it just is what it is. And I fear doing more damage than I have done with my life so far if I try to interpret that, and try to come up with some. . . . It's a simple, straightforward statement. If I try to make it mean something else, I'll wreck it.

Dave's trepidation reflected his awareness of how white masculinity has driven so many Black deaths throughout history. In this way, white people practice recognizing their place within the structures described in intersectionality, but rather than limiting that analysis to only the axes of oppression, they also identify axes of privilege.

For white women, in particular, this is an important distinction, since many white feminists are hyperfocused on gendered oppressions while ignoring the ways the traditional concept of gender was created with white women in mind.[56] Jo's[57] story is an excellent example of this. As she shared, "I only figured it out about six years ago that I was white and that it mattered. And so I've been working on that since then, because we just have to continuously work on what that means and what it is." She described receiving the results of her Harvard Implicit Bias Test and responding with, "This test is so stupid." She had expected the test to absolve her of any possibility that she discriminated against others, as if to confirm the concerns seasoned BLM activists have about the term "ally."

However, unlike those seeking confirmation of their racial innocence, Jo's initial reaction stuck with her. She said, "Upon realizing how ridiculous my response to that test was, I was like, 'I need to do some work.'" Jo combined her own self-reflection work with organizing in her predominantly white town with a population of 40,000. First, she created a Facebook page for the area's BLM supporters, then she "just showed up on the city square every day at twelve o'clock with a Black Lives Matter sign . . . I continued to stand mostly by myself on the street corner with this sign. . . . And the day before George Floyd's death there was eight people on the Facebook page. Now there's over 4,000, and people are showing up in droves." And yet, based on her self-reflection work, Jo realized that it was important for her to step back and take her cues from Black organizers. She said, "I'm one of the leaders of the [local BLM group], and also in the background because we do have Black admins that we are encouraging and asking to take the lead when they want to, so we're there for support."

We share Jo's story at length because it is, in many ways, a model for how BLM supporters in small predominantly white communities can approach activist work by blending the personal with the social. By beginning with a great deal of self-reflection, Jo could build an infrastructure that was then ready for others to join. But rather than coming to protests with an eye toward "screaming the loudest and . . . throw[ing] things at police," as O'Keefe feared in his Brooklyn protests, Jo realized the imperative to let Black activists lead while simultaneously providing the necessary support to make the movement successful.[58] Many other white people we spoke with shared similar perspectives to Hunter and Jo: they began with self-reflection, then developed ways they could help to educate, advocate, or lead others in their communities, particularly in smaller, predominantly white towns where there was no visible BLM presence.

In each of these cases, white presence highlights the role of the personal as well as the systemic. Certainly, the summer of 2020 saw many popular articles on the failings of white BLM supporters—white people who quickly labeled themselves allies but who were slow to participate in any meaningful way beyond "armchair activism." Many worried that white women, in particular, were on a crash course with activism burnout. As Lelia Gowland wrote for *Forbes* that summer, "I fear that white women who want to engage in this work will do so with fervor for a few weeks, only to burn out."[59] Certainly many white protesters, and likely many protesters across races, were energized by the massive public conversation following George Floyd's murder. It is difficult to imagine a moment in recent history that similarly galvanized so many institutions to speak out about systemic injustice, including news outlets, educational institutions, and even corporations. It felt as though everyone was talking about systemic racism, which made BLM activism seem like a particularly alluring—even trendy—pastime.[60] We don't doubt that some white people used the cultural "trendiness" of BLM as a way of centering themselves over the goals of the movement. And we suspect that at least some of the supporters we spoke with that summer have declined to participate in ongoing initiatives.

Yet, at least for that summer, the white supporters we spoke with recalled a period of careful self-reflection and interrogation. The personal, in the case of these new and seasoned participants, was absolutely crucial to understanding the tenor of urgency surrounding BLM activism during the summer of 2020. As Elaine[61] succinctly stated, "Our elected officials need to know—our entire government needs to know—this is not just a Black issue. I am an older white lady, and I feel strongly about Black Lives Matter because Black lives matter."

Conclusion

In an example that bears quoting at length for its eloquent blending of intersectional thought with self-care, Amy[62] told us that she sees the meaning of activism as expansive, particularly for Black women. She said,

> I guess I'll say that for me, participation doesn't have to be out in the forefront, it doesn't have to mean that you're marching, it doesn't have to mean that you can make the rally, make the meeting, make the Zoom call, make the phone call. You know what I'm saying? We think that showing up and participating, it has to be just outright physical, but I think it can be very existential too, right? Just being a Black woman and existing from day to day every few moments

and deciding to wake up, brush my teeth, put on some clothes—or decide I'm not going to put on clothes today, because self-care and I don't feel like doing the things. I think that is very important to highlight as well. Just existing, right?

Amy's comment encapsulates the sentiment that the personal is political. This idea, popularized by second wave feminists, remained salient in the summer of 2020. But as cultural conversations focused on the idea of intersectionality within a variety of social movements, that sentiment seemed to morph into a way of imagining the personal as intersectional, and the intersectional as personal. By articulating their own position within a matrix of intersecting oppressions and identities, BLM supporters focused their work around their positionalities. Necessarily, this meant that Black participants and white participants approached this task differently, with white participants tending to focus on reflecting on their privilege and Black activists focusing more on self-care. Those who felt equipped to make marches more inclusive did so, often through the time afforded by middle- or upper-class positioning. Younger participants focused on their comfort with newly popularized language while older participants focused on sharing their experiential knowledge of history. Across all of these activities, the connections were highly personal and based on their specific racial, gendered, class-based, and other identity positions.

These activities, even when protesters explicitly approached them through a lens of intersectionality, sometimes fell short. Achieving true political intersectionality is difficult. And yet, BLM participants demonstrated a commitment to learning and growing from past missteps and failures. These supporters focused on the ways their personal experiences—when compared with others' personal experiences—demonstrated the complex structures of privilege and oppression. In doing so, they brought an intersectional lens not only to their analyses of current social issues, but also to their visions for creating stronger political blocs. The personal is political, and the political is intersectional, they told us. As Regina[63] noted, "That's what we need to be working with, is receiving *me*, who *I* am, who *we* are. . . . Let's talk about the fact of getting people to understand how we can come together so that these various pieces can come together so that we can move forward."

Chapter 4

"IT'S AN EXTENSION OF MY FAITH"

The Role of Faith, Religion, and Spirituality
in the BLM Movement

On June 1, 2020, President Donald Trump briefly addressed the nation amid the ongoing unrest over George Floyd's murder.[1] He said that "all Americans were rightly sickened and revolted by the brutal death of George Floyd. My administration is fully committed that for George and his family, justice will be served." However, after promising justice for Floyd and his family, Trump shifted to address the "angry mobs" that drown out the voices of those "peace-loving citizens in our poorest communities." He vowed that he would "keep them safe" and "fight" to protect them. That day, he declared that he was the "president of law and order and an ally of all peaceful protesters to protect you."

He blamed the unrest on "state and local governments" that had failed to take "necessary action to safeguard their residents." To address this, Trump promised that if a "city or state could not take the necessary actions" to "defend life and property of their residents," then he would "deploy the United States military and quickly solve the problem for them." He also said that he would take "swift and decisive action to protect Washington, DC." Lamenting that he believed the actions of some of the protesters the previous night were a "total disgrace," Trump claimed to have "dispatched thousands and thousands of heavily armed soldiers, military personnel, and law enforcement to stop the rioting, looting, vandalism assaults and wanton destruction of property."

However, while the president addressed the nation, the National Guard and law enforcement officials fired "flash-bang shells, gas, and rubber bullets" into a crowd of peaceful protesters gathered in Lafayette Square. The crowd would soon understand why they were forcibly removed: to clear a path for Trump and other government officials to walk over to St. John's Episcopal Church for what simply became a photo op. Noted Evan Osnos, writing for the *New Yorker*:

> Trump stalked across the park, weaving past the monuments, with his security detail skittering around him. When he reached the sanctuary, he did not go inside. Instead, he turned toward the camera, and members of his entourage assembled into a tableau so bizarre that it took a moment to understand what was unfolding. He held up a Bible and posed with it for the cameras, clasping it to his chest, bouncing it in his hand, turning it to and fro, like a product on QVC.[2]

However, the Reverend Gini Gerbasi, the church's rector, described the scene that allowed Trump his photo op. "Trails of smoke [came] from Lafayette Square, followed by clouds of acrid smoke billowing through the crowds," Gerbasi wrote.[3] "People began to run north on 16th Street and onto the St. John's patio, some coming for eyewash, wet paper towels, or water. The first flash grenade rang out, sounding like gunfire, and some people dropped to the ground, thinking the police were shooting."[4]

She continued:

> Minutes later, the intensity of the flash grenades and gas clouds increased as the police began pushing protesters out of the park and onto H Street. More people ran in our direction, crying from

the smoke and from fear. Someone yelled "rubber bullets," and I looked up from washing someone's eyes to see a man holding his stomach, bent over. He moved his arms, and I saw marks on his shirt. When I looked over his shoulder, I couldn't believe my eyes. A wall of police, in full riot gear, was physically pushing people off the St. John's patio, maybe 15 feet away from me.[5]

She continued through the crowds and noticed how the police continued to "push them back." She said they never "intended to be on the front lines, but the police had literally pushed the front line across the park, then H Street, then the patio of St. John's."[6] There were "more flashes, more smoke, more panic."[7] She admitted that she was scared and had had enough. So, when she ran out of water, she gave the BLM medical staff the rest of her eyewash bottle and left. When she got home, her "church seminarian," Julia, texted her: "Did we really just get gassed for a PHOTO OP?" Upon reading the message, Gerbasi said, "My revulsion was immediate and strong, the reality of what happened sinking in: The president had used military-grade force against peaceful protesters, so he could pose with a Bible in front of the church. I sat in my driveway and wept."[8]

If Trump's photo op intended to show that he was a person of faith that grounds his leadership decisions in his faith and perhaps get a boost in the polls, it failed miserably. Other clergy spoke out against the president and his (mis)use of religious symbols. The Right Reverend Mariann Budde, the Episcopal bishop of Washington, DC, told CNN that she was "outraged" by Trump's action. "Let me be clear," she said, "the president just used a Bible, the most sacred text of the Judeo-Christian tradition, and one of the churches of my diocese, without permission, as a backdrop for a message antithetical to the teachings to Jesus."[9] Earlier, she addressed people of color specifically:

And in particular, that of the people of color in our nation, who wonder if anyone ever—anyone in public power will ever

acknowledge their sacred words. And who are rightfully demanding
an end to 400 years of systemic racism and white supremacy in our
country. And I just want the world to know, that we in the diocese
of Washington, following Jesus and his way of love . . . we distance
ourselves from the incendiary language of this president. We follow
someone who lived a life of nonviolence and sacrificial love.[10]

The Right Reverend Michael Curry, the presiding bishop of the
Episcopal Church, also criticized the president.

> This was done in a time of deep hurt and pain in our country, and
> his action did nothing to help us or to heal us. We need our presi-
> dent, and all who hold office, to be moral leaders who help us to
> be a people and nation living these values. For the sake of George
> Floyd, for all who have wrongly suffered, and for the sake of us all,
> we need leaders to help us to be "one nation, under God, with liberty
> and justice for all."[11]

The next day, Trump doubled down on his religious photo op by
visiting the Saint John Paul II National Shrine. According to reports,
the president and Melania Trump "posed for photos in front of a
statue of Pope John Paul II outside the shrine and stood silently
for a few minutes, hands clasped in front of them."[12] Washington
Archbishop Wilton Gregory criticized the president's visit, telling reporters that he found it "baffling and reprehensible that any
Catholic facility would allow itself to be so egregiously misused and
manipulated in a fashion that violates our religious principles"—
principles, he added, that "call us to defend the rights of all people,
even those with whom we might disagree."[13]

As a disputed inspector general's report from the Park Police
one year later suggested that plans to clear the square were already
underway before the president walked from the church,[14] the photo
ops at St. John's Episcopal and the Saint John Paul II National Shrine

spoke volumes. When taken together with his antiprotester, law-and-order speech, Trump communicated a particular understanding of faith grounded in what Kristin Kobes Du Mez called "militant masculinity."[15] In her book *Jesus and John Wayne: How White Evangelicals Corrupted a Faith and Fractured a Nation*, she argued that militant masculinity is an "ideology that enshrines patriarchal authority and condones the callous display of power, at home and abroad. the need to show force and that Trump was in control."[16] In short, when protests raged throughout the country to highlight what many believed was an injustice, Trump responded by tapping into his evangelical base by appealing to their religious values. Those values, however, according to Du Mez, were not those that "privilege humility" and elevate the "least of these," but "one that derides gentleness as a province of wusses. Rather than turning the other cheek, they'd resolved to defend their faith and their nation, secure in the knowledge that the ends justify the means."[17]

As the president communicated and performed a version of religiosity and faith, so were many of the protesters gathered that day in Lafayette Square. Many were out that day supporting Black Lives Matter because they understood faith and how it should operate. As we did in our previous work, we focused on our participants' use of religious narratives to describe their own understandings of religion, faith, and spirituality that led them to become involved with BLM. Just as before, while many participants understood spirituality as central to their connection to BLM, this heightened after Floyd's murder. We discovered that for many participants, the movement had not only inspired and energized people of faith in Christian traditions, but it has also inspired many in other religious traditions to reexamine their own faith journeys. In short, for some, their faith and religious grounding helped them to cope with Floyd's murder and compelled them to get active. Others, however, discovered after Floyd's death that their faith traditions could not address the feeling they were experiencing. They had to draw on something else.

The Role of Faith in the Black Lives Matter Movement

In the beginning, many people saw Black Lives Matter more as a secular movement than a spiritual one. Often compared to the civil rights movement in which Black church and religious leaders figured prominently, BLM was not often discussed as a spiritual or faith-inspired movement early on.[18] Many argued that the (Black) church was silent during those early days of the movement and that the lack of participation especially from Black churches marked BLM as "something different" from the oft-compared civil right movement.[19] Other reasons given for the lack of faith or spirituality in the movement ranged from the belief that since Black Lives Matter embraced a "Marxist oriented philosophy," it worked "against a Christian paradigm"[20] to the fact that the movement founders were Black women and were not products of the Black church and two of them self-identified as queer women.[21]

However, this antireligious narrative surrounding BLM was not entirely true. One of the first books that described BLM's role in religion, spirituality, and faith on the streets of Ferguson was Leah Gunning Francis's *Ferguson and Faith: Sparking Leadership and Awakening Community*. In the book, Francis argued that many of the BLM activists and protesters in the streets of Ferguson "demonstrated a very particular kind of embodiment of scripture and faith" and that activists "sought meaning through scripture in connection with their work for justice."[22] In short, Francis's book pushes back against the antireligious, antispiritual, antifaith narrative of BLM adherents. Indeed, reading the narratives collected in *Ferguson and Faith*, readers began to see the "role of faith in contemporary racial justice organizing."[23]

Recently, however, especially after Floyd's murder, there has been a move to be more intentional in pushing back against not only the antireligious, antifaith, and antispirituality of BLM but to offer a corrective. Many are beginning to argue that BLM, since its inception, was and has always been a spiritual movement. For instance,

Black Lives Matter-Los Angeles cofounder Melina Abdullah argues that despite people framing BLM as a secular movement, there has always been a component of spirituality in the movement. In an interview with KCRW, Abdullah said, "I think that we may not have recognized explicitly the spiritual power and groundedness of Black Lives Matter and that may have happened in earnest. The recognition of it may have happened in earnest about six months to a year in. But I think that it was always there. It was always foundational to who we were."[24] In an interview with *Religion Unplugged*, Hebah Farrag, who has been researching the role of spirituality in the BLM movement since 2014, maintains that "the fight for Black Liberation has always been a faith movement, and BLM is no different. It's just a different and newer faith." She further contends that the movement acts as a 'home for the spiritually wounded." She continues, "There is a deep sense of hurt you can often feel from BLM activists. Relics of spiritual pain and abuse. Many were raised in traditional faiths and kicked out because some aspects of their identity didn't fit."[25]

For long-time activist and public theologian Ruby Sales, the spirituality of Black Lives Matter is similar to what she calls "Black folk religion." Drawing on Albert Raboteau's notion of "slave religion" and the "invisible institution," Black folk religion is a de-institutional—or even anti-institutional—faith tradition that unites Black religiosity and Black social and political thought. It is a religion predicated on justice and right relations." It maintains that "Black spirituality and Black resistance, and their practices, are co-constitutive."[26]

Michael Battle argues in his essay "Black Lives Matter: A Spiritual Response" that the Black Lives Matter movement paradoxically sheds "light" on negative racial construction in Christian spirituality."[27] In many ways, Battle argues, the Black Lives Matter movement, with "its calls for non-violence civil disobedience against police brutality, and all racially motivated violence against Black people," has done a "better job than our institutional churches speaking for God."[28] This, he suggests should call all people of faith to "humility"—a humility not grounded in the "false kind in which we deflect accomplishments or compliments" but one that "urges us away from anxiety and into constructive action."[29]

Biko Mandela Gray argues that BLM has "religious undertones through its celebration of Black life as sacred." He suggests that "BLM offers a vision of Blackness as irreducibly sacred, as Blackness disrupts the normative significance of the contemporary world" in order to establish "the basis for a more general moral order" based upon "love and care over against the violence of distinction-making constitution."[30]

Christopher Cameron and Philip Luke Sinitiere remind us in their book *Race, Religion, and Black Lives Matter: Essays on a Moment and a Movement* that "contrary to general perceptions" of Black Lives Matter, "religion has been neither absent nor excluded from the movement's activities."[31] In the book, Cameron and Sinitiere argue that "religion is an important thread in BLM and has indelibly shaped and impacted the movement."[32] By adopting a "capacious rendering of religion," Cameron and Sinitiere were able to "broadly define religion" and also "highlight the religious pluralism" in the movement.[33]

We would agree with Cameron and Sinitiere's assessment of BLM and religion because we found similar findings in our book, *The Struggle Over Black Lives Matter and All Lives Matter*. For instance, in highlighting the role of the Black church and social justice movements in the past, we wrote that "despite the apparent rift between the traditional role of the Black church in racial justice organizing and the contemporary BLM movement, the historical role of spirituality in Black liberation movements bubbles beneath the surface of BLM adherents' understandings of their activism."[34] Moreover, we stated that early on, "many BLM participants understand spirituality as central to the connection with the movement and Black liberation more generally. Though BLM arose as a secular movement, we argue that this does not mean that participants were 'non-religious' or 'anti-religious.' Instead, many participants' positions within the church and the movement were mutually constitutive."[35]

Drawing from Andrew Wilkes's notion of Pentecostal Piety,[36] we argued that "proponents of this type of spirituality are not locked into the rigid confines of religious orthodoxy. In many cases, people practicing this brand of spirituality are not affiliated at all with any religious institution."[37] Furthermore, we wrote, "Pentecostal Piety prioritizes prophetic action, framing particular approaches to activism as a subversive civil religion." Prophetic, in this context, "refers to the crucial role of religion in offering a critical perspective on justice, oppression, and the contours of a moral society in general."[38] We thus argued that BLM "is part of the long African American prophetic tradition."[39] When understood in this way, "the role of religion in social justice organizing does not limit the inclusivity of a movement, but rather is well-aligned with an intersectional analysis that seeks to uncover all of the many and varied ways anti-Black racism influences contemporary society."[40]

BLM and Its Egalitarian Approach to Faith

While people of faith have been a part of the Black Lives Matter movement since its inception, some told us that religion played no role in their involvement with BLM. For instance, some, like Peter,[41] had no religious affiliation or connection. When asked about the part of faith in his participation with BLM, he told us: "I'm not religious. Yeah, I just never really grew up as Christian or anything. I'm totally interested in different cultures. My boyfriend is interested in Judaism. So, I think that's totally interesting. I love reading about different intersections of what it means to be Black and Jewish or Black and Muslim, but personally, I just don't really have that connection." It is this egalitarian approach that Desiree[42] spoke about as well. When we asked Desiree about the role of faith and BLM, she told us that some would prefer that religion not play a role in the movement. While in her community, people of faith were out at rallies, she told us there is a "big pushback" from folks who suggest this is not a "faith-based movement at all." She told us that people in her community support BLM and believe it should not be a religious-based movement at all. She told us that there were some in her community who would argue that

> [BLM] is not a religious-based movement at all, and we shouldn't center Christian thought or Christian opinion in any of this, and if we're going to allow Christian thought and Christian opinion to have a voice at the microphone or to have a voice with the megaphone, then we also need to make sure that we are getting as many non-Christian faiths up in front of that space as well.

While not all in her community desire BLM to be a "faith-based movement," her quote above opens that door for a more egalitarian involvement with people of faith. In short, it seems as if Desiree[43] would prefer that BLM be a non-religious movement, but she definitely does not want to see it as a Christian-only faith-based movement.

Scott[44] told us that in his community, there was a "fight over BLM and over social justice that is inextricably linked to religiosity." He continued:

> In terms of the way that it's locally focused here, it is very much a generational split between a group of, I'm going to say Southern Baptists, but I generally mean white Evangelicalism . . . [or] at worse, straight up anti-Black white Christianity, meaning, "We don't want any part of those kinds of things." But then the actual pro-BLM folks who are students very much ground their religious identity within a "BLM is part of who I am as a religious person . . ." While it's mostly Christian, I've also seen it in Muslim students. I've also seen it in self-described, "I'm spiritual but don't follow any particular thing" students, that they very much describe their identities as inextricably linked between religiosity and antiracism.

Peter's relationship to religion, or lack thereof, Desiree's community's preference that the BLM movement does not anchor itself in faith or belief, and the multifaceted faith traditions spoken of by Scott reflect what Religious Studies scholar Anthony Pinn calls BLM's "egalitarian approach." Pinn argues that BLM offers a "greater appreciation for the separation of church and state that affords a more robust and expansive narrative of justice not strangled by restrictive theological categories and limitations." Moreover, he continues, "the more egalitarian approach of Black Lives Matter opens and urges a greater sense of accountability and responsibility. There are no special skills, no divine callings serving as a litmus test for authentic voice. There is something more organic and synergistic about this de-centralizing of leadership."[45]

Katlyn[46] told us that her faith is in everything she does, including participating in Black Lives Matter. However, she offered a warning.

> Well, I believe that God is in everything and that you can pray without ceasing. So every time you're worried about something, you're praying about it. So to separate your spirituality from anything is a bit arid, desert, scary, lack of water. However, I think that Black Lives Matter should be allowed to be open without the tags of religion. It should not be, "Well, this is my Christian Black Lives Matter group, and this is my Muslim Black Lives Matter group." I'm intersectional in that way as well.

This egalitarian approach also makes room for people of faith to participate in the Black Lives Matter movement. As we found in our previous study of BLM participants, many come to the movement with their faith intact. For instance, Jennifer's[47] role in BLM found resonance in her reading of the Gospel narratives and how the Gospels speak out against injustice. She maintains that in her understanding of the Gospels, she sees how Jesus "felt about those who were on the margins." For her, those interactions demonstrate how "Jesus reached across all kinds of lines to show radical love." She continues:

I just think, as a person of faith, it's important that whenever we see other people treated unjustly, just like the woman who was caught in adultery, and the Pharisees were pointing the fingers at her, I think whenever we see that happening, we have a responsibility to speak up and to say, "No, her life matters. His life matters. Whomever." But I know specifically because of my own context, because I am a Black woman, I definitely want to say that our lives matter. So, I think there's a responsibility in terms faith, especially if we look at the radical love of Christ in the Gospel narratives, to speak out when we see injustice.

Jennifer[48] grounded her understanding of faith in the Gospels and how Jesus "felt about those on the margins." The radical love that Jesus showed manifested itself in the BLM movement because, again, for her, the movement speaks and stands with those that Jesus would have spoken and stood for: those on the margins. She explains her understanding of this by sharing with us the story of the "woman caught in adultery."

Referring to the story found in the Gospel of John (8:1–11), Jennifer sees this woman as one who was "treated unjustly" by the "Pharisees" who "were pointing fingers at her." In the story, Jesus was teaching the people at the temple when the "scribes and Pharisees" brought a woman who had been "caught in adultery" and made to stand before all the people there. The woman's accusers referred to the law that "commanded them" to "stone such women." They wanted to know Jesus's position in hopes of testing him on the law. However, Jesus turned the test back on them by declaring, "Let anyone among you who is without sin be the first to throw a stone at her." After hearing this, the woman's accusers went away, and when no one was left to "condemn" this woman, Jesus did not condemn her and sent her on her way.

Jennifer sees the woman in this story as a victim, and she sees Jesus as speaking up for the woman. For her, this woman's life matters, as do the lives of all women, especially the lives of Black women.

This understanding, grounded in this radical love of Christ, leads her to participate in the Black Lives Matter movement and speak out against injustice.

For Akira,[49] Black Lives Matter intersects with her faith because of her upbringing in the church. She told us that the way that her family, pastor, and church members taught her Christianity was to "love everybody." She has a "responsibility to love everybody, treat everybody equally." For Cheryl,[50] Black Lives Matter connects with her faith because it helps her to see the "divine" within her; she believes there is a "divineness" in Black Lives Matter.

The whole ethic of love for people of the Christian faith grounds itself on another Gospel teaching: loving neighbor as yourself.[51] BLM activists emphasize loving oneself as an essential and radical act. From the beginning of the movement, Alicia Garza called on Black people to "love ourselves."[52] That love letter helped launch the BLM movement, and since then, affirmations of Black life, Blackness, and self-love have always been a part of the movement. As Johnson argues, the "most radical love is self-love. In fact," he continues, in "order to love others, one must be able to fully love oneself" because it is the foundation on which "all other love is based and grounded."[53] It is the same type of love that Black Power advocates talked about and the same love that James Cone wrote about in his earlier versions of Black Theology.[54] Implied in loving God and neighbor, Johnson writes, "is a self-love that anchors it all."[55]

For Elaine,[56] BLM was not just an extension of her faith or spirituality but a way to actualize her faith. What she meant by this was that Black Lives Matter as a movement allowed her to put her faith in action. Desiree[57] echoed this when she described how she and others in her community put their faith into action:

[I]n the actual sort of public demonstrations, the question of faith has been super-, super-prevalent. In the instances where we get either counter-demonstrators or where we get other groups demonstrating that just don't agree with us, like they didn't show up

to counter-demonstrate us, but they have shown up to demonstrate and they don't agree with us, it's always communities of faith,
always, a hundred percent. We have folks drive by with militia insig-
nia that yell, "All lives matter," and stuff like that, so there's other
resistance, but when there's somebody else on the square, they're
there for their own purpose but very much not for our purpose, it's
always folks of faith.

Green[58] told us that her faith was critical in supporting BLM because
she felt that "we are all God's people and that we should act out of
love." For Green, the foundation of her faith (Christianity) grounded
itself in love, and she could not understand why other Christians
did not have this type of understanding. "This type of racism and
injustice" placed on Black people, she told us, "I feel like that's hate.
I'm trying to figure out where . . . how can this be? Racism is spewed
by people who claim to be Christians when I know that's not what
the Bible says. I know that's not what God says. I also feel like the
injustices and what's being done to us, not just Black people, but
folks that are being oppressed [is wrong.]"

To better grapple with this, Green turns to apocalyptic rhetoric to
help her find meaning. When talking about the racism and oppression Black people face daily, Green says:

I feel like that's only to make us stronger and I know because . . .
history just repeats itself. That there will be a day of reckoning, we
will rise up. . . . My faith tells me that, and I know that I've been in
some situations, like I said in the past, that God has brought me
out of and God calmed my fears, and that's how I was really able to
lean on my faith and my understanding of God and my spirituality and my relationship with God to know that . . . whom shall I
fear? There's no way that I should be fearing another human being
and what they could potentially do to me. So, definitely feel that
the Black Lives Matter movement is an extension of my faith and
what I believe in.

Bright Eyes[59] sees her relationship with Jesus as foundational to her role in Black Lives Matter. "I keep going back to Christ," she asserts. "[T]he pain of one member is the pain of us all. The joy is the joy of us all. And so, our concern should individually be to help people who are downtrodden, who are underprivileged, to increase in stature." She continued:

> The church has to teach that if there is to be salvation for you, then that salvation is tied to how you embrace the stranger, how you embrace someone that you think is the other. . . . The church cannot be silent. The church has to play a role in where we're going in the future. We can't preach on Sunday and sit in our homes and do nothing on Monday through Saturday. It can't be like that anymore because the Black church has always been instrumental in the growth of Black society from the civil rights movement, but they lost their way.

Here, Bright Eyes notes the importance and relevance of the (Black) church. For her, the church acknowledges the pain and suffering of others, as well as the joys and celebrations. The church should also "help people who are downtrodden, who are underprivileged, to increase in stature." She ties this into salvation itself—in how we "embrace the stranger" and the "other," and that for me to "be saved," I must help others "be saved." For Bright Eyes, by doing this, the church plays a role in where the people would head in the future. However, when she nears the end of her comment, she reveals that the church she spoke of was in the past, during the civil rights movement, because today, she feels, the church has lost its way.

This critique of the Black church, especially in relationship to BLM, is nothing new. Early in the movement, even some Black pastors lamented the lack of involvement and the "strange silence" from Black churches regarding the Black Lives Matter movement. Some even wondered how the Black church could be a part of the movement without taking ownership. In *The Struggle Over Black Lives*

Matter and *All Lives Matter*, we wrote that "for many the apparent lack of formal participation from Black churches around the country marked BLM as something different from the mid-twentieth-century civil rights movement, for better or for worse."[60]

However, Bright Eyes's participation in the (Black) church and BLM highlighted something else for us. As we discovered in our previous work, while participants did not believe that the Black church was a full participant in the BLM movement, or at least not at the level that would have satisfied them, many agreed that the faith they learned in the church was one of the primary reasons for their involvement with BLM. It was through the church that "had lost its way" that some participants still found a way to join the movement and ground it in their faith experience. This speaks to the history and legacy of the Black church. It also speaks to the preaching and teaching of the Black church and the "legacy of activism birthed from the church that bore witness to the issues germane to African Americans across a variety of places and times."[61] In short, even though Bright Eyes argued that the church had lost its way, there was enough of the church's tradition to help her see that her faith is indispensable in carrying out the work of Black liberation.

Faith, Blackness, and BLM

For some respondents, their understanding of Blackness itself and their own Blackness helped shape their understanding of faith. In speaking of her Blackness and being created in the image of God, Cheryl[62] told us:

> That it is the is-ness of my Blackness, or the Blackness of my people, or Afro-diaspora persons being created in the image of God, and therefore their humanity, their dignity, and all of that which God has created in them has value and has meaning and it has purpose and it's part of God's plan. And that, that thing, it must be lifted

up. Because it continues, time after time after time after time, and time and time again, consistently being destroyed, or decimated. Disappeared. Erased. Not just in the physical form, but in history, and everything else. And so, when we talk about Black Lives Matter, or at least when I talk about it for me, I'm talking about the very essence of a people, and everything that we bring to the table.

Thus, for Cheryl,[63] her value and meaning are wrapped up in her understanding of what it means to be made in the image of God as a Black woman. Blackness for her is not a bad or evil thing. It is how she was made in the image of God. It is part of God's plan and needs to be lifted and celebrated.

Regina[64] echoes much of what Cheryl said by expanding on it more. Her faith, as well as her Blackness, plays an essential role in her support of the Black Lives Matter movement. Pointing to the T-shirt she wore on the day we talked with her that read, "Humanize Being Black," she told us:

You see my T-shirt 'Humanize Being Black'? It is definitely part of my faith, and part of the reason it's part of my faith is not just because of the church that I attend, but because in life when we talk about that connection that God created us, we have to know that God didn't make a mistake when God made us Black. And that's something that I've had to share. And that's part of the theology that's come out and it's free. And it's that liberation theology that says, "God didn't make a mistake when God made some of us have a little bit more melanin than the other one. And it's okay."

She further shared:

So yeah, it's important, because a lot of people have had that white liberal theology that says they're less than. And so therefore when they're struggling and going through various situations, they don't really think God loves them, because why would God allow me to

be abused? Why would God allow me to be homeless? Why would
God allow me to be assaulted and all of these other things? So yes,
my theology says I have to put in Black Lives Matter because right
now [Black] lives are being negatively impacted.

First, we did not find any of these responses surprising. In our previous work, several respondents identified the same. BLM's focus
on affirming *all* Black lives and their contributions to society and
Black people's resilience in facing oppression[65] gave our respondents
a greater appreciation of their own Blackness. Many Black people
of faith see this Blackness as a gift from God.

While Autumn[66] did not talk directly about her Blackness and
BLM, she did talk about the importance of discernment. Autumn
told us that because she was a Christian, she had no choice but to
bring her faith into her activity with BLM. She further told us that
her relationship with her faith and God helped her discern "when
to post something, when not to post something, [and] what would
be more impactful."

> It's like He [God] quickens my spirit to know what to do and what
> not to do. And it's great when you have God's supernatural on the
> natural because something can move forward further. So, I feel as
> though if others who believe and have faith will put their faith too
> into the Black Lives Matter movement, it will go further. And if we
> magnify God in the process, He said, if we would bring Him up, He
> will draw all men unto thee. So, I feel as though if we would bring
> God into the Black Lives Matter Movement and let people know
> that this is a worthy course, but also that we support Christians in
> the process and everything, and lift up God in the process with this,
> then the movement will go further.

Autumn's[67] faith is more than simply spiritual: she believes that people of faith can directly affect the movement's success and progress.

In his book *The Reverend Albert Cleage Jr. and the Black Prophetic Tradition: A Reintroduction of the Black Messiah*,[68] Earle Fisher argues that the Reverend Cleage similarly argued the same point during the Black Power movement. Grounded in an understanding that Christians should worship a Black messiah, Fisher maintains that Cleage saw the people leading and participating in the Black Power movement as already doing the work of God. Fisher argues that the "Black Christianity" that Cleage promoted was "independent of the institutional church."[69] Arguing that the Black messiah Jesus did not "build a church, but a movement," Fisher writes that Cleage situated the Black Church as a location for Movement and (Nation) building."[70]

Cleage further maintained that the "[Black Power] Movement was the Christian Church in the 20th century and that the Christian Church cannot be the church until it also becomes the Movement."[71] Cleage even went so far as to suggest that the church ordain people in the movement:

> You could be ordained in this church as civil rights workers if we could somehow do away with the distinctions which exist in people's minds between what's religious and what's not religious. To ordain civil rights workers for civil rights work would declare that the Christian Church believes that this is what Christianity is all about, that individuals who gave their lives in the struggle for human freedom are Christian and that the Movement is not only Christian, but that the Movement is the Church.[72]

Thus, Fisher argues that "Cleage's rhetorical aim [was] to speak into existence the liberation of Black people, the transformation of the Black church, and a reconciliation of Black people to the Black church. The ordination of young Black radicals [was] a strategy to achieve those goals."[73] For many activists and adherents of BLM, this is done by first situating Blackness as a gift from God.

"It Can't Be of God": Rethinking Religion, Faith, and Spirituality

While much of the study of religion and social movements centers on how members of the movement perform their faith within the movement or how it already speaks to members' faith commitments, social movements can also challenge and expand members' faith. For some, BLM has "prompted a crisis of moral conscience" and, according to Professor Drew Hart, forced people of faith to do some "social-change work."[74]

One such person was Pastor Brenda Salter McNeil. McNeil, who describes herself as a Black evangelical, told the *New Yorker* that prior to BLM, she would "explicitly avoid talking about aspects of structural racism, such as the racial wealth gap, or the high death rate of Black mothers during childbirth."[75] She would preach sermons that she felt were "rooted in the Bible" and not in what she thought were just "politics." When she gave workshops, she would focus on "inspiring personal stories" but "left listeners with few practical tools to root out racism in their communities."[76]

However, that all began to change when she and other evangelical ministers arrived in Ferguson in 2014, asking the people there how the church could help. What they found were activists disillusioned with the church. After listening to them, she understood that she was on the "wrong side of justice" and began to reexamine her own theology. She earnestly believed that if she could have convinced "evangelical Christians that reconciliation was not some politically motivated agenda, but a Biblical calling rooted in Scripture, they would pursue racial justice." She now believes she was naïve in her thinking. She now thinks religious leaders and people of faith must "actively campaign against systematic racism if they are to effect change."[77]

Some participants also told us that BLM was challenging their faith, religion, and spirituality, causing them to grow. An example of this was Cerise, who told us:

I think I grew up with religious tolerance for other people who were religious. So, I can be Baptist. You can be Episcopalian. You can be AME, but I didn't grow up with the same appreciation of people who weren't religious at all. So, that's something that I'm having to. . . . As I get older and rethink my own spiritualities, a lot of people are spiritual but not religious, and that's okay too, and ways to engage and bring people in versus . . . because in many ways, in the South, one of the first things they'll ask you . . . I think with my white friends and colleagues is, "What do you do?" [With] Black [people, it's], "Where do you go to church?"

Virginia[78] also agrees that BLM challenges perceptions of religion and faith and helps bring people to awareness.

I do think it's changing, and I think the Black Lives Matter movement has brought people's awareness. I know that this is so small. I mean, it's so embarrassingly small, but one of my daughters is at a church in middle Tennessee. She's a pastor, and they have started reading one of these books like *White Fragility* or *How to Be an Antiracist* in their Sunday school class. Now, I know these are tiny little baby steps, but they weren't doing it before, and they are doing it now, and I'm sorry. I know I'm going on too much, but one thing that I think the church has done that looks good on the outside but doesn't change anything. All the years that the mainline churches have two things, have sent missionaries to foreign countries to "bring the natives to Christ," which is the natives have a better idea of fair play than we do.

Others, such as Hannah,[79] wrestled with some contradictions she found in her support of BLM. As a person of faith and a chaplain, Hannah told us that she struggled with "making those theological connections, and what does that say about who we are as a people? If there's such violence and hatred and division. . . . How can people speak out in such a just terrible, hateful way and yet read scripture in the same sentence? And it's just so pervasive. It's so pervasive."

Hannah offers as an example some Christian groups who actively pray against people who are working "towards justice."

> But I guess, part of what I've been trying to dissect, for almost fifteen years now, even having to do with BLM, but also before, is what happens when we have Christians that pray against other Christians? What does that look like in the spiritual realm? Because you're literally.... It can't be of God, right? So, what does that look like? And are people taking part in really something sinister when they really think that they're doing something positive? And so, I've been really wrestling with that for a while on how to have conversations, theological conversations, on prayer and justice and to be really aware of the intent and just really make it a point for people to pray for protection.

Hannah's frustration reminds us of our findings from our previous study of white people of faith who supported Black Lives Matter. Our research showed that white participants found it increasingly difficult to reconcile their faith with their support of Black Lives Matter. Hannah's struggle with making "theological connections" to justice movements speaks to an understanding of faith not rooted in liberation. However, through her "wrestling" and "dissecting," something pulls her to see the BLM as a just movement. It also has her questioning other Christians who actively pray against the movement. Thus, for Hannah, BLM provides space and a place to activate her faith and mold and shape her faith as well.

However, while Hannah is free to explore her newfound faith commitments within her faith tradition, others are not. One such example was Alan,[80] who told us that even mentioning Black Lives Matter at church or within one's own denomination could lead to a backlash. In his "more conservative denomination," saying "Black Lives Matter could potentially keep me from getting ordained, so it's one of those things that I'm treading lightly."

However, he was quick to add that the BLM movement was something that he could not simply "ignore what [was] happening," but he is still wrestling with his feelings.

Macy[81] echoed Alan and went further, saying,

I grew up Southern Baptist, [so] the answer is no. In the summer of 2016, when the Southern Baptist Convention condemned the Confederate flag, I was shook. I'm talking about I called everybody I knew, I was sending the article to people because I was like, you all what, because that was the wildest thing to me because Southern Baptist culture as a whole is extremely—I hate how we talk about conservatives in the form of, like, it's so sad that it correlates to doesn't care about human beings. But if your Jesus is not about liberation and if your Jesus is literally not about humanitarian aspects of life, we're not talking about the same one.

For Macy, this led him to leave the church, but as he explains, he is still spiritual. "I'm not a churchgoing human, but me and Jesus are good, and that's kind of how I describe my religion and my spirituality. Because the racism and sexism and everything in churches really bothered me, I just couldn't do it. I could not deal with the institution of the church and I've had people who are heavy churchgoing Christians block me, because I was like, that was problematic." When faced with disagreements with his former churchgoing acquaintances, Macy attempted to explain his newfound positions on the faith, but those discussions got "really feisty." He had many of his friends block him on social media, even though he tried to speak "calmly" so they could not say he was angry. He then summed up his conversations with them this way:

There are people who are so, I don't know the word that I'm looking for, but they're so into the culture of their church, as opposed to what is actually being said within the Bible that that is what is most important to them. They're blinded by church culture, as opposed to all the things in the Bible where God is literally talking about taking care of the poor and marginalized identities and literally, the entire book of Exodus, Him yelling because people aren't taking care of people. He's literally yelling at people, He's like, "Oh, you got a second house, you won't live in it." The culture is where people are more so at from my experience.

Brian[82] also echoed many of these sentiments. While he and his family are very outspoken about the BLM movement, he admits that many in other "Christian" institutions are not. He bluntly asserts that "they don't want to talk about it" and offers reasons for their reluctance. "They don't want to talk about it," he continues, "either because it's a lack of understanding or, to me, they fit into the category." His remedy for the reluctance is to have dialogue. "So, what we need to do is, find a way to speak intelligently without argument because once you argue, neither side is going to win."

Jo,[83] while a supporter of Black Lives Matter, admits that her church and denomination were slow to respond positively to BLM. "So, I'm not going to lie and say that our religion has always been in a hurry to worry about Black Lives Matter," she said, "because we have not. It's only been in the past four years. We started examining who we are as a faith [community] and what we really want our imprint on this world to be. And we came to the conclusion that as a denomination, we really do need to be doing work on Black Lives Matter."

However, she quickly told us that there was pushback from members of the church. "There's a part of our movement who are angry that we're doing this work because they think that we're being too politically correct. And it's not a large movement, but they're loud. So, they're really stirring up a lot of crap. And one of our ministers published a book two years ago now that called for the division of our [denomination]."

However, some had to leave their faith due to embracing Black Lives Matter. Dave[84] told us bluntly, "I had to put the faith I was raised in behind me because it was not going to move where I needed to move. And, so, yeah. I'm post-faith tradition at this point."

Conclusion

As we did in our previous work, in this chapter we focused on our participants' use of religious narratives to describe their own understandings of religion, faith, and spirituality that led them to become involved with BLM. Many of our findings echoed our previous research. First, as we noted before, the "long tradition of Black Churches being involved in social justice issues and concerns" allowed many Black participants to draw from the "legacy of civil rights history as well as their own personal histories in the church."[85] As before, the Black religious tradition for our participants gave them license "to rethink, reshape, and reimagine what spirituality would look like in the BLM movement."[86] It allowed them to contemplate and celebrate their Blackness, rooting that Blackness in something holy, acceptable, and good. It was a reminder that even in religious discourse, Black people always had to "put forth narratives that not only included them but also reminded them that their lives matter."[87]

Second, as we noted before, white people of faith struggled at times to reconcile their faith to the BLM movement. We previously wrote that "BLM members who worshipped in white evangelical churches had to reexamine those traditions and find spiritual homes outside the traditions."[88] Shaped in their "legacy of racist and sexist ideologies and structures,"[89] what many white participants began to understand was that their previous theological understanding did not or could not support their participation in the BLM movement. Therefore, they had to reexamine and self-reflect on what it meant to be a person of faith in this contemporary moment and be "born again" by the "anti-racist and anti-sexist messages of the movement."[90]

However, in our present study, we discovered that many participants appreciate BLM's egalitarian approach to faith. While there are people of faith in the movement, the movement also welcomes people with no relationship to religion or who practice a blend of religious traditions. This egalitarian approach provides avenues for people to explore their own Blackness and how that Blackness is shaped and performed. It creates an opening for people to reexamine and explore different versions, notions, and attitudes about faith. It also allows for growth and diversity of religious expression—giving people an opportunity to offer critique or even be challenged by previous religious presuppositions. Moreover, it gives license and provides a way out of toxic religious and spiritual relationships that are not life-affirming.

This egalitarian approach became all the more important after Floyd's murder. As BLM was quickly becoming the largest social movement in the history of the United States, it proved advantageous not to see the movement as a religious one but as one open to an eclectic diversity of religious expressions—a movement that does not highlight or focus on one particular brand of faith, but one that allows any or no expression of faith to move a people in unison to declare that Black Lives Matter.

Chapter 5

"IT'S HOW WE PICK OUR ENEMY"

BLM and the Role of Electoral Politics

On May 7, 2016, President Barack Obama delivered the commencement address at Howard University. While the speech included many elements of the typical commencement address, with the presidential election on the horizon, it also served as a chance for Obama to address the importance of participating in the electoral process. Directing his speech to the graduate class of 2016, Obama told them that they "have to go through life with more than just passion for change" and that they needed "a strategy."[1] He continued, "I want you to have passion, but you have to have a strategy. Not just awareness, but action. Not just hashtags, but votes."[2]

Obama argued that "change requires more than righteous anger. It requires a program, and it requires organizing."[3] Celebrating the efforts of Fannie Lou Hamer at the 1964 Democratic National Convention, Obama reminded his audience that while it was true that Hamer gave a "fiery speech," she "went back home to Mississippi and organized cotton pickers."[4] Invoking the legacy of Hamer offered Obama an opportunity to celebrate the "new guard of Black civil rights leaders who understand this. It's thanks in large part to the activism of young people like many of you," he continued, "from

Black Twitter to Black Lives Matter, that America's eyes have been opened—white, Black, Democrat, Republican—to the real problems, for example, in our criminal justice system."[5]

However, Obama offered a warning. To bring about the structural change that he perceived many in his audience wanted, being aware of a problem or issue was not enough. Passion only was not enough. A strategy was needed, including voting—"not just some of the time, but all the time."[6] While Obama conceded that fifty years after the Voting Rights Act, there were "still too many barriers to voting,"[7] he also reminded his audience that even if every barrier to voting would disappear, "that alone would not change the fact that America has some of the lowest voting rates in the free world."[8] After sharing the low turnout numbers in the 2014 midterms and explicitly targeting African American lower turnout in the same election, Obama critiques his audience:

> And you don't have to excuses. You don't have to guess the number of jellybeans in a jar or bubbles on a bar of soap to register to vote. You don't have to risk your life to cast a ballot. Other people already did that for you. [Applause.] Your grandparents, your great-grandparents might be here today if they were working on it. What's your excuse? When we don't vote, we give away our power, disenfranchise ourselves—right when we need to use the power that we have; right when we need your power to stop others from taking away the vote and rights of those more vulnerable than you are—the elderly and the poor, the formerly incarcerated trying to earn their second chance.[9]

For Obama, voting is a "duty," and he challenges his audience to accept this duty every chance they get:

> So you got to vote all the time, not just when it's cool, not just when it's time to elect a president, not just when you're inspired. It's your duty. When it's time to elect a member of Congress or a

city councilman, or a school board member, or a sheriff. That's how we change our politics—by electing people at every level who are representative of and accountable to us. It is not that complicated. Don't make it complicated.[10]

Also noteworthy in the speech is Obama's appreciation of the work of BLM activist and Campaign Zero cofounder Brittany Packnett. When she joined Obama's Task Force on 21st Century Policing, Obama reminded his audience that "some of her fellow activists questioned whether she should participate."[11] However, Packnett "rolled up her sleeves and sat at the same table with big city police chiefs and prosecutors. And because she did, she ended up shaping many of the recommendations of that task force. And those recommendations are now being adopted across the country—changes that many of the protesters called for."[12] He closed this part of the speech by saying, "If young activists like Brittany had refused to participate out of some sense of ideological purity, then those great ideas would have just remained ideas. But she did participate. And that's how change happens."[13]

Obama's commencement speech at Howard and his directed comments about voting foreshadowed an article in the *Washington Post* a little over a week later. Titled "Despite Black Lives Matter, Young Black Americans Aren't Voting in Higher Numbers," the article noted that despite younger African Americans "pushing criminal justice issues and institutional racism to the forefront of the presidential election," those efforts have had "little effect at the ballot box" during the primary season.[14] Citing exit polling across twenty-five states, Vanessa Williams and Scott Clement noted that Black voters younger than forty-five made up 11 percent of voters in 2008 but only 10 percent in the 2016 primary season. They cited Obama's commencement address and argued that Obama only echoed concerns that "some young Black activists involved in the current wave of political action do not share the belief in the critical importance of the right to vote."[15]

Reniqua Allen took issue with the *Washington Post* article. Writing for *The Nation* magazine, Allen called the headline and the story "unsurprising and frustrating, a disturbing affirmation that, for all of the talk about Black America in the media, we're still far from understood."[16] She continued, "Unlike white millennials, we aren't allowed to deviate from norms, to be untraditional. We have to follow strict standards and conventions. We have to be acceptable and respectable. We can't have nuanced views and ideology, and if we have the nerve, the audacity to be angry, we better have something to show for it."[17] Allen argued that Black Lives Matter "never claimed to represent all Black youth or be responsible for mobilizing an entire generation at the polls. Black Lives Matter organizers," she noted, "have repeatedly said that "voter mobilization isn't a priority and that they were not endorsing a presidential candidate in this election."[18]

Indeed, Melina Abdullah, a Black Lives Matter activist in Los Angeles, told Amy Goodman in March 2016 that "we're [BLM] are not telling people not to vote," but was saying that they would not endorse "any presidential candidate." For Abdullah, she maintained that BLM's focus was "recognizing where we want to put our time and energy is in the development of people to act in their own interests and on their own behalf."[19]

Abdullah echoed BLM cofounder Alicia Garza when she told the Associated Press in September 2015 that "Black Lives Matter as a network will not, does not, has not, ain't going to endorse any candidates." Garza maintained that, "if activists within the movement wanted to do that independently, they should feel free, and if that's what makes sense for their local conditions, that's fantastic. But as a network, that's not the work we're engaged in yet."[20] However, Garza did not write off becoming more "involved with candidates and [political] parties" and maybe even "run candidates in the future," but added, "we're not there yet."

However, after the election of Donald Trump as president in 2016 and seeing many of the reforms BLM advocated abandoned by the Trump administration, and most noticeably, the Trump administration's response to Floyd's murder, many Black Lives Matter advocates and activists did an about-face regarding elections and politics. Leading up to the 2020 election, not only did BLM conduct massive get-out-the-vote campaigns aimed at getting Black people to the polls but partnered with the Working Families Party in producing a progressive agenda that included, among other things, universal healthcare and a jobs program. BLM also created its own political action committee (PAC).

Created in October 2020, the Black Lives Matter PAC planned to endorse a "slate of candidates ahead of the general election, paying special attention to mayoral, county sheriff, and district attorney races."[21] In an interview with *Politico*, cofounder Patrisse Cullors said that BLM wanted to be able to not only speak in "get-out-the-vote language" but also to "talk directly to voters about who we think that they should be voting for and what we think they should be voting on."[22] Cullors further noted that the BLM political action committee would allow the "movement to hold elected officials accountable."[23] In addition, the PAC would push for policy change and "wield greater influence from the inside."[24] Seeing the connection between movement work and electoral politics as crucial, Cullors said that the goal of the PAC was to "put more candidates who align with Black Lives Matter's goals in office."[25]

With this in mind, we wanted to know if this shift toward electoral politics resonated with local activists and proponents of Black Lives Matter. Therefore, in this chapter, we examine the role of the BLM movement in electoral politics. In short, we wanted to know whether being a part of the BLM movement makes a person more prone to participate in the electoral political process. In asking this question and others like it, we wanted to determine if there is a direct connection between the street politics that movements engage in and the electoral politics of registration, supporting candidates, and voting. Our findings show that while many participants see a connection between the two, the debate is still far from over.

BLM, Politics, and the Electoral Process (BT: Before Trump)

In 2015, during the Democratic presidential primary campaign, many BLM activists challenged the party to prioritize their issues in the upcoming 2016 presidential election. Some would even show up at campaign events to offer criticism to the candidates. For instance, at the progressive Netroots Nation convention in July, BLM activists booed and heckled Martin O'Malley and Bernie Sanders.[26] Later at a Sanders campaign stop in Seattle, activists rushed the stage and shut down the event.[27] In Keane, New Hampshire, BLM activists, after trying to disrupt one of Hillary Clinton's campaign events, did get an audience with her afterward to share their grievances.[28] At another event, activist Ashley Williams interrupted a Clinton fundraiser in Charleston, South Carolina, to demand an apology for Clinton calling young Black men "superpredators" and the "need to bring them to heel" in the 1990s.[29]

At the time, BLM cofounder Alicia Garza supported the Seattle activists' efforts to disrupt the Sanders campaign. Garza argued that the strategy was "part of a very localized dynamic, but an important one," adding that "without being disrupted, Sanders wouldn't have released a platform on racial justice."[30] Sanders released a statement on civil rights, hired Symone Sanders, an African American woman, to be his national press secretary, and began mentioning "Black Lives Matter" on the campaign trail.[31]

In hopes of defusing criticism and affirming their position on Black Lives Matter, the Democratic Party passed a resolution at its summer meeting in August of 2015 in support of the Black Lives Matter movement. The resolution read in part:

> Therefore, BE IT RESOLVED that the DNC joins with Americans across the country in affirming "Black lives matter" and the "say her name" efforts to make visible the pain of our fellow and sister Americans as they condemn extrajudicial killings of unarmed African American men, women and children.
>   and

BE IT FURTHER RESOLVED that the DNC renews our previous calls to action and urges Congress to adopt systemic reforms
at state, local, and federal levels to prohibit law enforcement from
profiling based on race, nationality, ethnicity, or religion, to mini-
mize the transfer of excess equipment (like the military-grade vehi-
cles and weapons that were used to police peaceful civilians in the
streets of Ferguson, Missouri) to federal and state law enforcement;
and to support prevention programs that give young people alternatives to incarceration.[32]

However, if the DNC had hopes that affirming Black Lives Matter
would taper criticism aimed at the party, they were sadly mistaken.
In a response posted on their Facebook page, Black Lives Matter
took issue with the resolution. They first wanted to separate themselves from the resolution by letting readers know that the DNC's
"endorsement that Black lives matter, in no way implies an endorsement of the DNC by the Black Lives Matter Network."[33] Further,
they wanted readers to know that the DNC did not consult them
before making the resolution public. BLM reminded the public that
they have "not now, nor have we ever, endorsed or affiliated with
the Democratic Party, or with any party."[34] BLM argued that the
"Democratic Party, like the Republican Party and all political parties, have historically attempted to control or contain Black people's
efforts to liberate ourselves. True change," they continued, "requires
real struggle, and that struggle will be in the streets and led by the
people, not by a political party."[35]

In critiquing the effort from the DNC, BLM argued that a resolution would not "bring the changes"[36] that members wanted.
"Resolutions without concrete change are just business as usual,"
they maintained, and "promises are not policies."[37] The demand as far
as Black Lives Matter was concerned was "freedom for Black bodies, justice for Black lives, safety for Black communities, and rights
for Black people."[38] The movement demanded "action, not words,"
from those who would stand with them. They closed their response

by writing, "While the Black Lives Matter Network applauds political change towards making the world safer for Black life, our only endorsement goes to the protest movement we've built together with Black people nationwide—not the self-interested candidates, parties, or political machine seeking our vote."[39] A heavy disdain for electoral politics is understandable for some in light of what they see daily in their communities. They ask the question that Keeanga-Yamahtta Taylor asks in her book *From #BlackLivesMatter to Black Liberation*: "How do we explain the rise of a Black president, along with the exponential growth of the Black political class and the emergence of a small but significant Black economic elite, at the same time as the emergence of a social movement whose most well-known slogan is both a reminder and an exhortation that 'Black Lives Matter'?"[40]

According to Taylor, that answer lies in an over-dependence in the electoral process, especially regarding Black elected officials. "After forty years of this electoral strategy," writes Taylor, "Black elected officials' inability to alter the poverty, unemployment, and housing and food insecurity their Black constituents face casts significant doubt on the existing electoral system as a viable vehicle for Black liberation."[41]

According to political scientist Theodore Johnson, part of the problem is that while the gains of the "Great Society" legislation benefitted many educated and middle-class Americans, it also began to produce the "biggest intraracial income inequality of any racial or ethnic group."[42] Moreover, while the "chasm between African Americans who have and those who have not" have created "different lived experiences, which, in turn, produced different politics," Johnson argues that "these different politics, however, did not change [African American] voting choices."[43]

After Obama's two terms in office, many African Americans who went to the polls to support Obama were frustrated with the president's color-blind, "a rising tide lifts all boats approach to policy."[44] That frustration led to a belief that electoral politics was not the answer. According to Johnson, when change "did not materialize as anticipated, slight despair set in that Black citizens' disparate American experience would never be a national priority."[45] For instance, younger Black Americans "became disenchanted." Their voter participation "dropped by nearly 10 points" in Obama's reelection in 2012. Many of them began to identify as independents, and their frustration gave birth, Johnson argues, to "campus protests, rejection of respectability politics, and inspired activist movements like Black Lives Matter."[46]

But then Donald Trump became president.

BLM, Politics, and the Electoral Process (AT: After Trump)

Many pundits and political experts were shocked when Donald Trump became the forty-fifth president of the United States. Many did not believe that Trump, who broke all political conventions in his campaign, would be competitive, let alone win over the favorite, Hillary Clinton. On November 15, 2016, Black Lives Matter responded to Trump's victory by releasing a statement. The statement not only reminded supporters of the vision of the movement but also what activists and supporters needed to do next.

BLM started the statement by reminding readers that the movement was still committed to "organizing and ending all state-sanctioned violence until all Black Lives Matter."[47] They framed Trump's victory around the historical backlash that typically comes when "black people and women build power, white people become resentful. Last week," they continued, "that resentment manifested itself in the election of a white supremacist to the highest office in American government."[48] They continued,

> Donald Trump has promised more death, disenfranchisement, and deportations. We believe him. The violence he will inflict in office, and the permission he gives for others to commit violence, is just beginning to emerge. . . . But we ask ourselves—how do we reconcile our

vision for future generations' prosperity with the knowledge that more than half of white voting Americans believe a white supremacist can and should decide what's best for this country? We organize.[49]

For BLM, "civic engagement is one way to engage democracy," but they quickly reminded supporters that "our lives don't revolve around election cycles."[50] They suggest that the election of Trump proves that America needs and deserves "an elaborate strategy to eradicate both white supremacy and implicit bias towards it."[51] Further, they maintain that the country "must reckon with the anti-blackness of America's history that led to this political moment."[52] For BLM, they will continue to "operate from a place of love for our people and a deep yearning for real freedom" and "center the most marginalized and look to them for leadership."[53] While they are "committed to practicing empathy for one another in this struggle," BLM reminds readers that they "do not and will not negotiate with racists, fascists or anyone who demands we compromise our existence." They close by reminding their supporters that "the work will be harder, but the work is the same."[54]

However, while much of the work remained the same, the work was in some ways different. The election of Donald Trump forced BLM and its supporters to reexamine their strategy and some long-held beliefs. For instance, one of the first gatherings of BLM activists and supporters after the election was at the "Facing Race Conference" held in Atlanta, Georgia, November 10–12. Many attendees lamented Trump's election and wondered what it would mean for the movement dedicated to lifting and affirming Black lives. Alicia Garza called for "keeping watch on the overlapping ways oppression operates."[55] For Garza, this new reality meant that groups "already on the social and political fringes" could not afford to "retreat into enclaves to protect [their] own, but—especially at a time like this," she declared, "we have to keep a close watch on the overlapping ways in which oppression operates. We're all being attacked, and our movement needs a broader front," she noted, because, Black or Brown, "we're all going down together."[56]

Roxanne Gay called out "part-time progressives," taking white liberals to task for "allow[ing] themselves the distance of allyship."[57] As Brandon Tensley argued in his write-up of Gay's comments, the author and political commentator was through with "what she sees as the performative allyship of white progressives."[58] Tensley summarized her comments by maintaining that "white allies ought to walk the walk" and "have those prickly conversations with other white people."[59] They could also "donate money to groups looking to extinguish racism and not focus exclusively on whiteness when talking about post-election anxieties when people of color are the ones who have been feeling the stab of these anxieties most."[60] Gay also argued that the movement needed to reconsider elective office, a strategy she referred to as "infiltrating" spaces that have been historically white. "We need to think about running for office. Run for city council. Become a member of Congress. Get inside and suck it up."[61]

As the Trump administration began rolling back Obama-era recommendations on policing and police reform and instituting anti-immigration policies and Muslim bans, many activists associated with BLM started to see electoral politics—coupled with street protest and pressure—as one way to achieve movement aims. For instance, leading up to the midterms in 2018, while not necessarily supporting any particular candidate, BLM activists and supporters began pushing targeted campaigns centered around the election of district attorneys and other local offices. Activists even ran for office. One well-known activist, DeRay McKesson, ran in 2018 for mayor in his hometown of Baltimore. While unsuccessful, the campaign signaled to political operatives that activists were no longer content with just protesting in the street but were ready to engage fully with the electoral process.

BLM and the Ballot

With the shift in focus for BLM and the 2020 presidential election in full swing, we wanted to know how our participants saw electoral

politics as a part of the Black Lives Matter movement. We first asked
participants if they thought voting and engaging in the electoral
process was a part of the Black Lives Matter movement. For some
participants, the question was an easy one. For instance, Carlton[62]
answered the questions, "Yes and yes." He told us that "Black Lives
Matter affects life in all aspects. And that includes engaging the
civic process of voting." Akira[63] told us that she thought it would
be a "little bit self-hypocritical for the activists to do everything,
they're out there, and they're protesting, and they're trying to get
you to go out there and make change and a difference too, but they
don't go vote?" Jerry[64] answered the question quickly. "Yes," he told
us, because even though we are "out there in the streets, there are
still policies and procedures that we have to adhere to," and it is the
"lawmakers we have to deal with."

Bright Eyes[65] sees voting as a "parallel objective of the Black Lives
Matter movement" because, as she puts it, "we cannot change things
if we don't vote." She argues the importance of voting from history.

Hannah[66] admits that she does not know if BLM had an "actual
voting objective," but she sees BLM's role in the electoral process is to fight against "disinformation." She sees BLM as active in
fighting against laws that hinder and suppress the vote of African
Americans, saying,

> Just recently, up in Detroit, two white guys got caught making
> 180,000 phone calls to people in Detroit, Chicago, and Baltimore
> saying that if they went to vote then their records were going to
> be checked to see if they had warrants. It was just like, wait, what?
> I mean, just the sheer people doing poll watching that go down
> there to do nothing but intimidate. In Texas, they passed to where
> only one location per county was going to be allowed to drop off
> mail-in ballots. So when you have four or five million people in a
> county, you have one box. Come on. For people that don't have cars
> or transportation, or they're elderly. I think Black Lives Matter is
> pointing toward the violence and oppression that people exist or

that people experience and exist in. And so I think they're intrinsically related to politics and voter suppression is an ongoing thing.

We asked participants whether they thought involvement in the BLM movement would lead to greater electoral participation from those who participate. Many participants said yes. For instance, Cerise[67] noticed that the protests and rallies she attended featured "a lot of voter registration drives and education about the electoral process." The more she attended BLM protests, the more they reminded her to make sure you are "registered to vote," or if you were, "make sure you are still on the rolls."

Salted Plum[68] suggested that we focus on get-out-the-vote efforts, even driving people to the polls to enable them to vote. Her advocacy for this came from being a part of the movement and learning about the "high rate of incarceration of African American men" and how that is also part of voter suppression campaigns across the country.

Some participants saw voting as an extension of the movement. Amy[69] offered a poignantly felt empowered more so now than before the movement. After being part of the movement, she felt empowered to question "what it means to be a citizen?" While, for her, Black Lives Matter is a "nonpartisan" movement, the issues that she fights for and supports are very partisan. "I want everybody to vote Democrat," she told us. "I don't want people to [just to] vote. I want you to vote Democrat, okay? I'm just going to keep it real. If you're not voting Democrat, just forget it." When one of her fellow respondents asked her why, she offered this response:

> I'm a tell you why? I'm Black and female . . . so I'm going to say, "If you're not voting Democratic then you might as well not even show up, okay?" Because what's happening is these Republican governors are saying, "No, I'm not going to allow you to get an extension for the ballots. . . . Then some folks Latinx, Arab, queer, Black, women, 56 percent of white women [still vote for them], so then

let's talk about self-hate. But now it's an increasing population of people of color writ large that are voting Republican. That stems from wanting to enter into a space in which [one] can be respectable, right? Black Lives Matter supports voting, but for me, as far as my thoughts about it, vote blue.

For some participants, President Trump was reason enough to vote him and his policies out of office. Salted Plum[70] told us:

Yes, we've got to vote because I'm not shocked and horrified. I am shocked and horrified that someone like Trump exists. What really upsets me is that there were so many people who voted for this person. There are so many people who voted for this horrible, horrible, sociopathic, narcissistic, crazy shit person. He's not a politician. He thinks he's still in *The Apprentice*. He's still in a reality TV show.

While voting and participating in electoral politics are important for BLM activists, our participants lamented that many do not feel the same way. Cheryl[71] told us that she just simply does not know if many of the activists who support BLM actually participate in the electoral voting process. She puts it this way:

Do I believe that activists vote? That these activists are out here voting as much as they're championing and calling for everybody else to vote? I want to say yes. I want to say yes. I want to say yes. . . . But I don't know. And maybe it's because there are people whose posts on social media have indicated that, for all of their activism, they do not desire either one of the particular presidential candidates, or any of the choices that have been made available to them in their particular congressional district. And so they're either going to vote for somebody else, or they're going to sit it out. And the question becomes, "Then how many other people are they influencing, based on what they have already said?" Even though they are activists, and even though they are calling for equality and justice and equity and inclusion and diversity, but because they don't particularly care for the candidates who are running. So, yes and no. They do and they don't. And that's scary!

Dave[72] shared that he heard "some articulation in protest events of the notion that national politics are not nearly as important." While he did find those arguments "compelling," he also said that it would not stop him from voting in the national election.

Educating and (Re)educating

For some participants, BLM has been directly instrumental in educating people about the importance of voting. For Malcolm,[73] being part of the BLM movement was the first time that he really "embraced" the idea of voting. Kim[74] told us about some of the people in her community:

> I think in my community it's gotten a lot of people out and to care about . . . who maybe wouldn't care about voting so much. I know a lot of people feel very defeated in this area already because it's such a red state that it's hard to know whether or not your vote's going to matter. But . . . there have been minor successes that are big successes really, like Doug Jones getting into office. That's huge . . . beating Roy Moore. So knowing that our vote can count even if we feel like a minority. [As a white woman] that's a really weird thing for me to say, and I'm sorry. But I think it's [BLM] helped get people out and to care.

However, while celebrating the success of BLM to help "get people out and care," she also laments the assumption that if a person advocates for Black Lives Matter, one is "automatically assumed to be a Democrat." She told us that people assumed that if you say "human rights" or you "believe in human rights and social justice and Black

Lives Matter and people of color matter, all of a sudden, it became a political thing. I don't think saying a life matters ever was supposed to be [political]. I think this should be a bipartisan movement, and I don't understand why it's not."

Mr. Kirchfield[75] also agreed that the Black Lives Matter movement inspired many to vote. "I think that getting people out to vote, in fact, people to vote, certainly Black Lives Matter has had something to do with that." However, he added that the other main reason people were ready to vote was the actions of the Trump administration.

> I think probably more than anything else that is pushing people to get out to vote and making it easier to encourage people to vote is this present administration and the idea of not seeing him there again for another four years is motivation enough, that I don't think anything else really has to be said. It's just what we see and hear every day just motivates us to want to vote. I've never been so anxious to go cast my vote than I have this year.

For Peter,[76] it was the heightened awareness of the voter suppression campaigns nationwide. In speaking about voter suppression, he told us, "I think it's one of those things . . . directly from the poll tax at voting booths from a long time ago. It's just the language has changed, so now you can't look at it and say, 'That's explicit racism.'"

For Ashley,[77] BLM helped her to understand the issue of voter suppression and how widespread it is. She told us, "I did not realize how much voter suppression we have, especially in the South. I mean, that is awful. How are we having those issues again? Or always? That was something I was truly utterly ignorant about because I live in a rural area."

Natalie[78] told us that the Black Lives Matter movement has helped her and other white people acquire the "motivation" to become "radicalized in their political opinions" and to become "radical agents of change." She continues,

I think that BLM has woken up a lot of, especially younger white people, thirty and younger, to the importance of voting and to the connections that exist between who your political representatives are and what the reality of your lived experience and your community is. I think that before Trump, while we had Obama, I think there were a lot of white people who were very sort of comfortable in their existence, and then we got Trump into office, and we got this horrible person who was doing what he does, being very vocal about his racism, being very out in front of cameras and on Twitter about his racial dog whistles and all of that sort of stuff, and it has. . . . Yeah, it's given a lot of younger people an excuse to not be so jaded, for lack of a better way of putting that.

However, some respondents also thought that BLM should focus on educating people about the electoral process and the positions people run for during election season. For example, while Green[79] suggested that politics is and should be a big part of BLM's efforts, she also said that "there needs to be some education and some mode about what actually is happening with politics." She argues that some people don't want anything to do with politics because they simply do not understand how it works.

Pragmatic Politics

There is a belief that BLM and their supporters promote a radical politics that, in the end, cannot produce election wins. However, our research indicates that BLM supporters and activists can be and are pragmatic with the expectations. Malcolm[80] is a good example. In speaking about how BLM got him to embrace the 2018 election and take the vote seriously, he also learned that it was equally important to hold elected officials accountable and expect them to get results. For example, in speaking about politicians and the issues that he supports, he told us:

AOC [Alexandria Ocasio-Cortez], I love you; I love your ideas. But you got to do a little more than put on some red lipstick and talk [about] the Green New Deal. You got to start putting together bills that Congress can pass, that the Senate can pass, that can help not only your community, but my community. . . . Not only do we have to put them there, but now we got to hold their feet to the fire, we got to make sure that we put them there with our interests at heart, not your own.

Malcolm continued with this line of thinking on accountability. "And that's the big thing is that we have to keep moving forward. We have to take this and keep going forward with it," he told us. In speaking about what he and other supporters of BLM learned, he said,

We can't just be happy with, "Yay, Biden is in office." That's not enough. And we should have learned that lesson in 2008, 2012. Barack [Obama] wasn't enough. As great as he was, that wasn't enough. Now we've learned what happens when the Senate is ran by a conservative majority. You have what Mitch McConnell pulled out in 2016? Like, "Hey, no, we're not going to see a Supreme Court justice." And in the last three and a half years, [how many] Supreme Court justices got put on the court? Three. That's what happens.

For Malcolm, while the momentum and movement around Floyd's murder are getting people to reexamine their own politics and political beliefs, he warns that this could be another fledgling moment. "We can't let this momentum die, as we often see it do," he told us. "We had momentum after Trayvon for change, and it just kind of went away. We had momentum after Mike Brown; it kind of went away. We got this momentum. Honestly, this is the first time I feel like the ball is still rolling."

He continued:

We can't let up. We just can't back off of it. We just can't. We can relax for a day or two. We can take the week off. I'll give it that. But that following week, we got to go right back to the grind. And it shouldn't be and I'm I pray every time that it isn't another Black or Brown body killed by police that puts us back on a grind again.

Bonnie[81] sees BLM as instrumental in helping keep the momentum Malcolm speaks of going by getting involved locally in the 2022 midterm elections. She told us in 2020 that she was already working on the local district attorney race that would highlight her local elections. She also will focus on voter restoration efforts as well. She told us,

One of my major targets is voting restoration because one in five Black people in Tennessee cannot vote due to felony disenfranchisement. One in five. I have met tons of them. Because I do a voter registration drives. I wish I could tell you how many people have told me after talking to me, who have confessed to me that they cannot vote because of a felony disenfranchisement. They haven't been able to vote five years, ten years, fifteen years, thirty years—these people cannot vote. I was devastated. Beyond words, devastated. And then they explained to me what they'd been doing for the last X number of years they couldn't vote. So many of them tell me, "Well, I'm buying my house. I'm putting my children, my grandchildren, my great-grandchildren, I'm putting away money for their college fund." They can't vote so they're building for the next generation. Oh my God. And all they want to do is vote.

Black Lives Matter chapters from around the country continued to meet via Zoom during the pandemic. For Bonnie,[82] this was great because she learned so much about organizing. Bonnie told us about BLM and what those meetings taught her about organizing:

They [BLM] have hooked me up with phone banking, learning how to text message large groups of people. They have shown me how to organize a group that would make deliveries, home

deliveries of food banks. From food banks to people who can't
actually go in a car and pick up food. They have shown me how
to get a group together to deliver food to the disabled people who
don't have transportation, how to hook up into networks that
would bring produce and give it away free to homeless people.
They've taught me an awful lot, and I hope to be more valuable
in the future.

Being pragmatic also extended to some respondents sharing stories
of times when Black people thought that BLM may have pushed too
hard for change. Natalie[83] told us there was "definitely a generational
component to BLM." She continued,

> When I was working on the presidential elections earlier this year,
> I had an opportunity to speak to a lot of Black voters in the South
> who lived through the worst aspects of the civil rights movement
> and who were surprisingly, to my experience, pretty critical of BLM.
> There are a lot of older southern Black people who definitely harbor
> the opinion that pushing white people too hard or pushing society
> as a whole too hard is more detrimental than it is helpful.

She told us that this "divide" was coming up in "conversations
about Black people in the South overwhelming voted for Joe Biden,
and there was a lot of discussions among all the primary candidates
about exactly why that was."

> I think that it speaks to this sort of generational divide that exists.
> There are some older people down there in the South who definitely
> saw the worst, the most violent aspects, of that movement, and I
> think that a lot of them hold the opinion that the reason it got as
> bad as it did was because they pushed too hard. That was a really
> surprising thing for me to listen to from a lot of these people, but
> yeah, definitely there's this generational component there, for sure.

"Voting Is How You Pick Your Enemy"

Others, however, suggested that voting may be a component, but it is definitely not the only answer. Autumn[84] told us that many people her age had said to her that their vote wouldn't count and therefore did not see the need to vote. They thought the system was rigged, and since it is rigged, they wondered, "Why vote?" But she continued encouraging them because, as she told us, "We can't let [people] think things will be rigged anyway. We just have to push through and get our votes out there."

Hunter[85] told us, "If you look at the Black Lives Matter chapters across the country, obviously they're [BLM] pushing for certain candidates." He said he worries that people who believe voting is "everything" would say, "If we can just get Biden in office, everything's fixed." He suggested this would be the "absolute wrong and false" way to view it. He continued, "[Voting is] definitely a component, but not the answer; I mean, this work is going to continue. In some cases, it's going to be a harder road ahead, because some of these liberals who think electoral politics is the answer to the systemic problems."

Eric[86] put it this way:

It's absolutely an abomination to go out and march for Black Lives Matter and then don't vote because the marching brings awareness. But voting is where change is actually affected; it actually affects change. And when we get the right people in office, we can have policies that address, not just what's happening today, but what's happening in the systemic issues of racism. It's not just a matter of a police officer going out and killing a Black kid in the street, it's a matter of a system that allows that to happen, and until we switch it all up, and bring in people who are aware and who are concerned with everybody and not just making money, that's when change will really happen.

On the other hand, Malcolm[87] did not see voting as part of BLM. "I think that a social movement such as Black Lives Matter could be used as an organizational tool, a rallying tool to support different proposals and different candidates," he told us. However, he continued,

> I don't think that Black Lives Matter can be used until politicians are explicit in their racial appeals. And what that means is that candidates speak on race and racism. They don't just say, "African American voters." They talk about inequality. They talk about prejudice. They talk about racism. They talk about intolerance directly, not indirectly. They don't give small soundbites saying, "African American" or "immigrant" just to get votes. They actually have public and purposeful explicit statements, aligning themselves with marginalized groups of color. . . . Until we have candidates that are worth backing or are actually doing work for the proponents of Black lives, no. Black Lives Matter currently is not being utilized in that way. It could be, but right now, it's not.

However, Martin[88] offered a nuanced approach. Drawing from Hunter's and Eric's comments, he added:

> I think, we're basically dealing with both of those components. First, that voting is never going to be sufficient to do what we need to get done, and so one of the things that we're battling in Bloomington, Indiana, is that it is entirely liberals. There's no Republican candidates for anything. Everyone is a good white liberal and so they think, if we vote the right way, problem solved. So as Hunter says, that's actually not the case and so a lot of what we end up doing is saying, fine, go vote, but if that's where it ends, you are not helping us. The Democratic mayor who spent a quarter of a million dollars to buy a tank for the police department? What do you do, vote for the Republican instead? Like, electoral politics isn't the answer. But to Eric's point, you can make some changes and so basically, how we

ended up framing it here is, that voting is how you pick your enemy. Every politician is an enemy of Black people. There are no two ways about it. There's no other way around it.

We then asked whether you believe a person would be more committed to voting and participating in the electoral process if that person was active "on the ground" in the BLM movement. "I think that's split," Malcolm[89] told us. "I can't say yes or no because there are those who are part of the larger movement who are discouraging voting because they say it does not matter. But then, there are those who say that it's very important." However, Bright Eyes[90] could not see how someone active in BLM would also not vote. In a strongly worded response, she told us,

> I just can't imagine someone being associated with that movement and not voting. That seems asinine to me, so what are you doing? Why are you out there if you're not going to make your voice count? The vote is how we make our voices count. So, if you're out there, and you want to make your voice count, and you're not going to vote, especially where we are today, then you're wasting your time, if you're not encouraging people to vote, as opposed to discouraging people from voting. Too many people have died trying to vote. That's just the way I feel, so I can't imagine somebody else not wanting to vote. That's asinine.

However, Macy[91] pushed back on that line of thinking. She shared her frustration at how we shame people who do not vote. Further, he shared,

> Which is a problem because literally, some people can't vote, and some people don't have access to it, or it's not easily obtainable. You can't vote on Saturdays and Sundays, some people are literally having to choose between going to work and paying bills are going to vote, and that's a problem. And then you have people . . .

scrolling through Twitter really just makes me mad sometimes, because people are out here posting videos of people standing in the rain, we shouldn't be risking people's health, in a pandemic especially. Standing in the rain is already not good for your health, standing in the rain during a pandemic, even worse. . . . And so people are like glorifying it and being like, "Oh, look what these people are doing." It shouldn't exist, that shouldn't be happening. So why are we glorifying it, when we should be working to solve that situation?

Conclusion

In 2016, Black Lives Matter of Greater New York founder Hawk Newsome shocked many fellow activists when he declared, "I Ain't Voting Until Black Lives Matter."[92] He argued that Black people should "withhold their votes until a candidate adopted policies against police brutality" and promote policies such as having "independent prosecutors for police misconduct and jail time for cops who falsified reports."[93] Even though many tried to persuade him not to take the position, Newsome stuck with his convictions and did not vote.

However, in 2020, Newsome had a change of heart. In the presidential election between Biden and Trump, Newsome decided to vote and encourage other Black people to vote. He said that the difference was because he felt that politicians finally began understanding the power of the Black vote. He also highlighted that the Trump presidency was both a "curse and a gift" because it opened a lane for a more radical politics. It also helped that his sister was a candidate for office in the Bronx. He added that instead of his "I Ain't Voting" campaign, in the 2020 election, he would encourage Black to vote on the issues. "If I stand behind the issues and the person fails me," he said, "I can still sleep at night."[94]

While it may have taken BLM activist Newsome a Trump presidency to reconsider his position on voting, our findings show that
an overwhelming number of our participants saw electoral politics
as part of the BLM movement. They connected the social movement
with an understanding that while social movements are important
and necessary, so too are having elected officials sympathetic to
their cause. Many participants in BLM came to the movement with
an understanding that, as Bright Eyes[95] told us, "we cannot change
anything if we don't vote."

This understanding of the importance of the electoral process did
not come as a surprise to us. While many pundits and media blamed
activists for not showing up to the polls in the 2016 election that ushered in the Trump presidency, Jessica Byrd and others were busy creating the Electoral Justice Project in the movement for Black lives. It
aimed to figure out "how elections could be a meaningful tool for the
movement."[96] In an op-ed in the *New York Times*, Byrd wrote that "for
a new generation of Black activists, success lies in the process of making change—in politics, policies and social practices."[97] She continued:

> On the campaign trail, we hire managers and organizers who have
> experiences in common with their communities. We design field
> plans with an eye to year-round engagement rather than a month-
> long, extractive get-out-the-vote program. When we write cam-
> paign plans, we think about mutual aid and long-term governance.
> We want communications staff members who want to inspire and
> educate voters, not engage in the politics of fear. The ultimate goal
> of the ballot is to build and sustain coalitions of community mem-
> bers who can have a say in governance.[98]

"The ultimate goal of a new Black politics," Byrd writes, "is co-
governance where elected leaders are not the destination but the
vehicle to full civic participation."[99] What Byrd means by "co-gover-
nance" is more than just "representational politics." She argues that
it "requires elected leaders who are responsive to their constituents'

voices by creating transparency and real engagement."[100] In short, Byrd does not just want her candidates to win their respective races or even just to agree with the movement's demands. She argues that the movement aims to "build the collective political will to extinguish injustice and expand our ability to win in the long term."[101]

For several participants, BLM was where they became educated about politics and the issues that were important to them. For our white participants, not only being educated on issues in the public square but learning more about race and how racism functions in politics was a welcome experience. Another finding was that if people came to the movement ambivalent about voting or engaging in the electoral process, that quickly changed after being involved for a while in the movement. Many were led to become the radical change agents they felt were needed to make the changes many advocated.

Some were tepid about electoral politics but took a more pragmatic approach. Many still are not enamored with many of the candidates in elections. However, they decided to vote for the one candidate they could at least push to do the "right thing." Many quickly understood from the Trump administration that it doesn't matter how hard you move outside of politics; you need someone on the other side who would partner with you and pass legislation you support.

Lastly, our research also demonstrated something else. Before our interviews, we posited that more significant involvement in the BLM movement would lead to greater participation in the electoral process. For us, greater involvement meant attending protest events or being highly engaged in online posting of BLM events and actions. Based on our interviews with our participants, our assumptions were correct. While some did not fully trust the "just vote" message from politicians and pundits, all our participants told us that they had a greater appreciation for the electoral process since becoming active with the BLM movement. We suggest that this is important to highlight because if we want a higher voter turnout, maybe we should get people involved in social movements such as Black Lives Matter.

Chapter 6

"THIS IS LIVE? THIS IS REAL?"

Streaming a Movement

In the spring of 2021, we received a request for an interview from an Associated Press reporter. The reporter was working on a story about Derek Chauvin's impending trial, and he was hoping for some insights from us regarding the role of social media and citizen journalism in the growing movement for Black lives. "Isn't it great," he told us, "that these videos exist?" The reporter was referencing the videos of Black death that had been circulating throughout online spheres—seemingly without ceasing—for the past decade. We were not surprised by the reporter's perspective. The initial enthusiasm over social media's potential use in organizing often gives the impression that platforms like Facebook and Twitter are the unproblematic heroes of Black Lives Matter—that citizen journalism will be our savior in the fight for racial justice. Such a perspective is understandable. After all, Yarimar Bonilla and Jonathan Rosa remind us that the activism surrounding Mike Brown's murder was dramatically impacted by the relatively new technology of social media smartphone apps.[1] The very first week of the protests in

Ferguson saw approximately 3.6 million Ferguson-related tweets, as ordinary people and prominent activists documented the events on the ground in the St. Louis suburb. Within one month, the number of posts ballooned to exceed eight million. The Ferguson uprising was in many ways driven by social media.

However, social media, like all communication platforms, reflects the contexts of its design and use. Lisa Nakamura points out that early scholarly discussions of the internet tended to view online spaces as color-blind utopias.[2] After all, many scholars assumed, the lack of material presence on the internet must limit the risk of material harm. This assumption could not have been further from the truth, Nakamura writes, arguing that the internet was neither utopian in terms of universal access nor a universally egalitarian experience.[3] Of course, many rejected the assumption of digital space as egalitarian from the start. Many Black users, and other users of marginalized identities, realized well before white scholars that the lack of material presence online did little to mitigate the discrimination of the larger cultural context. As useful as social media is for spreading awareness, organizing rallies, coordinating messaging, and sharing images that might otherwise be buried by institutional powers, it can never fully overcome the differences in user experience that prompt us to interpret and feel messages differently based on our lived experiences. After our conversation with the journalist in spring 2021, he seemed to finally realize the trauma of Black death videos; for Black viewers, every video might easily have captured the death of a son, a cousin, a mother, or even themselves.

This chapter explores the shifting readings of the media landscape in the months following George Floyd's murder. Through the lens of participants' perspectives, we describe the cultural shifts in many Black Lives Matter supporters' attitudes toward social media. While early use of social media for social movements was largely met with enthusiasm, cultural shifts that include the increased preparedness of would-be citizen journalists, the rising hatred surrounding the 2020 presidential election, and the global pandemic made many participants wary of social media as a public good. In a cultural context saturated with discussions of systemic and structural racism, many began to apply these discussions to a more nuanced evaluation of social media use. And yet, this context offers few alternatives for activists wishing to recruit many people in a relatively short time period, making it seem, for many, a somewhat necessary evil. Thus, many participants maintained their social media accounts to allow them to stay in touch with rallies and actions in their area and nationally, despite their deep dread of the toxic discourses and traumatic images the platforms placed in front of their eyes.

The Ambivalent Online Sphere

In the summer of 2020, news media homed in on the meanings of protest by focusing on statistics and probabilities, emphasizing sweeping images of physical, in-person marches and rallies. Statistical analytics organization FiveThirtyEight conducted an analysis of cable and online news and found that BLM was typically covered in terms of protests, an expected framing that follows the traditional journalistic "protest paradigm." Protests were the central focus for Fox News, too, although the conservative network tended to describe demonstrations as "looting" and "riots," demonstrating what Janani Umamaheswar describes as the "public nuisance paradigm."[4] In both cases, traditional journalists tended to reduce BLM to protest actions, ignoring the many other forms of participation that supporters took in the fight for Black lives. Namely, many people also used social media to fight anti-Black racism, and often with an outsized psychological toll.

But the persistence of online discourse speaks to more than just smartphone culture—it also highlights the necessity of communal discourse within BLM and other social movements. It is not enough to acknowledge the logistical organizing function of hashtags like #BlackLivesMatter, as well as those that centered particular victims of state and other white supremacist violence. As Florini writes, a key aspect of Black online discourse surrounding the movement for Black lives is the shared and cooperative development of ideas.[5] Working together, BLM participants not only share information, but actually develop that information cooperatively. This situation, Jackson, Bailey, and Foucault Welles write, has historically been a constant component of democracy marked by "ordinary people challenging, redefining, and changing the terms of public debate."[6] This type of participation soared in the summer of 2020, with increasing numbers of participants across races coming together to participate in a variety of BLM-focused discourses.

Social media is integral to the initial and continuing spread of the movement for Black lives. While that's worth celebrating, it is also more complicated that it first appears. In her groundbreaking ethnographic study of professional content moderators, Sarah T. Roberts points out that online content, as most everyday users understand it, is enabled through personal trauma.[7] Since the early days of the internet, Roberts notes, community members carved out rules of engagement in ways that mimic processes of offline socialization. Yet, the larger these communities grow, the more room there is for disagreement on the particular cost-benefit analysis of sharing particular content.

We include this analysis because much of the literature on BLM's social media component takes a celebratory bent. Journalists and other popular press authors tend to applaud the ways online platforms allowed for the proliferation of race-based critical thinking, information sharing, and the community-based process of pulling back the curtain on centuries of anti-Black violence formerly buried by white supremacist documentation systems. And yet, as we wrote previously, the centrality of social media to BLM is not without its drawbacks, including surveillance by employers, family and friends, and even the government.[8] In the years since we discussed the issue of self-censorship in BLM communities, an even more sinister issue has arisen: as more and more non-Black supporters join the movement for Black lives, less attention is given to rules of online engagement that would center the mental health of Black participants. Graphic, traumatic images and videos regularly "go viral" in online spaces, justified by arguments about spreading awareness and associated, often, with the traditional journalistic idea of "newsworthiness." This situation exemplifies Andre Brock's important assertion that, "while the Internet doesn't offer the same physical potential for discrimination and racist violence against Black folk, there is still a pressing need for the curation of digital and online resources for Black folk seeking information and 'safe spaces.'"[9] As an information platform designed and implemented within a larger social system structured by white supremacy, online discourse often flows toward the conservative center, with tension building between Black online resistance and white digital reclamation.

Media—in terms of social media, online content, and traditional journalism—deserve a second look in the context of post-Floyd BLM. In this chapter, we trace the roles of various media platforms and participant approaches in the summer of 2020, from participant concerns about traditional journalism and media framing through to the crucial but under-discussed issue of Black death and the continual demand that Black people be continually subjected to trauma in online spaces in exchange for consciousness-raising, even when the issues being made more aware have been prominent in Black organizers' agendas for decades.

While social media consists of a relatively new set of platforms, the idea of taking alternative ideas to alternative discursive spaces is a traditional tenet of social movement activism. Jackson, Bailey, and Foucault Welles make this point eloquently. Drawing a connection between hashtag activism and the revolutionary work of Ida B. Wells, they write that "the alternative networks of debate created by marginalized members of the public . . . have always played the important role of highlighting and legitimizing the experiences of those on the margins even as they push for integration and change in mainstream spaces."[10] This description aptly summarizes social media's role in Black Lives Matter. As we have written elsewhere, Black Lives Matter began as a small, personal call for justice—shared first in a moment of despair by Garza.[11] From there, the hashtag not only exploded in activist spaces and in "Black cyber culture,"[12] but it also made its way into mainstream newsrooms.

Disconnected

While this transition marks a victory for activist efforts at gaining attention and spreading awareness, movements from counterpublic into mainstream consciousness are always ambivalent. We have written about this elsewhere, noting that white journalism has always been at odds with movements for civil rights.[13] Even in the era of Black Lives Matter, mainstream journalists have regularly written in tacit support of violence against Black lives by painting Black men and boys as criminals, even in the same publications that craft sympathetic headlines for white mass murderers.[14] With this history in mind, many Black Lives Matter supporters wisely approached news media coverage with skepticism. For example, Cerise[15] compared her experience with a local protest to the coverage of that same protest in the news:

> [W]hat I find very disheartening in many ways is the way that traditional "media" has covered some of the protests and rallies . . . it's over-coverage of ones where there may be violence, particularly property violence, but peaceful ones don't get the same media attention. . . . So, I think there's much more awareness that this go around of people with their camera phones and recording everything . . . [to compare with] the press footage being shown, which wasn't even a protest. It looked more like war footage. I'm like, "That's not even *this* protest."

In Cerise's case, the footage she saw on the news media so dramatically differed from what she saw in person that she had lost trust in traditional media.

This was Maria's[16] experience as well. Speaking with others in her group, she urged activists to take a systemic viewpoint on news coverage. "Let's talk about who is directing that," she said. "So the newsrooms are very white. The executives are all white. And so their description comes from their perspective. And so they're relaying the information as they understand it." Maria's analysis poignantly identifies the structural causes for current news misinformation, and it also stretches back to the time of Ida B. Wells reporting. When news media are run by white people, as is the case for 89 percent of newsrooms, the content released is not likely to be able to grapple with the lived realities of Black people.[17] Recalling an interview she had given to a local news outlet, Maria continued with righteous frustration, noting, "Here I am again giving perspective to the people who I should punch in the throat, but you have to understand your enemy, you have to understand the people who wouldn't care if you died. You have to understand them so that . . . you can't reach them if you don't understand them, if you don't know where they're coming from." For Maria, a systemic analysis of news media did not lead to an across-the-board rejection of the news or of journalists in general. Rather, her analysis led her to proceed with caution when discussing events with journalists. She recognized that not all journalists are willing or able to meld their white perspective on objectivity with the rhetoric surrounding social movements.

Often perspectives like these pressed participants toward social media. Many acknowledged that news media played an important role in spreading the word about BLM—as in Jerrica's[18] account of hearing BLM on the news, then turning to social media for further research. But overall, most supporters we interviewed saw social media and alternative news media as a much more reliable source for information about the movement. Cole[19] pointed out that many police shootings go unacknowledged by "CNN and Fox News and MSNBC." For Cole, it was a point of pride that his local BLM chapter had worked hard to bring attention to a local Latino man who had been murdered by police. He described his rallying call to his chapter as reminding members to "make sure that not only are we Black Lives Matter for the big things, we're Black Lives Matter for" our own city. Much of this type of effort, in Cole's case and others, occurred through social media outlets as well as in-person protests.

Most of our participants used social media to follow local happenings, at least to some extent. Hunter[20] pointed out that local government and news outlets will often "uplift certain people that do not seem to represent the movement and aren't doing the work." His recommendation for activists or those interested in joining activist circles was to find out "who those activists and organizers that are doing it" and to follow "their social media pages or their official group pages." However, Hunter cautioned, simply Googling protests or local social movements could set people on the wrong track. In his community, searching for protests in the search engine would bring up "a pattern of certain critical thinking abilities [but leave open questions of] what are they actually doing? Who are they? Are they a prop?" This type of ambivalence characterized our conversations around social media. Virginia[21] told us, "as much as I get irritated with Facebook and Twitter and all the social media, I think those platforms have opened the door for all kinds of information— a lot of which nobody wants to hear, but a whole lot is extremely valuable." She not only spoke to her annoyance with the platforms, but also highlighted the tensions that can arise on social media platforms when activists share news and perspectives related to the movement. These ideas, after all, are part of a movement because they are oppositional to the status quo. Thus, while social media may be a new way of communicating these ideas, BLM's online messages are not immune to the backlash culture that has met every social movement across history.

Writing of the social media channels for social movement organizing, Jackson, Bailey, and Foucault Welles write that "using relatively inexpensive equipment, and with limited technical knowledge, ordinary people can engage in public speech and actions without mediation by the mainstream media or other traditional sources of power."[22] This is true to the extent that social media posting does not require one to have editorial power within a newsroom or the ability to call a massively followed press conference on a moment's notice. However, as those we spoke to point out, the use of social media for organizing purposes is imperfect at best. In conversation with our participants' analyses, Jackson, Bailey, and Foucault Welles raise a crucial question: to what extent are the social media actions of activists able to function outside the mediating forces of traditional power structures? Certainly individual users escape some of the traditional power traps of broadcast and cable news programming, but the ambivalence our participants demonstrated blur the lines between power structures in a traditional sense, and the ways those structures seep through platforms like Google, social media, and other activist organizing spaces.

Educate Yourself

For those whose support and activism took them into online spaces, often with a noticeable psychological toll, the summer of 2020 marked a focus on antiracist education. "Educate yourself" became a mantra in online spheres, which were particularly central given the spikes in COVID-19 infections and the resulting quarantines of this time period. Calling on white people to educate themselves about racism predates the summer of 2020, but it took on a new meaning as an unprecedented number of new supporters scrambled to join a conversation that they had ignored or overlooked for decades. During this time, articles like *Time*'s "Books to Read to Educate Yourself" filled the digital sphere.[23] Resource lists like *USA Today*'s "100 Resources to Take Action Against Racism" spread through social media.[24] And mainstream publications which had previously published under a mantra of color-blindness suddenly produced suggestions for readers interested in learning about "how to help."[25] In all, the moment centered the need for white people to figure things out for themselves—or with the help of other white people. Well-meaning white people, in contrast to those who explicitly supported violence against protesters, were both invited to join the fight for Black lives and asked to avoid getting in the way of movement work. Realizing that many white people needed to begin that journey from the ground up, online culture took seriously the call to circulate educational resources among new BLM adherents.

The call to "educate yourself" aligns neatly with two standard motivations for social media use: learning new things and rallying others toward a cause. A Pew study conducted during the summer of 2020 showed that, for Black social media users in particular, social media represented an outlet for politically engaging expression.[26] Seventy percent of users polled noted not only that they had posted a photo or hashtag in support of the movement for Black lives, but also that they believed they might change people's minds about racial injustice by posting to social media. The rate of agreement for white users was slightly lower, at around half of the people surveyed. This conversation was particularly salient at the moment of the Pew study, which coincided with our conversations. During this time period, as more and more non-Black supporters were joining BLM, a dominant charge was for white people to educate themselves about the history of race in the US. The Ad Council, for example, ran an article entitled "Anti-Racism Resources to Help Educate Yourself,"[4] *Time* offered a reading list for new movement participants, and numerous libraries, literary presses, and educational institutions offered antiracist reading lists.

Many saw social media as a natural extension of this push to educate movement novices. Ashley[27] reported sharing a reading list she had seen posted by a professor she admired, and Jerrica[28] noted that she "consistently post(s) things on social media . . . showing what being an antiracist means and how we need to have those discussions and work with people more. Just showing people, you may not feel like you're a racist, and I'm not saying that you are one, but by reading these things, and learning more about it, you can open your eyes and become more understanding of other people's lives that you may not have known about." Ashley's and Jerrica's comments speak to the growing attention to scholarship on race, and particularly the wave of interest in Ibram X. Kendi's[29] work on antiracism and the history of race in the US as well as books by other authors like Ijeoma Oluo[30] and Robin DiAngelo.[31] It is worth noting that, in this case, social media was being used not as an alternative to traditional publishing mechanisms, but rather as a way to turn others back to print books distributed through traditional platforms. Actions such as these, which Hunter[32] described as "trying to re-educate myself out of racism," speak to an impulse to address the system of white supremacy that undergirds anti-Black police violence—and that extends into the cultural and psychological frameworks of activists as well as the general population.

Many noted that they were cognizant of those who used articles shared on social media, keeping their audience and purpose in mind. Macy[33] tried to keep her posts simple and accessible, noting, "I try to make sure the articles I'm sharing are not overloaded with academia, and just language that people are not going to understand. And there's a lot of really good, like, Instagram accounts, they'll share very basic images, where it's very clear on what they are saying, and it's not all of these big words that people don't know. I have a master's degree and half the time I'm like, 'What are you saying?'" Autumn[34] told us that she is always thinking about where the information she shares might take readers. She noted, "[I] give them the information of the Black Lives Matter movement and why supporting and why they should support it. And then it's up to them to follow through on whether they want to support the movement as well."

However, Autumn acknowledged that many of the people she interacts with online are not initially supportive of the movement for one reason or another. This resistance to the movement can come from a variety of previous experiences, as we wrote about in our previous book. This was clear in responses from participants from older generations, including Cheryl,[35] who told us that her "target audience usually has to do with people who are older, and are trying to understand the dynamics of the Black Lives [Matter] movement . . . they're not always engaged on social media." Cheryl's typical readers often compared BLM with the midcentury civil rights movement, a trend that can create generational- and class-based rifts in support from contemporary movement goals. As we discussed in chapter 3, differences in generation, class, and region naturally create different perspectives among Black people in terms of more controversial messaging such as "defund the police," a slogan and policy initiative that was popular during the summer of 2020.[36] And yet, Cheryl found social media a useful tool, even if her primary readers were not typically on social media, and even though many disagreed with some of the movement's goals and messages. "I'm just out there talking about it," she said.

The people we interviewed offered ample evidence that "just . . . talking about it" was a useful tool in raising awareness, particularly when posts and comments led to further research. Coming to the movement through Colin Kaepernick's activism, Cole[37] told us that he would watch the now-former NFL player talk about issues of police violence and think to himself, "'What is he seeing that I'm not?' . . . When he would talk about statistics and data and he would [name the source], I'd write down really quick what that thing was from, and then go to it and pull up that stat." For Cole, this process became a series of educational tasks that felt like "another thread, another rabbit hole," in a way that helped him to learn more about issues of anti-Black violence from police. Peter,[38] too, noted that social media posts often prompted him to do more research. He told us, "I tend to want to dive a little bit more into listening to the news, listening to podcasts about politics or something, trying to figure out what can be done and what might be done." The responses of Cole and Peter reflect a growing awareness that all opinions, even those grounded in statistics, are not equal. Many supporters spoke with an awareness that information from traditional news outlets was not always reliable, and that these pieces of information could be twisted and slanted in misleading ways. Lakelyn's[39] comment was telling in this instance, as she believed in "sharing things on social media, but with a critical and intentional mindset . . . and not just blindly sharing things on social media, but making sure the resources are beneficial, and making sure what I'm posting is educational and that I follow [it] myself."

And yet, many raised questions of whether using social media to prompt further research and inward self-reflection was politically powerful or even useful at all. As sociologist Crystal Fleming noted, the centuries-long prominence of anti-Black violence "is not something that an antiracist reading group will fix."[40] While Fleming was supportive of white self-reflection, she noted that readers would need to act on their newfound education. Activists were ready to prompt this type of investment from the flood of newly interested would-be allies.

Social Ambivalence

Since the early days of the internet, popular sentiment has positioned online spaces as pro-Democratic hubs where those without a traditional speaking platform can share their ideas and experiences. Though such assumptions have long been discarded by digital media scholars, the idea that social media offers marginalized populations (mostly) unfettered access to a public platform lingers for many in the public and scholarly imaginary. And yet, many of our participants felt ambivalent about social media, noting that they regularly experienced fatigue, anger, and other disturbances to their mental health as a direct result of their social media use. In our previous book, we noted that many movement participants use self-censorship to protect themselves from online hate, even as they continually used private and direct messages in attempt to change others' minds.[41] Activists in the summer of 2020 likewise found themselves struggling to maintain boundaries against hateful responses, but with an increased sense of intentionality and self-awareness.

A relatively new movement participant, Christy[42] told us that she is new to Facebook and has struggled with the responses of her peers to her posts. Since, like many who joined the movement following Floyd's murder, she has only been involved in BLM for a short time, her feed is still full of many who do not sympathize with the movement for Black lives. She told us that she tries to "forward and post and add things, and I do get hate back, but I'm trying to better accept that that's someone else's hate. That's not a reflection of me." Her attitude to activism in the social media sense was that "all we can do is plant the seed and keep moving. It may not be watered now, but it may be down the line a little bit. All we could do is share what we can, and if they're not ready for it, they're not ready for it." She shared that she had initially self-censored, saying to herself, "Well, I'm not going to [post things like that] again," but ultimately decided that educating others was more important than her own peace. "Just because they're still full of hate doesn't mean that I'm wrong or the message is wrong," she concluded.

While many participants felt called to educate others through social media, others often felt drained and helpless. In one exchange, Cheryl[43] and Jennifer[44] spoke about educating others through the things they shared on social media. Akira[45] was more ambivalent: "Cheryl and Jennifer stated they use it as a tool to educate, but I also feel like, especially now, it's also a tool that we can use for misdirection. Especially from the other side. And it's really hard trying to—like, yeah, I get it's used as a tool for education and things like that, and it can be good for that; but the other side has access to that too." In response, Cheryl asked whether Akira felt that the online rhetoric calling BLM a "terrorist organization" made her feel as though the hateful responses "change the narrative of what the movement is all about," and Akira confirmed this reading. She ultimately felt that social media "serves, it's good, but the fact that the other side has access to it, too, and they can do just as much damage as we do to educate, it's kind of hard to like social media as the go-to for" antiracist education. In our conversations with participants surrounding social media, we noticed a shift in tone compared to those in our 2016 focus groups. Many felt more optimistic in the earlier years of BLM, believing that social media might be a helpful way to educate others and share the message of the organization. However, as social media's problems have become more commonly discussed in the public sphere, these messages have dampened the spirits of some who might use these platforms to spread awareness and nurture the organization. As Katlyn[46] said, "I find [it] utterly exhausting."

Still, those we spoke with were resourceful, and many had taken a hardline approach to their own mental health self-care. Just as Cheryl and Akira had spoken about the disinformation that labeled BLM a "terrorist organization," other participants shared similar conversations. Maria's[47] response was to report those who shared things like this. In these months just before Twitter and Facebook began to mark incorrect information and "fake news," Maria told us that reporting bogus posts was "one of my favorite things. I roll through Twitter doing that." Cole[48] was similarly worried about misinformation and disinformation, but he approached his role as a moderator for his local BLM chapter differently. As a condition of entering the group, he required that potential members write about their understanding of BLM. For Cole, those entering with the aim of being combative and fighting against one another was only a drag on the mental health of those in the group. He told us, "I literally have two questions to get into the group, and one of them is like, 'What is Black Lives Matter to you?' . . . I don't want combative terms [such as 'fighting' or 'ACAB,' meaning 'All Cops Are Bastards']. But if it is like standing with my Black and Brown brothers as an ally, to learn, to take part in, then I'm a little more open to it." For Cole, it was important to keep his group on target in terms of messaging as a way to ensure that the group functioned as an organized branch of a larger social movement. Limiting the membership of his BLM group allowed him to maintain control over the types of posts he saw as well as the volume of posts that required later moderation. In short, by liberally blocking, reporting, and rejecting, many activists felt more equipped to protect their own stamina and feelings of self-efficacy.

This strategy of limiting social media use—and limiting those whose posts are visible on an activist's social media feed—was widely referenced as a form of self-care. Finding himself totally overwhelmed, Charles[49] noted that he had to refrain from social media and the internet in general for "a string of years." While he currently uses social media as a tool for resistance, he noted that too much time online can leave a person "constantly angry, constantly hurt, constantly in fear, and that's like stress levels I could not tolerate for much longer." This phrasing speaks to a slew of articles released during the height of summer 2020's activist surge: articles that urged social media users to avoid sharing videos of Black death, and that encouraged Black people to consider how social media might be impacting their mental health.[50] And yet, as Balquiss[51] noted, staying away from social media was not nearly enough in a context where anti-Black violence was a constant topic of conversation. They noted, "a lot of times [social media detox] is not enough, and I end up in this little spiral of [asking], 'Why isn't the world a good place?'"

By the summer of 2020, it had become very clear that the online space was helpful for organizing rallies and raising awareness about issues of anti-Black violence. It was also clear that spaces of social movement organizing were not immune to infiltration and the massive disinformation attacks that had been launched at BLM in earlier years.[52] For many protesters, emotions were already heightened, and any additional stress from online encounters with strangers was a bridge too far, especially when they were well aware that many people who actively resisted their messaging were "trolls," as Maria[53] called them. And yet, even liberal patterns of blocking, muting, and reporting could not fully protect activists from the potential traumas of the social media environment.

Sharing Black Death

For many observers, including the journalist whose story opened this chapter, videos of police brutality against Black people have become a new form of protest journalism. Authors including Allissa V. Richardson and Kia Gregory have compared the documentation and circulation of these videos to Ida B. Wells's transformative journalism on lynching.[54] Considered in this light, videos shared on social media are a version of "Southern Horrors: Lynch Law in All Its Phases," updated for modern eyes. Certainly these videos have a similar cultural impact as Wells's revolutionary work. In the summer of 2020, in particular, it is difficult to imagine the BLM rallying cry rising to such prominence absent the video of George Floyd's public murder. But alongside the key political effect of police brutality videos is a disturbing side effect: repeated trauma. The prevalence of these videos can seem like a never-ending onslaught of violence that, particularly for Black viewers, is "now stuck in your head forever." To quote psychological Monnica Williams, "You carry that horror around with you."[55]

Williams's perspective is one that many felt deeply. Jennifer[56] stated this simply: "It felt like every day we were looking up and a video was emerging. And we were being re-traumatized with this experience of feeling almost like we're being hunted." Where Jennifer spoke about the experience specifically in terms of Black lives being "devalued," Maria[57] discussed the effect as dehumanizing. She shared that she refuses to watch these videos and does not understand why others share them. She told us, "I don't think people understand how traumatizing that is for people to see a person who looks like them have their life negligently or willfully erased and understand that there likely will be no consequence for it. That's almost harder, the knowledge that there will be no consequence is almost harder than the death itself because if they are not human and they look like you, then *you* are not human and it can happen to *you*." The trauma of dehumanization was apparent to those white participants who had

seen the fallout in their everyday lives. Katlyn[58] noted that she will
not watch the videos because she regularly "deal[s] with the fallout.
I take care of my people that are crying, my Facebook family and
friends that are screaming in agony. I don't have to see [the video]"
to call for justice. Katlyn went on to compare these videos to 9/11,
noting that people who lived through that experience, "don't need
to see the footage of the planes."

Some supporters actively asked that the videos not be shared
with them. Balquiss[59] had filtered their Instagram followers such
that they only followed those who "know not to post those types
of videos without trigger warnings." This process mirrors the
decision of many participants to filter their friends lists to avoid
arguments with those who did not see them as fully human. But
Balquiss goes on to point out another key issue in the sharing
of Black death videos: as an extra measure of protection against
traumatizing videos, they chose to change their Twitter settings
so that videos do not autoplay. This prevented them from seeing
videos they did not want to see, but did little to stop others from
sharing the videos in the first place. Cerise[60] took a more hands-
on approach, not only posting a plea for people to "stop sending
me stuff like that," but even writing a newsletter entry about the
harms of sharing traumatizing content online. Cerise noted that
many of her friends, acquaintances, and coworkers send terrible
imagery directly to her inbox. "It was from both people who were
also Black but then from my white friends and allies who were trying to learn more," she said. In addition to videos of Black death,
Cerise told us that many people shared images and videos of "the
George Floyd challenge," in which white people posed in reenact-
ments of the man's murder and posted the images online. She said,
"I was having nightmares, and then on top of that, people were
saying, 'What do you think of this George Floyd challenge? Don't
you think this is racist?' 'Yes. Why are you sending me this?' So, I
actually had to put a post out there like, 'Look, stop sending me
racist videos and videos of people literally dying to ask me what

I think. I think it's terrible. I think they're racist, videos of people dying or of people dying, showing how racist society still is.'"

Cerise's point was underscored by many of the white participants we spoke with who felt obligated to watch these videos, even feeling called to share them in hopes of convincing those on their friends lists who are not supporters of BLM. Ashley,[61] a forty-three-year-old white woman, told us that she does not like to see the same images or videos repeatedly, but that she does feel that she should not avoid them. She told us she will "usually watch or see pictures of it, and then I just immediately put it away after." However, she went on to say, "I think it is important for people to see that in a sense, because that's how jarring it is in real life. But I do think it's a certain group of people who need to really actively watch it, and I think those are the people that don't come into contact with it." The ambivalence in Ashley's[62] response is indicative of many white supporters who recognize both the rhetorical power of this imagery and the human suffering and death included. Katlyn[63] similarly noted that, while it is important to discuss issues of police brutality and murder, she "personally can't share those types of things."

Unlike Ashley, Katlyn explicitly noted that she refrains from recirculating the images "because I know that I have people of color and Black people who follow me, and I know it's a completely different level of trauma to see those types of things." Across the white participants we spoke with, there was a sense of ambivalence. Most did not want to watch the videos themselves, and most recognized the trauma these images can do to Black viewers, as well as to their own personal psyche. But many still clung to the importance of the videos, often feeling compelled to watch them, perhaps in hopes of narrowing the gap between their own lived experiences and those at the heart of BLM. Most white supporters acknowledged the limitations for white people in terms of understanding how Black people might experience images differently from themselves. Referencing her self-reflexivity in social media posts, Zoe[64] noted that "as a white woman, I'm not experiencing that oppression every day, and so [it's important to make self-reflection] an everyday practice to think about what I could be doing, and what I'm doing, and is it harmful." For many white people, thinking about whether to share these videos required energy, but, of course, that energy is incomparable to the energy of processing grief, trauma, and the experience of watching someone who looks like you and your family be gunned down in the street.

The fact that these videos continued to be shared speaks to a cultural ambivalence surrounding them. As common as it was for those we interviewed to explicitly mention the trauma of watching Black death, many also recognized that there is a more sinister component of this type of shared imagery. Seeming hesitant to even articulate the idea, Balquiss[65] told us, "I don't want to have to watch a Black person suffer for almost," she paused, "entertainment." Truly, the circulation of videos of Black death alongside social media's more typical cat videos and cooking demonstrations creates a disturbing situation that some have called "trauma porn."[66] Drawing a comparison to the imagery that helped to galvanize the midcentury civil rights movements, Atlanta lawyer Destiny Singh told CNN, "These videos and mass circulation of videos and photos of Black and Brown bodies being slain in the streets, have existed since the slaying of Emmett Till. So when people say we're doing this to raise awareness, what are we raising awareness about?" Balquiss[67] shared this sentiment, going on to say, "I already feel the pity. I don't need to watch it to feel the empathy for their family and just knowing that this is wrong and something needs to change." Speaking in a different group interview, Maria[68] agreed. She compared her refusal to watch these videos to another participant whose mother refused to watch the movie *Selma*, noting, "She doesn't need to [watch it], she lived it, right? I don't need to traumatize myself in that way." These responses raise a question about the efficacy of sharing the videos at all in a context that has already gathered more than adequate evidence of police violence against Black people.

Conclusion

Conversations about social justice and politics have been replete with discussions of "the media" for decades. Often this ambiguous entity is blamed for being too conservative or too liberal, depending upon the slant of the commentator. Or, in the era of social media, it is generally positioned as a boogeyman, responsible for a host of antisocial tendencies and a variety of mental health symptoms. While this conversation of media and culture is beyond the scope of this book, it does provide important context on the ways mediated communication forms converge in the era of BLM. On one hand, according to a Pew poll conducted in the fall of 2020, nearly one quarter of social media users reported changing their stance on "a political or social issue" based on something they saw online.[69] Add to this the frequent use of social media and other online platforms as tools for organizing rallies and demonstrations, and it becomes clear that "the media" has beneficial uses for social movements like BLM.

On the other hand, the importance of social media—as an educational tool, organizing platform, and hub for conversations surrounding everything from a particular protest event to general understanding of race in the US—meant that participants often felt overwhelmed and exhausted by their feeds. In the summer of 2020, social media became more than just a tool for those invested in social change. It became a responsibility. That that responsibility carried with it a level of screen fatigue with clear psychological, emotional, and even physical detriments. Black activists, in particular, experienced a very real trauma from watching videos of Black death, which seemed to circulate endlessly in May and June of 2020. Many of these videos circulated not only through individual users, but through the powerful influence of cable news outlets. Here, television media meets social media in a conglomeration of messaging that can feel difficult to avoid.

While the Associated Press reporter whom Andre spoke with was not able to—or chose not to—place his story, the anecdote is instructive. Media not only shapes everyday viewers' understanding of social movements; movements also shape media's functions. The reporter, who we believe had the best intentions, simply had not been trained in ethical social movement reporting. He was unaware that police reports of officer-involved shootings are often skewed in favor of the officer—if not completely falsified.[70] And he had not been pushed to immerse himself in the communities he wrote about. Put bluntly, he'd been trained in media's whiteness. Still, he reached out to us and was willing to listen. We received several such calls from journalists who wanted to get the story right, a striking departure from the norms of reporting in the early days of BLM. This situation speaks to the importance of mediated communication, and the necessity for social movements to talk back to journalists, pushing for accountability from those who report the stories of violence as much as those who commit the violence in the first place. Through this work, we can begin to develop just institutions that support the basic contentions of social movements like BLM—not as a result of "the media's" slant, but through its commitment to truth.

CONCLUSION

On April 20, 2021, a jury found Derek Chauvin guilty of unintentional second-degree murder, third-degree murder, and second-degree manslaughter.[1] Two months later, a judge sentenced him to twenty-two and a half years in prison.[2] Chauvin accepted a plea deal in May 2022, admitting that he violated Floyd's civil rights. The judge in the case, Paul A. Magnuson, sentenced Chauvin to twenty years in federal prison.[3]

Ten weeks before the official record of Chauvin's plea, a federal grand jury convicted former police officers Tou Thao, J. Alexander Kueng, and Thomas Lane for violating Floyd's civil rights.[4] Prosecutors argued that officers deprived Floyd of medical care, and while Chauvin placed his knee on Floyd's neck for over nine minutes, "Kueng knelt on Floyd's back, Lane held his legs and Thao kept bystanders back."[5] In this case, Magnuson, the judge that would later sentence Chauvin, sentenced Kueng to three years, Thao to three and a half years, and Lane to two and a half years in prison.[6] Lane would also plead guilty to the state charge of aiding and abetting second-degree manslaughter, while the state case for Thao and Kueng was delayed until January 2023.[7]

Despite the video seen around the world of George Floyd's murder at the hands (and knee) of Derek Chauvin—and despite the mountain of evidence, much of it from members of the Milwaukee police department who testified against their former fellow officer—guilty verdicts were far from expected. Many activists and supporters of Black Lives Matter had been down this road before. Sometimes they waited and hoped for justice, only to hear "not guilty." Others, the fight was derailed by a grand jury before it could even come to court. Before reading Chauvin's verdict, Philonise Floyd, the brother of George Floyd, prayed in the courtroom that the jury would find him guilty. He told a reporter, "As an African American man, we usually never get justice."[8]

Even at the height of BLM's popularity, some warned us not to get so caught up in the euphoria that was taking place. While some believed that the 2020 uprising, with its multiracial, multiethnic makeup and record number of protesters, signaled a coming change, many others braced for what Martin Luther King called the "white backlash."[9] Just weeks after Floyd's murder, Reggie Jackson published an op-ed in the *Milwaukee Independent* titled "The Inevitability of a White Backlash to the George Floyd Protests." He noted that it was "great that more whites are 'woke' but we've seen this before." After Dr. King's 1968 assassination, polls showed drastic shifts in white attitudes about race. The civil unrest and images of burning cities and angry Black people led significantly more whites to dismiss the efforts of civil rights leaders and groups. As is common when Black Americans make even a fraction of progress in this country, whites demonstrated their unhappiness by actively fighting to reverse those gains.[10]

Kali Holloway, writing for *The Nation*, echoed Jackson's sentiments. Citing an August 2020 NPR/Ipsos poll, Holloway lamented that it only took "two months for white Americans' support of Black Lives Matter—which climbed to an unprecedented peak in June, to tumble back toward pre-protest levels":

> It's always true that most white folks are unbothered and unmoved by anti-Black discrimination and violence; the steadfast endurance of American institutional racism proves that. It is also clear from history that white antiracism has always had a dangerously short

shelf life. Ignore the barrels of digital ink spilled lately about white people's new willingness to reckon with structural racism. When the pendulum swings toward Black equality and full citizenship, white supremacy mounts a counteroffensive.[11]

As time went on, those warnings proved right. First, overall Black Lives Matter support plummeted. Writing one year after Floyd's murder, Nathalie Baptiste, citing polling data from the *New York Times*, suggested that the surge in support for Black Lives Matter was in response to the "shocking nature of George Floyd's death" and not an "actual embrace of the Black Lives Matter Movement."[12] She maintained that this all "adds up to what appears to be yet another example of the inevitable backlash that occurs after a broad movement for racial justice takes place. It's a cycle that repeats itself throughout American history."[13]

Holloway, the journalist who warned of a white "counteroffensive" just months after Floyd's murder, continued to cover the state of the "promised racial reckoning."[14] As it turns out, her previous predictions were spot on.

Black demands for full citizenship and equality are being treated as entitlement, calls for white racial accountability redefined as white persecution, and antiracism falsely construed as anti-whiteness. To reestablish unchallenged white dominance, a movement of white resistance, or anti-antiracism, is working tirelessly to blot out what it sees as a problematic presence—purging Black folks from democracy by stripping voting rights, erasing Black struggle from history by banning the teaching of slavery and its legacy, and prohibiting protest that threatens the white supremacist status quo.

In the end, she concluded that the summer of 2020 was a "white lie."

After Trump's presidential defeat, conservatives in states such as Georgia passed new laws that, in effect if not intention, nullified Black votes. The John Lewis Voting Rights Act failed in the

Senate, offering more support for Holloway and others' predictions. Politicians moved to ban Critical Race Theory from schools. Laws were introduced to restrict protest. The George Floyd Police Reform Bill failed. The list unrolled endlessly, making the outpouring of love and concern over Floyd's murder a distant memory.

At the same time, BLM saw a different type of backlash, one that perhaps was unexpected by many prescient reporters, thinkers, and other public figures. The Black Lives Matter Global Network Foundation (BLMGNF), the entity "widely seen as a steward of the Black Lives Matter Movement," saw an infusion of donations after Floyd's murder.[15] Estimated at ninety million dollars, the influx of donations caused disharmony among local chapter activists as many called for financial transparency from the organization. These local activists lamented that, since 2013, most had received nothing from the central movement. For example, Mike Brown Sr., whose son was killed by former Ferguson police officer Darren Wilson, wondered aloud, "Why hasn't my family's foundation received any assistance from the movement?"[16] Samaria Rice, the mother of twelve-year-old Tamir Rice, who police shot and killed on a playground, and Lisa Sampson, the mother of Richard Risher, who police shot and killed in Los Angeles, said, "We don't want or need y'all parading in the streets accumulating donations, platforms, movie deals, et cetera, off the death of our loved ones, while the families and communities are left clueless and broken."[17] April Goggans, an organizer for BLM DC, spoke for many organizers when she said in an interview, "We are BLM. We built this, each one of us."[18]

In responding to the calls for transparency, BLM now has a page dedicated to their website titled "BLM Transparency Center."[19] As the title suggests, BLM aims to be more open, transparent, and accountable moving forward. Understanding that the movement is going down a path never charted before, they write, "We understand our responsibility, and we are here to continue intentionally building trust so we can forge a path that sustains Black people for generations."[20] They continue, "We will continue to unveil new initiatives to increase transparency and accountability and will continue to disrupt what philanthropy looks like in service of Black people. BLMGNF is working diligently to increase operations transparency, including tightening compliance operations and growing the board to help steer the organization to its next evolution."[21] The site includes the latest updates, posted 990 form, its board of directors listing, and a Frequently Asked Questions section.

One of these questions regards the purchase of "Creator's House." In an article published in the *Intelligencer* by Sean Campbell, he details the purchase of the house—more the "6500 square feet with more than a half dozen bathrooms, several fireplaces, a soundstage, pool, and a bungalow" at the cost of nearly "six million dollars."[22] The property was purchased, in cash, with donations to BLMGNF. Campbell wrote,

> The transaction has not been previously reported, and Black Lives Matter's leadership had hoped to keep the house's existence a secret. Documents, emails, and other communications I've seen about the luxury property's purchase and day-to-day operation suggest that it has been handled in ways that blur, or cross, boundaries between the charity and private companies owned by some of its leaders. It creates the impression that money donated to the cause of racial justice has been spent in ways that benefit the leaders of Black Lives Matter personally. . . . Even if everything about the house is above board, the general air of secrecy is out of step with the transparency that is expected of charitable or tax-exempt organizations. The size of the acquisition could expose the group to criticism.[23]

When this story came out, several of BLM's local activists were livid. Ferguson Activist Tory Russell said he "felt depressed" when learning about the purchase. He called it a "waste of resources."[24] Russell spoke about national BLM leaders: "They shouldn't be walking around, no Black people, no Black communities. They should be somewhere in shame."[25] Karen Attiah, writing for the *Washington*

Post, also criticized the purchase and its surrounding lack of transparency as "a serious betrayal":

> Do they think we're stupid? For years, people marched, got teargassed, donated, and literally put their lives on the line in the hopes of Black emancipation—not a Black influencer McMansion. . . . During the Trump years, many of us wanted to protect the movement from attacks by the right. But we can't defend a BLM national leadership that arrogantly refuses to be accountable to Black victims and communities.[26]

In response to criticism about purchasing the house, BLMGNF wrote that they bought the house as a "space of their own, with the intention of providing housing and studio space for recipients of the Black Joy Creators Fellowship."[27] They also wrote that they would announce other plans for the house when they have "further built out internal infrastructure and staff."[28] Despite giving over twenty million dollars in the form of grants to Black-led frontline organizations, BLM chapters, Impacted Family foundations, and COVID relief programs, in hindsight, BLMGNF would probably have handled the purchase of the house differently.

Looking Forward

In our previous work, we argued for the real-time documentation of social movements and the recording of developments as they unfold. Media and rhetoric scholars depend upon texts, we argued. We draw from the valuable histories of social movements, often explored well after the fact, scrambling decades later to piece together the minute building blocks of major historical events. If we bear the responsibility to tease out the nuanced mechanisms of communication that bring these movements to the cultural fore, we should also participate in their preservation.[29]

We stand by those statements. As we demonstrated in chapter 1, by focusing on the movement's everyday participants, we outlined how Floyd's murder helped reshape their understanding and meaning of BLM. While as many of half of BLM protesters had no previous involvement with the movement, Floyd's murder provided a catalyst for involvement. But, if half of the movement's supporters were new, half had trod this road before. The new surge of support reminded many of what Black Lives Matter always stood for: exposing police brutality and corruption. The longevity of the movement further provided nuance and a space to reflect on the deeper philosophical and spiritual meanings of both the phrase and the movement itself.

And yet, the experience of protesting during the summer of 2020 was neither easy nor comfortable. In chapter 2, we explored how protesters coped with the threats of police, increased surveillance, white supremacist violence, and the COVID-19 pandemic. Many openly faced the risks involved in physical actions because they felt it was more important to protest this injustice, while others found creative ways to participate while protecting their mental and physical health. Despite the consistent gaslighting and name-calling, those who protested in the streets and found alternative ways to protest brought an ethic of love and community. The stories they shared with us painted a picture of care that flew in the face of media reports emphasizing intentional, orchestrated, movement-led violence and property destruction.

In chapter 3, we explored the concept of intersectionality and how it became a rallying cry in the Black Lives Matter movement. On becoming the largest social movement in the history of the United States, BLM activists became astutely aware of the need for coalitional politics, leading many in the movement to push for increased inclusiveness. Many supporters articulated their understanding of intersectionality through a lens of the personal, speaking to the push for self-care that surged alongside the increased interest in the concept of intersectional thinking. This tactic personalized the movement's meaning for individual participants but, at times, it also led to ambivalence in terms of coalition-building.

The sense of love, care, and community that participants shared led many to share religious narratives. In chapter 4, drawing on our findings of the intersectionality of the movement, many people of faith appreciated BLM's egalitarian approach, emphasizing the sense of inclusiveness they felt, not only for Christians, but with other denominational affiliations, more spiritual approaches to faith, and even atheism and agnosticism. As many shared that their faith was, in fact, part of why they were involved, Floyd's murder led some to reexamine their faith journeys. As we noted earlier in the chapter, it proved advantageous not to see the movement as religious but as one open to an eclectic diversity of religious expressions.

In chapter 5, we examined the role of electoral politics within the BLM movement. As we noted earlier in the chapter, while many participants see a connection, the debate is far from over. However, we discovered that more significant involvement in the BLM movement leads to greater participation in the electoral process. Therefore, we suggest that if we want a higher voter turnout, we should get people involved in social movements such as Black Lives Matter.

Lastly, in chapter 6, we explored BLM supporters' use of social media. The chapter highlighted how activists use social media as an educational and organizing tool to motivate and move large masses of folks on an issue. However, we also explored the dread of the toxic discourses and traumatic images the platforms placed in front of their eyes. We explored how many activists deal with the joys and pain of social media, and how they handle images of Black death that are shared over the platforms, as well as how those images seep into culture beyond social media, influencing—and being influenced by—more traditional journalistic formats.

Despite the backlash and transparency issues, the summer of 2020 left a lasting impression on the country. In the summer of 2020, we saw a man die at the hands of police with our own eyes. No matter how hard we tried, we could not look away. We could not deny that Derek Chauvin placed his knee on George Floyd's neck and killed him, as other officers helped. The facts were undeniable. So was the history of police violence in the United States.

Chauvin's murderous actions activated millions worldwide to protest Floyd's death during a worldwide pandemic. It changed how we saw and understood Black Lives Matter. While there was debate about the campaign to "defund the police," it did force us to talk about policing and public safety issues that we never had before. The summer of 2020 pressured corporations, professional and college sports teams, media outlets, and other businesses and institutions to reexamine how white supremacy influenced their operations. The summer of 2020 even led to some changes in our colleges and universities. Many college presidents and department heads released statements acknowledging their shortcomings regarding race and the issue of racism. Many began to address those shortcomings with cluster faculty hires and the establishment of DEI committees. Like never before, these organizations donated money, platformed speakers, and published messages in support of racial justice.

However, while the lasting impacts of those changes are always debatable, the summer of 2020 made one thing clear: Black Lives Matter protests shifted public discourse around race. As lead researcher Zachary Dunivin noted, "Black Lives Matter got people to pay attention when people weren't paying attention. The protests got people to care, and that has changed the way people are talking and thinking about race."[30] Co-researcher Jelani Ince notes, "Black Lives Matter is providing an alternative route to the social problems society has created. These protests aren't just trying to make noise but to reimagine what community can do."[31]

This reimagining unfolded over the course of a single summer. Millions of people stood on the right side of history as part of America's largest social movement. And as they took to the streets across the country—and around the world—to protest the injustice they witnessed, they dared to hope that things could change.

ACKNOWLEDGMENTS

Like social justice organizing itself, writing a book about the participants in a dynamic social movement like Black Lives Matter demands investment from a lot of people. We argue in this book that a movement is its people, and we owe the ideas in this book to the people who supported them, encouraged them, and shared them with us. First, we thank the participants who engaged with us and each other openly and in good faith. The perspectives given freely by participants in the BLM movement were gifts that blessed us tremendously. We were indeed honored that they agreed to spend time with us to share their stories and involvement in the movement.

The task of gathering participants together and researching for the book was greatly aided by a Research Cultivation Grant from the National Communication Association and a grant from the Waterhouse Family Institute for the Study of Communication and Society. Without their financial support, this book would not exist. We also thank the National Communication Association and the Rhetoric Society of America for allowing us to preview some of our material from the book on the podcasts *Communication Matters* and *RSA Remote*. The work of our research assistants contributed to this project as well. Thank you to DiArron M. Curtis Chamblee, Solomon Cochren, and Peter Boyd for your work and support of this project. We also want to thank members of our WriteOn writing group, who, despite navigating a pandemic, met virtually on Friday afternoons and held us accountable.

We are grateful for Emily Bandy's work as our editor and the wonderful people at the University Press of Mississippi. We thank the anonymous reviewers who offered quality feedback both on the full manuscript and through various conferences to which we submitted along the way. Early versions of this work were presented at the National Communication Association, Southern States Communication Association, and Rhetoric Society of America. Feedback at these venues was instrumental in shaping the ideas in this book.

On a personal note, Andre would like to thank his wife and partner, Lisa, for her insight, wisdom, and activism. Also, he would like to thank his Gifts of Life Ministries church family for allowing him to write, research, protest, and still serve as pastor. Finally, he would like to thank Amanda Nell Edgar for being his "write or die" partner, fellow coconspirator, and friend. Despite dealing with the pandemic and other issues that came up, she helped us to stay focused and committed to the task at hand. Andre is grateful and thankful that he knows you.

Amanda would like to thank her incredibly supportive partner, Aaron Dechant, as well as the friends and family who encouraged her throughout the project. Much of this project was written and revised during Friday writing groups and 311Love summer writing retreats, and she is grateful to the members of those groups who celebrated and commiserated at RP Tracks and the Dollhouse in Cape Girardeau. Last, she thanks Andre E. Johnson for his wisdom, candor, and unwavering commitment to justice. The timeline of this project took us through some of the highest highs and the lowest lows. Thank you for your friendship and uplifting energy. I am always trying to be more like you.

NOTES

Introduction: One More Long, Hot Summer

1. Participants are named using either their real name or a pseudonym, depending on their preference, and their basic demographics are reported in the notes throughout the book. Cerise is forty-three, female, African American, and a professor.

2. These are the names of the sixty-two Black men and women killed by police across the United States between the murders of Ahmaud Arbery and George Floyd:

Kenneth Sashington	Dewayne Curtis Lafond	Said Joquin
SanJuan Migayle	Joshua Dariandre Ruffin	Demontre Bruner
Thomas	Zyon Romeir Wyche	Qavon Webb
Matthew Felix	Jonathan Lee Adams	Jah'Sean Iandie Hodge
Justin Lee Stackhouse	Goldie Bellinger	Dreasjon Reed
Anthony Taylor	Jasman Washington	McHale Rose
Elijah Jamaal Brewer	Derick L. Powe	Adrian Medearis
Tyler M. Jones	Steven Taylor	Finan H. Berhe
Barry Gedeus	Willie J. Hampton	Yassin Mohamed
Donnie Sanders	Virgill Thrope	David Tylek Atkinson
Darwin Foy	Chase Rosa	Rayshard Scales
William Simpkins	Elmer L. Mack	Robert Johnson
Harold Spencer	Joshua Johnson	Randy Roszell Lewis
Lebarron Ballard	Fred Brown	Wilbon Cleveland
Mycael Johnson	Marlon Aaron Bonds	Woodard
Kamaal Koby Edwards	Roy Joiner	Terry Caver
Alvin Lamont Baum	Jonas Joseph	Tobby Wiggins
Gerald Johnson	Malcolm Xavier Ray	Willie Lee Quarles
Tyrell Fincher	Williams	Maurice S. Gordon
Etonne Tanzymore	William Debose	Christopher Clark
Nathan R. Hodge	Shaun Lee Fuhr	Dion Johnson
Idris Abdus-Salaam	Brent Martin	

3. https://www.pewresearch.org/fact-tank/2021/09/27/support-for-black-lives
-matter-declined-after-george-floyd-protests-but-has-remained-unchanged-since/.

4. S. Harlow, "Journalism's Change Agents: Black Lives Matter, #Blackout-
Tuesday, and a Shift Toward Activist Doxa." *Journalism & Mass Communication
Quarterly* 99, no. 3 (2022): 742–62, https://doi.org/10.1177/10776990221108648.

5. Ibid.

6. I. X. Kendi, *How to Be an Antiracist* (Random House, 2020); R. J. DiAngelo,
White Fragility: Why It's So Hard for White People to Talk about Racism (Beacon
Press, 2020).

7. Robert L. Scott and Donald K. Smith, "The Rhetoric of Confrontation,"
Quarterly Journal of Speech 55, no. 1 (1969).

8. Ibid.

9. Robert S. Cathcart, "Movements: Confrontation as Rhetorical Form," *Southern Speech Communication Journal* 43, no. 3 (1978), doi: 10.1080/10417947809372383.

10. Ibid., 362–63.

11. Ibid., 366.

12. Ibid., 367.

13. T. O. Haakenson, "1968, Now and Then: Black Lives, Black Bodies," *Cultural
Critique*, 103, no. 1 (2019), 75–83, https://doi.org/10.1353/cul.2019.0022.

14. Carlos Morrison and Jacqueline Trimble, "Still Work to Be Done: The
Million Man March and the 50thAnniversary Commemoration Selma to Montgomery March as Mythoform and Visual Rhetoric," *Howard Journal of Communication* 28, no. 2 (2017): 141, https://doi.org/10.1080/10646175.2017.1287609.

15. Robert S. Cathcart, "Movements: Confrontation as Rhetorical Form."

16. Carlos Morrison and Jacqueline Trimble, "Still Work to Be Done: The
Million Man March and the 50th Anniversary Commemoration Selma to Montgomery March as Mythoform and Visual Rhetoric," *Howard Journal of Communications* 28, no. 2 (2017): 132–43, doi: 10.1080/10646175.2017.1287609.

17. Alicia Garza, *The Purpose of Power: How We Come Together When We Fall
Apart* (One World, 2020).

18. Ibid.

19. Amanda Nell Edgar and Andre E. Johnson, *The Struggle Over Black Lives
Matter and All Lives Matter* (Lexington Books, 2018), 47.

20. Ibid.

21. Morrison and Trimble, "Still Work to Be Done."

22. "Home—Black Lives Matter," n.d., https://blacklivesmatter.com/.

23. Edgar and Johnson, *The Struggle Over Black Lives Matter and All Lives
Matter*, 47.

24. Garza, *The Purpose of Power*, xi.

25. S. J. Jackson, M. Bailey, and B. F. Welles, *#Hashtagactivism: Networks of Race
and Gender Justice* (MIT Press, 2020).

26. Ibid.

27. Armond R. Towns, "Black 'Matter' Lives," *Women's Studies in Communication* 41, no. 4 (2018): 349–58, doi: 10.1080/07491409.2018.1551985.

28. Ibid.

29. J. Bailey and D. Leonard, "Bailey_leonard Black Lives Matter Post-Nihilistic Freedom Dreams," *Journal of Contemporary Rhetoric* 5, nos. 3–4 (2015).

30. Ibid.

31. Towns, "Black 'Matter' Lives."

32. Bailey and Leonard, "Bailey_leonard Black Lives Matter Post-Nihilistic Freedom Dreams."

33. J. O'Neil, A. E. English, and J. Lambiase, "After the Killing of Atatiana Jefferson: Black Stakeholder Experiences within a Municipal Listening Structure. *Journalism & Mass Communication Quarterly* 99, no. 3 (2022): 802–25, https://doi .org/10.1177/10776990221105588.

34. Ibid.

35. Pollyanna Ruiz, "Covid Publics and Black Lives Matter: Posts, Placards and Posters," *Javnost—The Public* 29, no. 2 (2022): 165–78, doi: 10.1080/13183222.2022 .2042787.

36. Ibid.

37. Ibid.

38. By Leopold and Bell.

39. E. Zuckerman, J. N. Matias, R. Bhargava, F. Bermejo, and A. Ko, "Whose Death matters? A Quantitative Analysis of Media Attention to Deaths of Black Americans in Police Confrontations, 2013–2016," *International Journal of Communication* (2019), https://ijoc.org/index.php/ijoc/article/view/8782.

40. Harlow, "Journalism's Change Agents: Black Lives Matter, #BlackoutTuesday, and a Shift Toward Activist Doxa."

41. M. Mundt, K. Ross, and C. M. Burnett, "Scaling Social Movements through Social Media: The Case of Black Lives Matter," *Social Media + Society* 4, no. 4 (2018), https://doi.org/10.1177/2056305118807911.

42. Garza, The *Purpose of Power.*

43. Ibid.

44. Ruiz, "Covid Publics and Black Lives Matter: Posts, Placards and Posters."

45. Ibid.

46. Sarah Florini, *Beyond Hashtags: Racial Politics and Black Digital Networks* (New York University Press, 2019); Edgar and Johnson, *The Struggle Over Black Lives Matter and All Lives Matter.*

47. L. F. Holt and D. Carnahan, "Which Bad News to Choose? The Influence of Race and Social Identity on Story Selections within Negative News Contexts," *Journalism & Mass Communication Quarterly* 97, no. 3 (2019): 644–62, https://doi .org/10.1177/1077699019892632.

48. Ibid.

49. Chrysalis Wright, Kwame Gatlin, Damaris Acosta, and Christopher Taylor, "Portrayals of the Black Lives Matter Movement in Hard and Fake News and Consumer Attitudes Toward African Americans," *Howard Journal of Communications* (2022), doi: 10.1080/10646175.2022.2065458.

50. Zuckerman, Matias, Bhargava, Bermejo, and Ko, "Whose Death Matters?"

51. Ibid.

52. Ruiz, "Covid Publics and Black Lives Matter."

53. V. Williamson, K.-S. Trump, K. L. Einstein, "Black Lives Matter: Evidence that Police-Caused Deaths Predict Protest Activity," *Perspectives on Politics* 16, no. 2 (2018): 400–415. https://doi.org/10.1017/s1537592717004273.

54. Ibid.

55. Alexander H. Updegrove, Maisha N. Cooper, Erin A. Orrick, and Alex R. Piquero, "Red States and Black Lives: Applying the Racial Threat Hypothesis to the Black Lives Matter Movement," *Justice Quarterly* 37, no. 1 (2020): 85–108, doi: 10.1080/07418825.2018.1516797.

56. Edgar and Johnson, *The Struggle Over Black Lives Matter and All Lives Matter.*

57. Andre E. Johnson and Anthony Stone, "The Most Dangerous Negro in America: Rhetoric, race, and the Prophetic Pessimism of Martin Luther King Jr.," *Journal of Communication and Religion* 21, no. 1 (2018): 8–22.

58. Lotz, "Assessing Qualitative Television Audience Research"; Michael Kackman and Mary Celeste Kearney, *The Craft of Criticism: Critical Media Studies in Practice* (Routledge, 2018).

59. Alfred L. Martin Jr. "For Scholars . . . When Studying the Queer of Color Image Alone Isn't Enough," *Communication and Critical/Cultural Studies* 17, no. 1 (2020): 69–74, doi: 10.1080/14791420.2020.1723797; Rukmini Pande, *Squee From the Margins: Fandom and Race* (University of Iowa Press, 2018).

60. Amanda Nell Edgar and Ashton Toone, "'She Invited Other People to That Space': Social Justice and Place in Beyoncé's *Lemonade* Fan Communities," *Feminist Media Studies* 19, no. 1 (2017), doi: 10.1080/14680777.2017.1377276.

61. John W. Creswell, *Research Design: Qualitative, Quantitative, and Mixed Methods Approaches*, 3rd ed. (Sage Publications, 2009).

Chapter 1: "I Saw the Video": George Floyd and the Meaning of Black Lives Matter

1. "Whatever Happened to Black Lives Matter?" *The Economist*, May 21, 2020, https://www.economist.com/united-states/2020/05/21/whatever-happened-to -black-lives-matter.

2. "Whatever Happened to Black Lives Matter?"

3. Ibid.

4. Ibid.

5. Ibid.

6. Thiede and Wigdahl, https://www.kare11.com/article/news/local/reactions -to-death-of-george-floyd-restrained-by-minneapolis-police/89-baecfa83-0729 -4182-a371-86d40ab5f0f0.

7. Dana Thiede and Heidi Wigdahl, "Reactions to the Death of George Floyd," KARE11, https://www.kare11.com/article/news/local/reactions-to-death-of-george -floyd-restrained-by-minneapolis-police/89-baecfa83-0729-4182-a371-86d40a b5f0f0 (para. 4–5).

8. Tommy Call III, "Steph Curry Voices Outrage About Death of George Floyd with Instagram Message," *Warriors Wire*, May 27, 2020, https://warriorswire .usatoday.com/2020/05/27/steph-curry-voices-outrage-about-death-of-george -floyd-with-instagram-message/.

9. "Kurt Helin, LeBron James, Others Around NBA speak out After Death of George Floyd," NBCSports.com, May 27, 2020, https://nba.nbcsports.com /2020/05/27/lebron-james-others-around-nba-speak-out-after-death-of -george-floyd/.

10. Editorial Board, "Opinion: Another Unarmed Black Man Has Died at the Hands of Police. When will it End?" *Washington Post*, https://www.washingto npost.com/opinions/another-unarmed-black-man-has-died-at-the-hands-of -police-when-will-it-end/2020/05/26/7c426b88-9f80-11ea-9590-1858a893bd59_ story.html.

11. Andrea Torres, "Miami Police Chief: No Training Teaches Deeply Disturb-ing Action in George Floyd's Death," Local 10, May 27, 2020, https://www.local10 .com/news/local/2020/05/27/miami-chief-to-officers-no-training-teaches-deeply -disturbing-action-killing-george-floyd/.

12. "Texas Police Chiefs Speak Out About Death of George Floyd," May 29, 2020, https://www.reformaustin.org/public-safety/texas-police-chiefs-speak- out-on-death-of-george-floyd/#:~:text=Austin%20Police%20Chief%20Brian%20 Manley,breathe%20but%20to%20no%20avail.

13. Ibid.

14. Round Rock police chief Allen Banks expressed similar sentiments. Banks posted on Twitter, "We in law enforcement CAN'T look at the George Floyd case and turn a blind eye! There is NO justification for these actions! We MUST hold officers accountable for atrocious decisions!" The University of Texas at Austin police department chief David Carter also took to Twitter and wrote: "I sadly must again address my officers and ask how they felt about the unlawful homi-cide of George Floyd, an American citizen in Minneapolis. Police leaders must confront the failures of our profession, or we are doomed to repeat them and cast further doubt on our legitimacy."

15. According to their website, the Major Cities Chiefs Association (MCCA) is a professional organization of police executives representing the largest cities in the United States and Canada. The mission of MCCA is to provide a forum for police executives from large population centers to address the challenges and issues of policing, to influence national and international policy that affects police services, to enhance the development of current and future police leaders, and to encourage and sponsor research that advances this mission (https://majorcities chiefs.com/).

16. "Major Cities Chiefs Association (MCCA) Statement Regarding the Death of George Floyd," May 27, 2020, https://majorcitieschiefs.com/wp-content /uploads/2021/01/NEWS-RELEASE-Statement-regarding-Death-of-George -Floyd.pdf.

17. Andy Mannix, "Minneapolis Chief Cite 'Fluid' Situation for Troubling Mis-information released After George Floyd Death," *Minneapolis Star Tribune*, June 3, 2020, https://www.startribune.com/mpls-police-still-haven-t-explained-mis information-after-floyd-s-death/570970152/.

18. John Elder, "Investigative Update on Critical Incident," Internet Archive, May 26, 2020, https://web.archive.org/web/20200526183652/https://www .insidempd.com/2020/05/26/man-dies-after-medical-incident-during-police -interaction/.

19. Forty, female, white, teacher.

20. Sixty-two, female, white, disabled.

21. Thirty-four, male, Black, editorial assistant.

22. Eric Silver, Kerby Goff, and John Iceland, "Social Order and Social Justice: Moral Intuitions, Systemic Racism Beliefs, and Americans' Divergent Attitudes Toward Black Lives Matter and Police," *Criminology* (2022): 4, doi: 10.1111/1745-9125.12303.

23. Lydia Saad, "Black American Want Police to Retain Local Presence," Gallup, August 5, 2020, https://news.gallup.com/poll/316571/black-americans-police -retain-local-presence.aspx.

24. https://www.nnw.org/.

25. "Social Order and Social Justice," 2.

26. Akira: twenty-two, female, Black teacher.

27. Jennifer: thirty-seven, female, Black pastor.

28. Forty, male, white, carpenter.

29. Sixty-one, female, white, consultant.

30. Forty-four, female, African American, teacher.

31. Forty-three, female, African American, professor.

32. Thirty-six, trans female, white, occupation n/a.

33. Thirty-four, male, Black.

34. Thirty-four, male, Black, editorial assistant.

35. Eighty-four, female, white, retired.

36. Twenty-six, female, white, student affairs professional.

37. Sixty-two, female, white, disabled.

38. https://www.forbes.com/sites/jemimamcevoy/2020/07/22/sales-of-white-fragility-and-other-anti-racism-books-jumped-over-2000-after-protests-began/?sh=46af336b303d.

39. https://www.blacklivesmattersyllabus.com/.

40. Florini, 3.

41. Sixty-one, female, African American, consultant.

42. Thirty-eight, female, Caucasian, English professor.

43. Thirty-four, female, Black, ministry.

44. Twenty-two, female, Black, teacher.

45. Andre E. Johnson, "Confrontational and Intersectional Rhetoric: Black Lives Matter and the Shutdown of the Hernando De Soto (I-40) Bridge," in *The Rhetoric of Social Movements: Networks, Power, and New Media*, ed. Nathan Crick (Routledge, 2001), 98–115.

46. Thirty-seven, female, white, professor.

47. Fifty-five, male, white, retail.

48. Sixty-two, female, white, disabled.

49. Sixty-six, female, Asian, associate professor.

50. Edgar and Johnson, *The Struggle Over Black Lives Matter and All Lives Matter*, 6.

51. Herstory, "Black Lives Matter," https://Blacklivesmatter.com/about/herstory/.

52. https://www.nytimes.com/interactive/2020/07/03/us/george-floyd-protests-crowd-size.html.

53. Forty-three, female, African American, professor.

54. Thirty-seven, female, Black, pastor.

55. Twenty-six, female, white, teacher.

56. Fifty-nine, female, Afro-Latina, student/clergy.

57. Edgar and Johnson, *The Struggle Over Black Lives Matter and All Lives Matter*.

58. Forty-five, female, Anglo, energy professional/political candidate.

59. Twenty-two, female, Black, teacher.

60. Twenty-three, female, Black, caregiver.

61. Twenty-seven, male, Black, student.

62. Sixty-two, female, African American, attorney.

63. Twenty-seven, male, African American, recruiting specialist.

64. Forty-five, male, Black, teacher.

65. Sixty-six, female, Asian, associate professor.

66. Thirty-five, female, Black, food scientist.

67. Forty, female, white, teacher.

68. Forty-seven, female, Black, lawyer.

69. Twenty-six, female, white, elementary school teacher.

70. Thirty-four, female, Black, ministry.

71. Bianca DiJulio, Mira Norton, Symone Jackson, and Mollyann Brodie, Kaiser Family Foundation/CNN Survey of Americans on Race, November 2015, https://files.kff.org/attachment/report-survey-of-americans-on-race.

72. Gary Langer, "63% Support Black Lives Matter as Recognition of Discrimination Jumps," ABC News, July 21, 2020, https://abcnews.go.com/Politics/63-support-black-lives-matter-recognition-discrimination-jumps/story?id=71779435.

73. https://www.nytimes.com/interactive/2020/07/03/us/george-floyd-protests-crowd-size.html.

74. https://www.nytimes.com/interactive/2020/07/03/us/george-floyd-protests-crowd-size.html.

75. Larry Buchanan, Quoctrung Bui, and Jugal K. Patel, *New York Times*, July 3, 2020, https://www.nytimes.com/interactive/2020/07/03/us/george-floyd-protests-crowd-size.html.

76. Nancy Armour, "Drew Brees Needs to Do More than Apologize for Comments on Protests," *USA Today*, June 4, 2020, https://www.usatoday.com/story/sports/columnist/nancy-armour/2020/06/04/george-floyd-drew-brees-needs-do-more-than-apologize-comments/3144320001/.

77. Leah Asmelash, "In Reactions to Roger Goodell's Mea Culpa, Most Seized on What he Didn't Say," CNN, June 6, 2020, https://www.cnn.com/2020/06/05/us/colin-kaepernick-roger-goodell-statement-trnd/index.html.

78. Sean Gregory, "College Athletes Are Realizing Their Power Amid the George Floyd Protests and Covid-19," *Time*, June 18, 2020, https://time.com/5855471/college-athletes-covid-19-protests-racial-equality/.

79. Vanessa Romo, "U.S. Soccer Lifts Ban on Kneeling During National Anthem," NPR, June 10, 2020, https://www.npr.org/sections/live-updates-protests-for-racial-justice/2020/06/10/874531497/u-s-soccer-lifts-ban-on-kneeling-during-national-anthem.

80. Leigh Brownhill, "The Emancipatory Politics of Anti-Racism," *Capitalism Nature Racism* 31, no 3 (2020): 4–15.

Chapter 2: "Face the Fear and Do It Anyway": Protesting in the Face of Compounding Threats

1. Tom Cotton, "Send in the Troops," *New York Times*, June 3, 2020, https://www.nytimes.com/2020/06/03/opinion/tom-cotton-protests-military.html.

2. Grace Segers, "Senate Republicans Block Commission on January 6 Insurrection," CBS News, May 29, 2020, https://www.cbsnews.com/news/january-6-commission-bill-capitol-riot-senate-republicans-block/.

3. Greg Sargent, "Opinion: Trump and Tom Cotton Are Losing the Argument. New Polls Confirm it.," *Washington Post*, June 5, 2020, https://www.washington post.com/opinions/2020/06/05/trump-tom-cotton-are-losing-argument-new -polls-confirm-it/?utm_campaign=wp_main&utm_medium=social&utm_ source=twitter.

4. "Protestors' Anger Justified Even If Actions May Not Be," Monmouth University Polling Institute, https://www.monmouth.edu/polling-institute/reports /monmouthpoll_us_060220/.

5. Quoted in Dhrumil Mehta, "National Media Coverage of Black Lives Matter Had Fallen During the Trump Era- Until Now," *FiveThirtyEight*, June 11, 2020, https://fivethirtyeight.com/features/national-media-coverage-of-black-lives -matter-had-fallen-during-the-trump-era-until-now/.

6. Ibid.

7. "Demonstrations & Political Violence in America: New Data for Summer 2020," ACLED, September 2020, https://acleddata.com/2020/09/03/demonstrations -political-violence-in-america-new-data-for-summer-2020/.

8. Patrice Khan-Cullors and asha bandele, *When They Call You a Terrorist: A Black Lives Matter Memoir* (New York: St. Martin's Griffin, 2020), 6.

9. Victor J. Blue "The World Is Watching: Mass Violations by U.S. Police of Black Lives Matter Protestors' Rights," Amnesty International, accessed June 30, 2021, https://www.amnestyusa.org/worldiswatching/.

10. Ibid.

11. "Police Brutality as BLM Protests," BLM Protest, accessed July 2, 2021, https://blmprotests.forensic-architecture.org/.

12. "USA: Law Enforcement Violated Black Lives Matter Protesters' Human Rights, Documents Acts of Police Violence and Excessive Force," Amnesty International, August 4, 2020, https://www.amnesty.org/en/latest/news/2020/08/usa -law-enforcement-violated-black-lives-matter-protesters-human-rights/.

13. "Health Equity Considerations and Racial and Ethnic Minority Groups," *Center for Disease Control and Prevention*, April 19, 2021, https://www.cdc.gov /coronavirus/2019-ncov/community/health-equity/race-ethnicity.html.

14. Ibid.

15. Dhaval M. Dave, Andrew I. Friedson, Kyutaro Matsuzawa, Joseph J. Sabia, & Samuel Safford, "Black Lives Matter Protests, Social Distancing, and COVID-19," Cato Institute, October 14, 2020, https://www.cato.org/research-briefs -economic-policy/black-lives-matter-protests-social-distancing-covid-19.

16. Whether or not Trump realized that he was quoting Walter Headley's threat against 1967 protesters in Miami, social media users quickly associated Trump's tweet with the historical racist remark. Twitter officially gave the reason for censoring the tweet as "glorifying violence" (Alex Hern, "Twitter Hides Donald Trump Tweet for 'Glorifying Violence,'" *The Guardian*, https://www.theguardian.com/tech nology/2020/may/29/twitter-hides-donald-trump-tweet-glorifying-violence).

17. Andrea Benjamin, "Polls Show Strong Support for the Protests—and Also for How Police Handled Them," *Washington Post*, June 11, 2020, https://www.washingtonpost.com/outlook/polling-protests-police-protesters-opinion/2020/06/11/987259fe-ab5a-11ea-9063-e69bd6520940_story.html.

18. Kellie Carter Jackson, *Force and Freedom: Abolitionists and the Politics of Violence* (University of Pennsylvania Press, 2020).

19. Tonya Mosley and Allison Hagan, "Violence as a Form of Protest," WBUR, *Here and Now*, https://www.wbur.org/hereandnow/2020/06/11/voilence-protests-racial-justice.

20. Carlos Morrison and Jacqueline Trimble, "Still Work to Be Done: The Million Man March and the 50th Anniversary Commemoration Selma to Montgomery March as Mythoform and Visual Rhetoric," *Howard Journal of Communication* 28, no. 2 (2017): 141, https://doi.org/10.1080/10646175.2017.1287609.

21. Thirty-five, female, Black, food scientist.

22. Thirty-five, female, Black, food scientist.

23. Thirty-four, male, Black, editorial assistant.

24. Declined questionnaire.

25. Thirty-four, male, Black, editorial assistant.

26. Sixty-nine, female, white, retired registered nurse.

27. Twenty-six, female, white, elementary school teacher.

28. Emily Stewart, "How to be a Good White Ally, According to Activists," *Vox*, June 2, 2020, https://www.vox.com/2020/6/2/21278123/being-an-ally-racism-george-floyd-protests-white-people.

29. Twenty-two, NB, Middle Eastern, student.

30. Helier Cheung, "George Floyd Death: Why Do Some Protests Turn Violent?," BBC News, May 31, 2020, https://www.bbc.com/news/world-us-canada-52869563.

31. Fifty-nine, female, Afro-Latina, student/clergy.

32. Forty-seven, female, Black, lawyer.

33. The next day, Fayetteville's police chief knelt with protesters in the town square, ignoring the massive escalation police brought to that Monday's protests.

34. Sixty-two, female, African American, attorney.

35. Olivia B. Waxan, "What Martin Luther King Jr. Said at the March on Washington About Police Brutality," *Time*, August 27, 2020, https://time.com/5882308/march-on-washington-police-brutality/.

36. Forty, male, white, carpenter.

37. Bryan Walsh and Alison Snyder, "Scientist Caught Between Pandemic and Protests," *Axios*, June 10, 2020, https://www.axios.com/black-lives-matter-protests-coronavirus-science-15acc619-33d-47c2-9c76-df91f826a73c.html.

38. Forty-two, male, Black, teacher.

39. Fifty-seven, male, Black, pastor/professor.

40. Tara Parker-Pope, "How Safe Are Outdoor Gatherings?," *New York Times,* June 3, 2020, https://www.nytimes.com/2020/07/03/well/live/coronavirus-spread -outdoors-party.html.

41. Fifty-two, female, African American, organizer and faith leader.

42. According to several studies cited throughout this chapter, protesters across the country seem to have been just as diligent as our participants.

43. Forty-two, male, Black, teacher.

44. Thirty-seven, female, Black pastor.

45. Twenty-eight, male, white, youth pastor/ denominational employee.

46. Thirty-seven, female, white, professor.

47. Matt Berger, "Why the Black Lives Matter Protests Didn't Contribute to the COVID-19 Surge," *Healthline,* July 8, 2020, https://www.healthline.com/health -news/black-lives-matter-protests-didnt-contribute-to-covid19-surge; Daniela Hernandez, Sarah Krouse, Brianna Abbott, and Charity L. Scott, "Early Data Show No Uptick in Covid-19 Transmission from Protests," *Wall Street Journal,* June 18, 2020, https://www.wsj.com/articles/recent-protests-may-not-be-covid-19 -transmission-hotspots-11592498020.

48. Dhaval M. Dave et al., "Black Lives Matter Protests and Risk Avoidance: The Case of Civil Unrest During a Pandemic," *National Bureau of Economic Research*, January 2021. Retrieved from https://www.nber.org/papers/w27408.

49. Thirty, female, white/Caucasian, attorney.

50. Larry Buchanan, Quoctrung Bui, and Jagal Patel, "Black Lives Matter May Be the Largest Movement in U.S. History," *New York Times,* July 3, 2020, https:// www.nytimes.com/interactive/2020/07/03/us/george-floyd-protests-crowd-size .html.

51. Forty-two, male, Black, teacher.

52. Forty-three, female, African American, professor.

53. Eighty-four, female, white, retired.

54. Fifty-five, male, white, retail.

55. See, for example, Laurel Dickman, "5 Ways to Make Protests Accessible and Truly Include Disabled Folks," *Huffington Post*, February 21, 2017, https://www .huffpost.com/entry/5-ways-to-make-protests-accessible-and-truly-include -disabled-folks_b_58acac38e4b02eb3a9832c78.

56. Eighty-four, female, white, retired.

57. See, for example, "Black Disabled Lives Matter Protest Best Practices," Detroit Disability Power, July 5, 2020, https://www.detroitdisabilitypower.org/blm.

58. Declined questionnaire.

59. Sixty-nine, female, white, retired registered nurse.

60. Thirty-six, trans female, white, occupation n/a.

61. Buchanan, Bui, and Patel, "Black Lives Matter May Be," 1.

62. Forty-four, female, African American, teacher.

63. Karma Chávez and Cindy Griffin, "Power, Feminisms, and Coalitional Agency: Inviting and Enacting Difficult Dialogues," *Women's Studies in Communication* 32, no. 1 (2009): 8, doi:10.1080/07491409.2009.10162378.

64. Garza, *The Purpose of Power*, xii.

Chapter 3: "What's More Important Is the Bigger Picture": Intersectionality as a Personal Investment

1. https://trends.google.com/trends/story/US_cu_IxEWyVUBAABgWM_en.

2. The previous record was set in July 2016 following the murders of Philando Castile and Alton Sterling.

3. Kimberlé Crenshaw, "Demarginalizing the Intersection of Race and Sex: A Black Feminist Critique of Antidiscrimination Doctrine, Feminist Theory and Antiracist Politics," *University of Chicago Legal Forum* 1, no. 8 (1989).

4. Patricia Hill Collins and Sirma Bilge, *Intersectionality: Key Concepts* (Polity Press, 2016), 2.

5. Sarah Kate Ellis, "GLAAD Statement: 'There Can Be No Pride If It Is Not Intersectional,'" GLAAD, June 1, 2020, https://www.glaad.org/blog/glaad -statement-black-lives-matter.

6. "Intersectional Feminism: What It Means and Why It Matters Right Now," UNWomen, July 1, 2020, https://www.unwomen.org/en/news/stories/2020/6 /explainer-intersectional-feminism-what-it-means-and-why-it-matters.

7. Kimberle Crenshaw, "Mapping the Margins: Intersectionality, Identity Politics, and Violence Against Women of Color," *Stanford Law Review* 43, no. 1 (1991): 1242.

8. Karma R. Chávez and Cindy L. Griffin, "Power, Feminisms, and Coalitional Agency: Inviting and Enacting Difficult Dialogues," *Women's Studies in Communication* 32, no. 1 (2009): 1–11.

9. Karma R. Chávez, in *Against Equality: Queer Revolution Not Mere Inclusion*, ed. Ryan Conrad (AK Press, 2014), 188.

10. Jennifer C. Nash, "Intersectionality and Its Discontents," *American Quarterly* 69, no. 1 (2017): 117, doi: https://doi.org/10.1353/aq.2017.0006.

11. "Tucker: The Never-Ending Car Crash of Intersectionality," YouTube, February 6, 2019, https://www.youtube.com/watch?v=XWCmQ8euRJM.

12. Nash, "Intersectionality and Its Discontents," 117.

13. Sara Salem, "Intersectionality and Its Discontents: Intersectionality as Traveling Theory," *European Journal of Women's Studies* 25, no. 4 (2018), 414doi/pdf /10.1177/1350506816643999.

14. Nash, "Intersectionality and Its Discontents," 126.

15. Vivian M. Mays, *Pursuing Intersectionality, Unsettling Dominant Imaginaries* (Routledge, 2015).

16. Collins and Bilge, *Intersectionality*, 85.

17. Patricia Hill Collins, "On Violence, Intersectionality and Transversal Politics," Ethnic and Racial Studies 40, no. 9 (2017), https://doi.org/10.1080/01419870 .2017.1317827.

18. Collins, "On Violence," 1465.

19. Collins, "On Violence."

20. Crenshaw, "Mapping the Margins," 1244.

21. Ibid., 1245.

22. Amber Johnson, "Gender Futurity at the Intersection of Black Lives Matter and Afrofuturism," in *The Routledge Handbook of Gender and Communication*, eds. Marnel Niles Goins, Joan Faber McAlister, and Bryant Keith Alexander (Routledge, 2020), 616–17.

23. Collins, "On Violence," 1465.

24. Johnson, "Gender Futurity," 619.

25. Johnson, "Gender Futurity," 617.

26. Christine Emba, "Intersectionality," *Washington Post*, September 21, 2015, https://www.washingtonpost.com/news/in-theory/wp/2015/09/21/intersectionality -a-primer/%3Ftid=a_inl%26utm_term=.aa49b841c868.

27. Twenty-one, male, Black, student.

28. Crenshaw, "Demarginalizing the Intersection of Race and Sex," 167.

29. Thirty-six, trans female, white, occupation n/a.

30. Thirty-seven, female, white, professor.

31. Fifty-two, female, African American, organizer and faith leader.

32. https://poor-peoples-campaign-a-national-call-for-moral-revival.myshopify .com/collections/forward-together-not-one-step-back-collection.

33. Thirty-eight, female, white, minister.

34. Dan Levin, "Generation Z: Who They are, in Their Own Words," *New York Times*, March 28, 2019, https://www.nytimes.com/2019/03/28/us/gen-z-in-their -words.html.

35. Forty-three, female, white, daycare teacher.

36. Twenty-three, female, Black, caregiver.

37. Dominic-Madori Davis, "The Action Generation: How Gen Z Really Feels About Race, Equality, and Its Role in the Historic George Floyd Protests, Based on a Survey of 39,000 Young Americans," *Insider*, June 10, 2020, https://www.business insider.com/how-gen-z-feels-about-george-floyd-protests-2020-6.

38. Deja Thomas and Juliana Menace Horowitz, "Support for Black Lives Matter Has Decreased Since June But Remains Strong Among Black Americans," Pew Research Center, September 16, 2020, https://www.pewresearch.org/fact-tank/2020 /09/16/support-for-black-lives-matter-has-decreased-since-june-but-remains -strong-among-black-americans/.

39. Garza, *The Purpose of Power*, 57.

40. Forty-three, female, white, daycare teacher.

41. Evette Dionne, "For Black Women, Self-Care is a Radical Act," *Ravishly*, March 9, 2015, https://www.ravishly.com/2015/03/06/radical-act-self-care-black -women-feminism.

42. Garza, *The Purpose of Power*, 285.

43. Garza, *The Purpose of Power*, 288.

44. Fifty-two, female, African American, organizer and faith leader.

45. Twenty-six, female, white, student affairs professional.

46. Twenty-eight, genderqueer/femme leaning, white, PhD student at UC Sociology.

47. Amanda Barroso and Rachel Minkin, "Recent Protest Attendees are More Racially and Ethnically Diverse, Younger than Americans Overall," *Pew Research Center*, June 24, 2020, https://www.pewresearch.org/fact-tank/2020/06/24/recent -protest-attendees-are-more-racially-and-ethnically-diverse-younger-than -americans-overall/.

48. Johanna C. Luttrell, *White People and Black Lives Matter: Ignorance, Empathy, and Justice* (Palgrave Macmillan, 2019).

49. Sixty-two, female, African American, consultant.

50. Brian Mann and Elizabeth Baker, "Black Protest Leaders to White Allies: 'It's Our Turn to Lead Our Own Fight,'" NPR, September 22, 2020, https://www .npr.org/2020/09/22/913094440/black-protest-leaders-to-white-allies-it-s-our -turn-to-lead-our-own-fight.

51. Mann and Baker, "Black Protest Leaders to White Allies."

52. Thirty-four, male, Black, editorial assistant.

53. Jesse Singal, "Does Asking White People for Moral Self-Reflection About Race Actually Work?," *New Yorker*, August 18, 2015, https://www.thecut.com/2015 /08/does-asking-whites-to-morally-self-reflect-work.html.

54. Forty, male, white, carpenter.

55. Fifty-one, male, white, professor.

56. bell hooks, *Ain't I a Woman: Black Women and Feminism* (Routledge, 2015).

57. Thirty-eight, female, white, minister.

58. Mann and Baker, "Black Protest Leaders to White Allies."

59. Lelia Gowland, "White Women: 3 Ways to Sustain Anti-Racism as a Lifelong Commitment," *Forbes*, June 25, 2020, https://www.forbes.com/sites /leliagowland/2020/06/25/white-women-3-ways-to-sustain-anti-racism-as-a -lifelong-commitment/?sh=b842152b39bc.

60. Daniella Mehlek-Dawveed, "Black Lives Matter is Not Just Some Trendy Post to Add to Your Timeline," *The Tide*, November 28, 2020, https://thermtide .com/12691/popular/black-lives-matter-is-not-just-some-trendy-post-to-add -to-your-timeline/.

61. Sixty-two, female, white, disabled.

62. Thirty-four, female, Black, ministry.

63. Fifty-two, female, African American, organizer and faith leader.

Chapter 4: "It's an Extension of My Faith": The Role of Faith, Religion, and Spirituality in the BLM Movement

1. Donald Trump, speech transcript, June 1, "Trump May Deploy US Military to Cities," June 1, 2020, https://www.rev.com/blog/transcripts/donald-trump -speech-transcript-june-1-trump-may-deploy-us-military-to-cities.

2. Evan Osnos, "'An Abuse of Sacred Symbols': Trump, A Bible, and a Sanctuary," *New Yorker*, June 2, 2020, https://www.newyorker.com/news/daily-comment /an-abuse-of-sacred-symbols-trump-a-bible-and-a-sanctuary.

3. Gini Gerbasi, "I'm a Priest: The Police Forced Me Off Church Grounds for Trump's Photo Op," *Washington Post*, June 3, 2020, https://www.washingtonpost .com/outlook/2020/06/03/priest-stjohns-church-trump/.

4. Ibid.

5. Ibid.

6. Ibid.

7. Ibid.

8. Ibid.

9. Paul LeBlanc, "Bishop at DC Church Outraged by Trump Visit: 'I Just Can't Believe What My Eyes Have Seen,'" CNN, June 2, 2020, https://www.cnn.com /2020/06/01/politics/cnntv-bishop-trump-photo-op/index.html.

10. Ibid.

11. "Beth Dalbey, Episcopal Priest 'A Force to Be Reckoned With' After Trump Photo," *Patch*, June 2, 2020, https://patch.com/district-columbia/washingtondc /episcopal-priest-force-be-reckoned-after-trump-photo.

12. David Jackson, Michael Collins, and Nicholas Wu, "Washington Archbishop Denounces Trump Visit to Catholic Shrine as 'Baffling' and 'Reprehensible,'" *USA Today*, June 2, 2020, https://www.usatoday.com/story/news/politics/2020/06/02 /george-floyd-trump-visit-catholic-shrine-amid-photo-op-criticism/3122549001/.

13. Ibid.

14. Aaron Rupar, "What the New IG Report About the Gassing of Protesters Around Lafayette Square Actually Says," *Vox*, June 11, 2021, https://www.vox. com/2021/6/11/22527796/ig-report-trump-bible-lafayette-square-protest.

15. Kristin Kobes Du Mez, *Jesus and John Wayne: How White Evangelicals Corrupted a faith and Fractured a Nation* (Liveright, 2020), 3.

16. Ibid.

17. Ibid.

18. Edgar and Johnson, *The Struggle Over Black Lives Matter and All Lives Matter*, 47.

19. Ibid., 47–48.

20. Lisa Robinson, "Some Honest Thoughts on #BlackLivesMatter, the Church and Real Reconciliation," Lisa Robinson: Thinking and Living Theological

Thoughts Out Loud, May 13, 2016, https://theothoughts.com/2016/05/13/some-honest-thoughts-on-Blacklivesmatter-thechurch-and-real-reconciliation/.

21. Christopher A. House, "Crying for Justice: The #BLACKLIVESMATTER Religious Rhetoric of Bishop T. D. Jakes," *Southern Journal of Communication* 83, no. 1 (2018): 1.

22. Leah Gunning Francis, *Ferguson and Faith: Sparking Leadership and Awakening Community* (Chalice Press, 2015), 63–64.

23. Francis, 47.

24. Jonathan Bastian, "The Role of Spirituality and Prayer in the Black Lives Matter Movement," KCRW, July 25, 2020, https://www.kcrw.com/culture/shows/life-examined/religion-slavery-black-lives-matter/black-lives-matter-blm-melina-abdullah-hebab-ferrag-interview.

25. Liza Vandenboom, "The Faith of the Black Lives Matter Movement," *Religion Unplugged*, July 10, 2020, https://religionunplugged.com/news/2020/7/10/the-faith-of-the-black-lives-matter-movement.

26. Ari Coston, Losing Religion: Black Lives Matter, the Sacred, and the Secular, *Canopy Forum*, August 12, 2020, https://canopyforum.org/2020/08/12/losing-religion-black-lives-matter-the-sacred-and-the-secular/.

27. Michael Battle, "Black Lives Matter: A Spiritual Response," *Spiritus*, no. 21 (2021): 20.

28. Ibid., 29.

29. Ibid., 30.

30. Biko Mandela Gray, "Religion in/and Black Lives Matter: Celebrating the Impossible," *Religion Compass*, no. 13 (2019): 5, https://doi.org/10.1111/rec3.12293.

31. Christopher Cameron and Philip Luke Sinitiere, *Race, Religion, and Black Lives Matter: Essays on a Moment and a Movement* (Vanderbilt University Press, 2021), 2.

32. Ibid., 3.

33. Ibid., 4.

34. Edgar and Johnson, *The Struggle Over Black Lives Matter and All Lives Matter*, 48.

35. Ibid., 48.

36. Ibid., 49–53.

37. Ibid., 52.

38. Ibid.

39. Ibid., 53.

40. Ibid.

41. Twenty-one, male, Black, student.

42. Thirty-seven, female, white, professor.

43. Thirty-seven, female, white, professor.

44. Forty-four, male, white, professor.

45. Anthony Pinn, "How Black Lives Matter Challenges Twentieth Century Models of Protest," Berkley Center for Religion, Peace & World Affairs, October 24, 2020, https://berkleycenter.georgetown.edu/responses/how-black-lives-matter -challenges-twentieth-century-models-of-protest.

46. Twenty-six, female, white, elementary school teacher.

47. Thirty-seven, female, Black, pastor.

48. Thirty-seven, female, Black, pastor.

49. Twenty-two, female, Black, teacher.

50. Fifty-nine, female, Afro-Latina, student/clergy.

51. Mark 12:31.

52. Carly Jennings, "The Love Note That Launched a Movement," *Footnotes* 48, no. 4 (July/August 2020), https://www.asanet.org/news-events/footnotes/jul-aug -2020/features/love-note-launched-movement.

53. Andre E. Johnson, *On Self-Love*, *The Feminist Wire*, September 8, 2013, https://thefeministwire.com/2013/09/self-love/.

54. James Cone, *Black Theology, Black Power: 50th Anniversary Addition* (Orbis Books, 2019).

55. Johnson, *On Self-Love*.

56. Sixty-two, female, white, disabled.

57. Thirty-seven, female, white, professor.

58. Thirty-five, female, Black, food scientist.

59. Sixty-one, female, white, consultant.

60. Edgar and Johnson, 48.

61. Ibid., 54.

62. Fifty-nine, female, Afro-Latina, student/clergy.

63. Fifty-nine, female, Afro-Latina, student/clergy.

64. Fifty-two, female, African American, organizer and faith leader.

65. Black Lives Matter, https://blacklivesmatter.com/about/.

66. Twenty-three, female, Black, caregiver.

67. Twenty-three, female, Black, caregiver.

68. Earle J. Fisher, *The Reverend Albert Cleage Jr. and the Black Prophetic Tradition: A Reintroduction of the Black Messiah* (Lexington Books, 2022).

69. Fisher, 107.

70. Ibid.

71. Quoted in Fisher, *The Reverend Albert Cleage Jr.*, 82.

72. Ibid., 111.

73. Fisher, 102.

74. Eliza Griswold, "How Black Lives Matter is Changing the Church," *New Yorker*, August 30, 2020, https://www.newyorker.com/news/on-religion/how -black-lives-matter-is-changing-the-church.

75. Ibid.

76. Ibid.

77. Ibid.

78. Eighty-four, female, white, retired.

79. Forty-five, female, Anglo, energy professional/political candidate.

80. Twenty-eight, male, white, youth pastor/denominational employee.

81. Twenty-six, female, white, student affairs professional.

82. Fifty-five, male, white, retail.

83. Thirty-eight, female, white, minister.

84. Fifty-one, male, white, professor.

85. Edgar and Johnson, 65.

86. Ibid.

87. Ibid.

88. Ibid., 66.

89. Ibid.

90. Ibid.

Chapter 5: "It's How We Pick Our Enemy": BLM and the Role of Electoral Politics

1. Barack Obama, "Obama's Full Remarks at Howard University Commencement Ceremony," *Politico*, May 7, 2016, para. 36. https://www.politico.com/story/2016/05/obamas-howard-commencement-transcript-222931.

2. Ibid.

3. Ibid.

4. Ibid.

5. Ibid.

6. Ibid.

7. Ibid.

8. Ibid.

9. Ibid.

10. Ibid.

11. Ibid.

12. Ibid.

13. Ibid.

14. Vanessa Williams and Scott Clement, "Despite Black Lives Matter, Young Black Americans Aren't Voting in Higher Numbers." *Washington Post*, May 14, 2016, https://www.washingtonpost.com/politics/despite-black-lives-matter-young-black-americans-arent-voting-in-higher-numbers/2016/05/14/e1780b3a-1176-11e6-93ae-50921721165d_story.html.

15. Ibid.

16. Reniqua Allen, "Note to Media: Black Lives Matter Is Not a 'Get Out the Vote Campaign,'" *The Nation*, May 20, 2016, https://www.thenation.com/article /archive/note-to-media-black-lives-matter-is-not-a-get-out-the-vote-campaign/.

17. Ibid.

18. Ibid.

19. "'We Are Pushing Real Revolution': Black Lives Matter on Why They Don't Have Faith in Any Candidate," *Democracy Now!*, March 9, 2016, https://www .democracynow.org/2016/3/9/we_are_pushing_real_revolution_black (para. 4).

20. "Black Lives Matter Movement Won't Endorse a Presidential Candidate," *PBS News Hour*, September 19, 2015, https://www.pbs.org/newshour/politics /black-lives-matter-movement-wont-endorse-presidential-candidate.

21. Maya King, "Black Lives Matter Launches a Political Action Committee," *Politico*, October 9, 2020, https://www.politico.com/news/2020/10/09/black-lives -matter-pac-428403.

22. Ibid.

23. Ibid.

24. Ibid.

25. Ibid.

26. Sam Frizell, "Sanders and O'Malley Stumble During Black Lives Matter Protest," *Time*, July 18, 2015, https://time.com/3963692/bernie-sanders-martin -omalley-black-lives-matter/.

27. Dan Merica, "Black Lives Matter Protesters Shut Down Sanders Event in Seattle," *CNN Politics*, August 10, 2015, https://www.cnn.com/2015/08/08/politics /bernie-sanders-black-lives-matter-protesters/index.html.

28. Maggie Haberman, "Hillary Clinton, Pressed on Race, Issues Her Own Challenge," *New York Times*, August 19, 2015, https://www.nytimes.com/2015/08/20 /us/politics/hillary-clinton-takes-on-civil-rights-generation-gap.html?_r=0.

29. Jelani Cobb, "The Matter of Black Lives," *New Yorker*, March 6, 2016. https://www.newyorker.com/magazine/2016/03/14/where-is-black-lives-matter -headed (para. 33).

30. Ibid.

31. Ibid.

32. Darren Sands, "DNC to Vote on Resolution Supporting Black Lives Matter," *Buzzfeed News*, August 27, 2015, https://www.buzzfeednews.com/article/darren sands/dnc-to-vote-on-resolution-supporting-black-lives-matter#.dk14OZjWA.

33. Black Lives Matter, statement, Facebook, August 30, 2015, https://www .facebook.com/BlackLivesMatter/posts/488330528004864.

34. Ibid.

35. Ibid.

36. Ibid.

37. Ibid.

38. Ibid.

39. Ibid.

40. Keeanga-Yamahtta Taylor, *From #BlackLivesMatter to Black Liberation* (Haymarket Books, 2016), 6.

41. Ibid., 103.

42. Theodore Johnson, "We Are Not Our Vote," *New America*, September 15, 2016, https://www.newamerica.org/weekly/we-are-not-our-vote/.

43. Ibid.

44. Ibid.

45. Ibid.

46. Ibid.

47. Aaron Morrison, "Black Lives Matter Issues a Statement on Trump's Election. Mic. November 15, 2016," https://www.mic.com/articles/159496/exclusive -black-lives-matter-issues-a-statement-on-trump-s-election#.dFUSeOdvg.

48. Ibid.

49. Ibid.

50. Ibid.

51. Ibid.

52. Ibid.

53. Ibid.

54. Ibid.

55. Brandon Tensley, "The 2016 Election Exposed Deep Seated Racism: Where Do We Go from Here," *Talk Poverty*, November 17, 2016, https://talkpoverty.org /2016/11/17/2016-election-exposed-deep-seated-racism-go/.

56. Ibid.

57. Ibid.

58. Ibid.

59. Ibid.

60. Ibid.

61. Ibid.

62. Twenty-seven, male, Black, student.

63. Twenty-two, female, Black, teacher.

64. Twenty-seven, male, African American, recruiting specialist.

65. Sixty-one, female, white, consultant.

66. Forty-five, female, Anglo, energy professional/political candidate.

67. Forty-three, female, African American, professor.

68. Sixty-six, female, Asian, associate professor.

69. Thirty-four, female, Black, ministry.

70. Sixty-six, female, Asian, associate professor.

71. Fifty-nine, female, Afro-Latina, student/clergy.

72. Fifty-one, male, white, professor.

73. Thirty-four, male, Black, editorial assistant.

74. Thirty, female, white/Caucasian, attorney.

75. Forty-five, male, Black, teacher.

76. Twenty-one, male, Black, student.

77. Forty-three, female, white, daycare teacher.

78. Thirty-six, trans female, white, occupation n/a.

79. Thirty-five, female, Black, food scientist.

80. Thirty-four, male, Black, editorial assistant.

81. Sixty-nine, female, white, retired registered nurse.

82. Sixty-nine, female, white, retired registered nurse.

83. Thirty-six, trans female, white, occupation n/a.

84. Twenty-three, female, Black, caregiver.

85. Forty, male, white, carpenter.

86. Fifty-seven, male, Black, pastor/professor.

87. Thirty-four, male, Black, editorial assistant.

88. Forty-two, male, Black, teacher.

89. Thirty-four, male, Black, editorial assistant.

90. Sixty-one, female, white, consultant.

91. Twenty-six, female, white, student affairs professional.

92. Wilbert L. Cooper, "I Ain't Voting Until Black Lives Matter: What Does an activist Radical Strategy Mean for 2020?," *The Guardian*, September 18, 2020, https://www.theguardian.com/us-news/2020/apr/18/i-aint-voting-till-black-lives-matter-what-does-an-activists-radical-strategy-mean-for-2020.

93. Ibid.

94. Ibid.

95. Sixty-one, female, white, consultant.

96. Jessica Byrd, "The Future of Black Politics," *New York Times*, September 1, 2020, https://www.nytimes.com/2020/09/01/opinion/black-lives-matter-election.html (para. 4).

97. Ibid.

98. Ibid.

99. Ibid.

100. Ibid.

101. Ibid.

Chapter 6: "This Is Live? This Is Real?": Streaming a Movement

1. Yarimar Bonilla and Jonathan Rosa, "#Ferguson: Digital Protest, Hashtag Ethnography, and the Racial Politics of Social Media in the United States," *American Ethnologist* 42, no. 1 (2015), http://doi.org/10.1111/amet.12112.

2. Lisa Nakamura, *Digitizing Race: Visual Cultures of the Internet* (University of Minnesota Press, 2008).

3. Ibid.

4. Janani Umamaheswar, "Policing and Racial (In)Justice in the Media: Newspaper Portrayals of the "Black Lives Matter" Movement," *University of California Press* 1, no. 1 (2020), https://doi.org/10.1525/001c.12143.

5. Florini, *Beyond Hashtags.*

6. Sarah J. Jackson, Moya Bailey, and Brooke Foucault Welles, *#HashtagActivism: Networks of Race and Gender Justice* (MIT Press, 2020).

7. Sarah T. Roberts, *Behind the Screen: Content Moderation in the Shadows of Social Media* (Yale University Press, 2019).

8. Edgar and Johnson, *The Struggle.*

9. Andre Brock, *Distributed Blackness: African American Cyberculture* (New York University Press, 2020).

10. Sarah J. Jackson, Moya Bailey, and Brooke Foucault Welles, *#Hashtag Activism: Networks of Race and Gender Justice*, (MIT Press, 2020).

11. https://www.pewresearch.org/internet/2016/08/15/the-hashtag-blacklivesmatter-emerges-social-activism-on-twitter/.

12. Brock, *Distributed Blackness.*

13. Edgar and Johnson, *The Struggle.*

14. Nick Wing, "When the Media Treat White Suspects and Killers Better Than Black Victims," *Huffpost*, December 6, 2007, https://www.huffpost.com/entry/media-black-victims_n_5673291.

15. Forty-three, female, African American, professor.

16. Forty-seven, female, Black, lawyer.

17. Rasmus Kleis Nielsen and Simge Andi, "Race and Leadership in the News Media 2020: Evidence from Five Markets," *Reuters Institute*, July 16, 2020, https://reutersinstitute.politics.ox.ac.uk/race-and-leadership-news-media-2020-evidence-five-markets.

18. Thirty-eight, female, Caucasian, English professor.

19. Declined questionnaire.

20. Forty, male, white, carpenter.

21. Eighty-four, female, white, retired.

22. Jackson, Bailey, and Welles, *#Hashtag Activism*, 2020.

23. Suyin Haynes, "Several Antiracist Books Are Selling Out. Here's What Else Black Booksellers and Publishers Say You Should Read," *Time*, June 2, 2020, https://time.com/5846732/books-to-read-about-anti-racism/.

24. Sara M. Moniuszko and Anika Reed, "100 Resources to Take Action Against Racism, Help Black Organizations and Learn to be Anti-Racist," *USA Today*, May 29, 2020, https://www.usatoday.com/story/life/2020/05/29/george-floyd-death-donations-resources-justice-petitions/5282539002/.

25. Rachel Epstein, "George Floyd Was Murdered. We Must Not Be Silent—Here's How to Help" *Marie Claire*, June 1, 2020, https://www.marieclaire.com/politics/a32712559/how-to-help-george-floyd-protests-donate/.

26. Brooke Auxier, "Social Media Continue to be Important Political Outlets for Black Americans," *Pew Research Center*, December 11, 2020, https://www.pewresearch.org/fact-tank/2020/12/11/social-media-continue-to-be-important-political-outlets-for-black-americans/.

27. Forty-three, female, white, daycare teacher.

28. Thirty-eight, female, Caucasian, English professor.

29. Ibram X. Kendi, *How to Be an Antiracist* (One World Publishing, 2019).

30. Ijeoma Oluo, *So You Want to Talk About Race* (Seal Press, 2019).

31. Robin DiAngelo, *White Fragility: Why It's So Hard for White People to Talk About Racism* (Beacon Press, 2018).

32. Forty, male, white, carpenter.

33. Twenty-six, female, white, student affairs professional.

34. Twenty-three, female, Black, caregiver.

35. Fifty-nine, female, Afro-Latina, student/clergy.

36. Aaron Ross Coleman, "How Black People Really Feel About the Police, Explained," *Vox*, June 17, 2020, https://www.vox.com/2020/6/17/21292046/black-people-abolish-defund-dismantle-police-george-floyd-breonna-taylor-black-lives-matter-protest.

37. Declined questionnaire.

38. Twenty-one, male, Black, student.

39. Twenty-five, female, white/Caucasian, graduate student.

40. Claire Fallon, "Can a Book Club Fight Racism?" *Huffpost*, August 19, 2020, https://www.huffpost.com/entry/can-a-book-club-fight-racism_n_5f3a80abc5b6e054c3fc9d44.

41. Edgar and Johnson, *The Struggle*.

42. Forty, female, white, teacher.

43. Fifty-nine, female, Afro-Latina, student/clergy.

44. Thirty-seven, female, Black, pastor.

45. Twenty-two, female, Black, teacher.

46. Twenty-six, female, white, elementary school teacher.

47. Forty-seven, female, Black, lawyer.

48. Declined questionnaire.

49. Declined questionnaire.

50. https://www.vox.com/recode/2020/6/11/21281028/before-sharing-images-police-brutality-protest-george-floyd-ahmaud-arbery-facebook-instagram-twitter; https://www.nytimes.com/2020/06/03/opinion/george-floyd-video-social-media.html; https://penntoday.upenn.edu/news/police-killings-and-black-mental-health.

51. Twenty-two, NB, Middle Eastern, student.

52. Patrice Khan-Cullors and asha bandele, *When They Call You a Terrorist: A Black Lives Matter Memoir* (St. Martin's Griffin, 2020).

53. Forty-seven, female, Black, lawyer.

54. Kia Gregory, "How Videos of Police Brutality Traumatize African Americans and Undermine the Search for Justice," *New Republic*, February 14, 2019, https://newrepublic.com/article/153103/videos-police-brutality-traumatize-african-americans-undermine-search-justice.

55. Quoted in "How Videos of Police Brutality Traumatize African Americans."

56. Thirty-seven, female, Black, pastor.

57. Forty-seven, female, Black, lawyer.

58. Twenty-six, female, white, elementary school teacher.

59. Twenty-two, NB, Middle Eastern, student.

60. Forty-three, female, African American, professor.

61. Forty-three, female, white, daycare teacher.

62. Forty-three, female, white, daycare teacher.

63. Twenty-six, female, white, elementary school teacher.

64. Twenty-eight, genderqueer/femme leaning, white, PhD student at UC Sociology.

65. Twenty-two, NB, Middle Eastern, student.

66. Ashlee Marie Preston, "Sorry, Consuming Trauma Porn Is Not Allyship," *Marie Claire*, June 9, 2020, https://www.marieclaire.com/politics/a32802688/stop-sharing-trauma-porn-black-deaths/.

67. Twenty-two, NB, Middle Eastern, student.

68. Forty-seven, female, Black, lawyer.

69. Andrew Perrin, "23% of Users in U.S. Say Social Media Led Them to Change Views on an Issue; Some Cite Black Lives Matter," Pew Research Center, October 15, 2020, https://www.pewresearch.org/fact-tank/2020/10/15/23-of-users-in-us-say-social-media-led-them-to-change-views-on-issue-some-cite-black-lives-matter/.

70. Harmeet Kaur, "Videos Often Contradict What Police Say in Reports. Here's Why Some Officers Continue to Lie," CNN, June 6, 2020, https://www.cnn.com/2020/06/06/us/police-reports-lying-videos-misconduct-trnd/index.html.

Conclusion

1. Laurel Wamsley, "Derek Chauvin Found Guilty of George Floyd's Murder." NPR, April 20, 2021, https://www.npr.org/sections/trial-over-killing-of-george-floyd/2021/04/20/987777911/court-says-jury-has-reached-verdict-in-derek-chauvins-murder-trial.

2. Bill Chappell, "Derek Chauvin is Sentenced to 22 ½ Years for George Floyd's Murder." NPR, June 25, 2021, https://www.npr.org/sections/trial-over-killing-of -george-floyd/2021/06/25/1009524284/derek-chauvin-sentencing-george-floyd -murder.

3. Hannah Knowles, "Judge Approves Derek Chauvin Plea Deal for Violating George Floyd's Rights," May 4, 2022, https://www.washingtonpost.com/nation /2022/05/04/chauvin-federal-plea-deal/.

4. Amy Forliti, Steve Karnowski, and Tammy Webster, "3 Ex-Cops Convicted of Rights Violations in Floyd Killing," AP News, February 24, 2022, https://apnews .com/article/death-of-george-floyd-george-floyd-minneapolis-race-and-ethnicity -racial-injustice-ab7a1e89268ac60a58ae8a317e0b6079.

5. Ibid.

6. Eric Levenson and Bill Kirkos, "Two Officers Who restrained George Floyd Sentenced to 3 Years and 3.5 Years in Federal Prison," CNN, July 27, 2022, https:// www.cnn.com/2022/07/27/us/tou-thao-kueng-george-floyd-sentence/index.html.

7. Cole Premo, "State Trial Delayed for Tou Thao, J. Alexander Kueng until January 2023," CBS Minnesota, June 6, 2022, https://www.cbsnews.com/minnesota /news/state-trial-delayed-for-tou-thao-j-alexander-kueng-until-january-2023/.

8. Wamsley.

9. Johnson and Stone, "The Most Dangerous Negro in America."

10. Reggie Jackson, "The Inevitability of a White Backlash to the George Floyd Protests," Milwaukee Independent, June 12, 2020, http://www.milwaukee independent.com/featured/inevitability-white-backlash-george-floyd-protests/.

11. Kali Holloway, "The Whitelash Next Time," The Nation, September 8, 2020, https://www.thenation.com/article/society/black-lives-matter-backlash/.

12. Nathalie Baptiste, "One Year After George Floyd's Murder, the Racial Reckoning Gave Way to a Backlash," Mother Jones, May 27, 2021, https://www.mother jones.com/politics/2021/05/one-year-after-george-floyds-murder-the-racial -reckoning-gave-way-to-a-backlash/.

13. Ibid.

14. Kali Holloway, "Our 'Racial Reckoning' Is Turning Out to Be a White Lie," The Nation, July 19, 2021, https://www.thenation.com/article/society/black -lives-matter-backlash-2/.

15. Aaron Morrison, "Black Lives Matter Opens Up About Its Finances," AP, February 23, 2021, https://apnews.com/article/black-lives-matter-90-million -finances-8a80cad199f54c0c4b9e74283d27366f.

16. Karen Attiah, "Black Lives Matter Needs to Get Its (Real Expensive) House in Order," Washington Post, April 11, 2022, https://www.washingtonpost.com /opinions/2022/04/11/black-lives-matters-needs-get-its-real-expensive-house -order/.

17. Ibid.

18. Morrison.

19. Black Lives Matter, BLM Transparency Center, https://blacklivesmatter
.com/transparency/.

20. Ibid.

21. Ibid.

22. Sean Campbell, "Black Lives Matter Secretly Bought a $6 Million House,"
Intelligencer, April 4, 2022, nymag.com.

23. Ibid.

24. Ibid.

25. Ibid.

26. Attiah.

27. BLM Transparency Center.

28. Ibid.

29. Edgar and Johnson, *The Struggle Over Black Lives Matter and All Lives
Matter*, 114–15.

30. Kim Eckart, "How Black Lives Matter Protests Sparked Interest, Can Lead
to Change," *UW News*, March 7, 2022, https://www.washington.edu/news/2022
/03/07/how-black-lives-matter-protests-sparked-interest-can-lead-to-change/.

31. Ibid.

BIBLIOGRAPHY

Allen, Reniqua. "Note to Media: Black Lives Matter Is Not a 'Get Out the Vote'
Campaign." *The Nation*, May 20, 2016. https://www.thenation.com/article
/archive/note-to-media-black-lives-matter-is-not-a-get-out-the-vote-campaign/.
Amnesty International. "USA: Law Enforcement Violated Black Lives Matter
Protesters' Human Rights, Documents Acts of Police Violence and Excessive
Force." Amnesty International, August 8, 2022. https://www.amnesty.org/en
/latest/press-release/2020/08/usa-law-enforcement-violated-black-livesmatter
-protesters-human-rights/.
Amnesty International USA. "The World Is Watching: Mass Violations by U.S.
Police of Black Lives Matter Protesters' Rights." Amnesty International USA,
n.d. https://www.amnestyusa.org/worldiswatching/.
Anderson, Monica. "3. The Hashtag #BlackLivesMatter Emerges: Social Activism
on Twitter." Pew Research Center, August 15, 2016. https://www.pewresearch
.org/internet/2016/08/15/the-hashtag-blacklivesmatter-emerges-social
-activism-on-twitter/.
Armour, Nancy. "Opinion: Drew Brees Needs to Do More than Apologize for
Comments on Protests." *USA Today*, June 4, 2020. https://eu.usatoday.com
/story/sports/columnist/nancy-armour/2020/06/04/george-floyd-drew-brees
-needs-do-more-than-apologize-comments/3144320001/.
Asmelash, Leah. "In Reactions to Roger Goodell's Mea Culpa, Most Seized on
What He Didn't Say." CNN, June 6, 2020. https://edition.cnn.com/2020/06
/05/us/colin-kaepernick-roger-goodell-statement-trnd/index.html.
Attiah, Karen. "Black Lives Matter Needs to Get Its (Real Expensive) House in
Order." *Washington Post*, April 11, 2022. https://www.washingtonpost.com/
opinions/2022/04/11/black-lives-matters-needs-get-its-real-expensive
-house-order/.
Auxier, Brooke. "Social Media Continue to Be Important Political Outlets for
Black Americans." Pew Research Center, December 11, 2020. https://www.pew
research.org/fact-tank/2020/12/11/social-media-continue-to-be-important
-political-outlets-for-black-americans/.

Bailey, Julius, and David Leonard. "Black Lives Matter: Post-Nihilistic Freedom Dreams." *Journal of Contemporary Rhetoric* 5, nos. 3–4 (2015): 67–77.

Baptiste, Nathalie. "One Year after George Floyd's Murder, the Racial Reckoning Gave Way to a Backlash." *Mother Jones*, May 27, 2021. https://www.mother jones.com/politics/2021/05/one-year-after-george-floyds-murder-the-racial -reckoning-gave-way-to-a-backlash/.

Barroso, Amanda, and Rachel Minkin. "Recent Protest Attendees Are More Racially and Ethnically Diverse, Younger than Americans Overall." Pew Research Center, June 24, 2020. https://www.pewresearch.org/fact-tank /2020/06/24/recent-protest-attendees-are-more-racially-and-ethnically -diverse-younger-than-americans-overall/.

Bastian, Jonathan. "Is Black Lives Matter a Spiritual Movement? Melina Abdullah on How Ritual Adds Energy to Collective Actions." KCRW, April 30, 2022. https://www.kcrw.com/culture/shows/life-examined/religion-slavery-black-lives -matter/black-lives-matter-blm-melina-abdullah-hebab-ferrag-interview.

Battle, Michael. "Black Lives Matter: A Spiritual Response." *Spiritus: A Journal of Christian Spirituality* 21, no. 1 (2021): 20–35. https://doi.org/10.1353/ scs.2021.0002.

Benjamin, Andrea. "Polls Show Strong Support for the Protests—and Also for How Police Handled Them." *Washington Post*, June 11, 2020. https://www .washingtonpost.com/outlook/polling-protests-police-protesters-opinion /2020/06/11/987259fe-ab5a-11ea-9063-e69bd6520940_story.html.

Berger, Matt. "Why the Black Lives Matter Protests Didn't Contribute to the COVID-19 Surge." *Healthline*, July 8, 2020. https://www.healthline.com/health -news/black-lives-matter-protests-didnt-contribute-to-covid19-surge.

Black Lives Matter. Statement. Facebook, August 30, 2015. https://www.facebook .com/BlackLivesMatter/posts/488330528004864.

Blacklivesmatter.com. "Herstory," n.d. https://blacklivesmatter.com/herstory/.

Blue Water Media. "National Neighborhood Watch | Crime Prevention Through Neighborhood Cohesiveness and Collaboration," n.d. https://www.nnw.org/.

Bonilla, Yarimar, and Jonathon Rosa. "#Ferguson: Digital Protest, Hashtag Ethnography, and the Racial Politics of Social Media in the United States." *American Ethnologist* 42, no. 1 (January 15, 2015). https://doi.org/10.1111/amet.12112.

Brock, André, Jr. *Distributed Blackness: African American Cybercultures.* New York University Press, 2020.

Brownhill, Leigh. "The Emancipatory Politics of Anti-Racism." *Capitalism Nature Socialism* 31, no. 3 (August 26, 2020): 4–15. https://doi.org/10.1080/10455752.2 020.1790714.

Buchanan, Larry, Quoctrung Bui, and Jugal Patel. "Black Lives Matter May Be the Largest Movement in U.S. History." *New York Times*, October 25, 2021. https:// www.nytimes.com/interactive/2020/07/03/us/george-floyd-protests-crowd -size.html.

Business Insider. "The Action Generation: How Gen Z Really Feels about Race, Equality, and Its Role in the Historic George Floyd Protests, Based on a Survey of 39,000 Young Americans," June 15, 2020. https://www.businessinsider.com/how-gen-z-feels-about-george-floyd-protests-2020-6?international =true&r=US&IR=T.

Byrd, Jessica. "The Future of Black Politics." *New York Times,* September 1, 2020. https://www.nytimes.com/2020/09/01/opinion/black-lives-matter-election.html.

Call, Tommy, III. "Steph Curry Voices Outrage about Death of George Floyd with Instagram Message." *Warriors Wire,* May 27, 2020. https://warriorswire.usa today.com/2020/05/27/steph-curry-voices-outrage-about-death-of-george -floyd-with-instagram-message/.

Cameron, Christopher, and Phillip Luke Sinitiere, eds. *Race, Religion, and Black Lives Matter: Essays on a Moment and a Movement.* Vanderbilt University Press, 2021.

Cathcart, Robert S. "Movements: Confrontation as Rhetorical Form." *Southern Speech Communication Journal* 43, no. 3 (September 1978): 233–47. https://doi .org/10.1080/10417947809372383.

Chappell, Bill. "Derek Chauvin Is Sentenced to 22 1/2 Years for George Floyd's Murder." NPR, June 25, 2021. https://www.npr.org/sections/trial-over-killing -of-george-floyd/2021/06/25/1009524284/derek-chauvin-sentencing-george -floyd-murder.

Chávez, Karma R., and Cindy L. Griffin. "Power, Feminisms, and Coalitional Agency: Inviting and Enacting Difficult Dialogues." *Women's Studies in Communication* 32, no. 1 (April 2009): 1–11. https://doi.org/10.1080/07491409 .2009.10162378.

Cheung, By Helier. "George Floyd Death: Why Do Some Protests Turn Violent?" BBC News, May 31, 2020. https://www.bbc.com/news/world-us-canada -52869563.

Cobb, Jelani. "The Matter of Black Lives." *New Yorker,* March 6, 2016. https://www .newyorker.com/magazine/2016/03/14/where-is-black-lives-matter-headed.

Coleman, Aaron Ross. "How Black Americans Really Feel about the Police, Explained." *Vox,* June 17, 2020. https://www.vox.com/2020/6/17/21292046/black -people-abolish-defund-dismantle-police-george-floyd-breonna-taylor-black -lives-matter-protest.

Collins, Patricia Hill. "On Violence, Intersectionality and Transversal Politics." *Ethnic and Racial Studies* 40, no. 9 (June 5, 2017): 1460–73. https://doi.org/10.1 080/01419870.2017.1317827.

Collins, Patricia Hill, and Sirma Bilge. *Intersectionality (Key Concepts).* 1st ed. Polity, 2016.

Colston, Ari. "'Losing Religion:' Black Lives Matter, the Sacred, and the Secular." *Canopy Forum,* August 12, 2020. https://canopyforum.org/2020/08/12 /losing-religion-black-lives-matter-the-sacred-and-the-secular/.

Cone, James. *Black Theology and Black Power: 50th Anniversary Edition*. Orbis Books, 2019.

Conrad, Ryan. *Against Equality: Queer Revolution, Not Mere Inclusion*. AK Press, 2014.

Cooper, Wilbert L. "'I Ain't Voting Till Black Lives Matter': What Does an Activist's Radical Strategy Mean for 2020?" *The Guardian*, April 18, 2020. https://www.theguardian.com/us-news/2020/apr/18/i-aint-voting-till-black-lives-matter-what-does-an-activists-radical-strategy-mean-for-2020.

Cotton, Tom. "Opinion | Tom Cotton: Send In the Military." *New York Times*, June 7, 2020. https://www.nytimes.com/2020/06/03/opinion/tom-cotton-protests-military.html.

Crenshaw, Kimberle. "Demarginalizing the Intersection of Race and Sex: A Black Feminist Critique of Antidiscrimination Doctrine, Feminist Theory and Antiracist Politics." *University of Chicago Legal Forum*, vol. 1989, no. 1, article 8.

Crenshaw, Kimberle. "Mapping the Margins: Intersectionality, Identity Politics, and Violence against Women of Color." *Stanford Law Review* 43, no. 6 (July 1991): 1241. https://doi.org/10.2307/1229039.

Creswell, John. *Research Design: Qualitative, Quantitative, and Mixed Methods Approaches, 3rd Edition*. 3rd ed. SAGE Publications, Inc., 2008.

Cullors, Patrisse, and Asha Bandele. *When They Call You a Terrorist: A Black Lives Matter Memoir*. St. Martin's Press, 2018.

Dalbey, Beth. "Episcopal Priest 'A Force to Be Reckoned With' After Trump Photo." *Patch*, June 2, 2020. https://patch.com/district-columbia/washingtondc/episcopal-priest-force-be-reckoned-after-trump-photo.

Dave, Dhaval. "Black Lives Matter Protests and Risk Avoidance: The Case of Civil Unrest During a Pandemic." NBER, June 22, 2020. https://www.nber.org/papers/w27408.

Dave, Dhaval, Andrew I. Friedson, Kyutaro Matsuzawa, Joseph J. Sabia, and Samuel Safford. "Black Lives Matter Protests, Social Distancing, and COVID-19." *Social Science Research Network*, December 31, 2019. https://doi.org/10.2139/ssrn.3631599.

DiAngelo, Robin. *White Fragility: Why It's So Hard for White People to Talk About Racism*. Beacon Press, 2018.

Dickman, Laurel. "5 Ways to Make Protests Accessible And Truly Include Disabled Folks." *HuffPost*, February 21, 2017. https://www.huffpost.com/entry/5-ways-to-make-protests-accessible-and-truly-include-disabled-folks_b_58acac38e4b02eb3a9832c78.

DiJulio, Bianca, Mira Norton, Symone Jackson, and Mollyann Brodie. "Kaiser Family Foundation/CNN Survey of Americans on Race." *Files.Kff.Org*, November 2015. https://files.kff.org/attachment/report-survey-of-americans-on-race.

Dionne, Evette. "For Black Women, Self-Care Is a Radical Act." *Ravishly*, March 6, 2015. https://www.ravishly.com/2015/03/06/radical-act-self-care-black -women-feminism.

Eckart, Kim. "How Black Lives Matter Protests Sparked Interest, Can Lead to Change." *UW News*, March 7, 2022. https://www.washington.edu/news /2022/03/07/how-black-lives-matter-protests-sparked-interest-can-lead -to-change/.

The Economist. "Whatever Happened to Black Lives Matter?" May 21, 2020. https://www.economist.com/united-states/2020/05/21/whatever-happened -to-black-lives-matter.

Edgar, Amanda Nell, and Andre Johnson. *The Struggle over Black Lives Matter and All Lives Matter*. Lexington Books, 2018.

Edgar, Amanda Nell, and Ashton Toone. "'She Invited Other People to That Space': Audience Habitus, Place, and Social Justice in Beyoncé's *Lemonade*." *Feminist Media Studies* 19, no. 1 (September 21, 2017): 87–101. https://doi.org /10.1080/14680777.2017.1377276.

Editorial Board. "Another Unarmed Black Man Has Died at the Hands of Police. When Will It End?" *Washington Post*, May 27, 2020. https://www.washington post.com/opinions/another-unarmed-black-man-has-died-at-the-hands-of -police-when-will-it-end/2020/05/26/7c426b88-9f80-11ea-9590-1858a893bd59 _story.html.

Ellis, Sarah Kate. "GLAAD Statement: 'There Can Be No Pride If It Is Not Intersectional.'" GLAAD (blog), June 1, 2020. https://www.glaad.org/blog /glaad-statement-black-lives-matter.

Emba, Christine. "Intersectionality." *Washington Post*, September 21, 2015. https:// www.washingtonpost.com/news/in-theory/wp/2015/09/21/intersectionality -a-primer/?tid=a_inl&utm_term=.aa49b841c868.

Epstein, Rachel. "George Floyd Was Murdered. We Must Not Be Silent—Here's How to Help." *Marie Claire*, July 1, 2020. https://www.marieclaire.com /politics/a32712559/how-to-help-george-floyd-protests-donate/.

Fallon, Claire. "Can A Book Club Fight Racism?" *HuffPost*, August 19, 2020. https://www.huffpost.com/entry/can-a-book-club-fight-racism_n_5f3a80abc 5b6e054c3fc9d44.

Fisher, Earle. *The Reverend Albert Cleage Jr. and the Black Prophetic Tradition: A Reintroduction of the Black Messiah*. Lexington Books, 2021.

Florini, Sarah. *Beyond Hashtags: Racial Politics and Black Digital Networks*. New York University Press, 2019.

Forensic Architecture. "Police Brutality at the BLM Protests," n.d. https://blm protests.forensic-architecture.org/.

Forliti, Amy, Steve Karnowski, and Tammy Webster. "3 Ex-Cops Convicted of Rights Violations in Floyd Killing." *AP News*, February 24, 2022. https://

apnews.com/article/death-of-george-floyd-george-floyd-minneapolis-race
-and-ethnicity-racial-injustice-ab7a1e89268ac60a58ae8a317e0b6079.

Fox News. "Tucker: The Never-Ending Car Crash of Intersectionality," February 7, 2019. https://www.youtube.com/watch?v=XWCmQ8euRJM.

Francis, Leah Gunning. *Ferguson and Faith: Sparking Leadership and Awakening Community*. Chalice Press, 2015.

Frizell, Sam. "Sanders and O'Malley Stumble During Black Lives Matter Protest." *Time*, July 18, 2015. https://time.com/3963692/bernie-sanders-martin-omalley
-black-lives-matter/.

Garza, Alicia. *The Purpose of Power: How We Come Together When We Fall Apart*, 2021.

Gerbasi, Gini. "I'm a Priest. The Police Forced Me off Church Grounds for Trump's Photo Op." *Washington Post*, June 3, 2020. https://www.washington
post.com/outlook/2020/06/03/priest-stjohns-church-trump/.

Google Trends. "Black Lives Matter," n.d. https://trends.google.com/trends/story
/US_cu_IxEWyVUBAABgWM_en.

Gowland, Lelia. "White Women: 3 Ways to Sustain Anti-Racism as A Lifelong Commitment." *Forbes*, June 25, 2020. https://www.forbes.com/sites/lelia
gowland/2020/06/25/white-women-3-ways-to-sustain-anti-racism-as-a
-lifelong-commitment/?sh=b842152b39bc.

Gray, Biko Mandela. "Religion in/and Black Lives Matter: Celebrating the Impossible." *Religion Compass* 13, no. 1 (2019): e12293. https://doi.org/10.1111
/rec3.12293.

Gregory, Kia. "How Videos of Police Brutality Traumatize African Americans and Undermine the Search for Justice." *New Republic*, February 13, 2019. https://newrepublic.com/article/153103/videos-police-brutality-traumatize
-african-americans-undermine-search-justice.

Gregory, Sean. "College Athletes Are Realizing Their Power Amid the George Floyd Protests and COVID-19." *Time*, June 18, 2020. https://time.com
/5855471/college-athletes-covid-19-protests-racial-equality/.

Griswold, Eliza. "How Black Lives Matter Is Changing the Church." *New Yorker*, August 30, 2020. https://www.newyorker.com/news/on-religion/how-black
-lives-matter-is-changing-the-church.

Haakenson, Thomas O. "1968, Now and Then: Black Lives, Black Bodies." *Cultural Critique* 103, no. 1 (2019): 75–83. https://doi.org/10.1353/cul.2019.0022.

Haberman, Maggie. "Hillary Clinton, Pressed on Race, Issues Her Own Challenge." *New York Times*, August 19, 2015. https://www.nytimes.com/2015/08/20/us
/politics/hillary-clinton-takes-on-civil-rights-generation-gap.html?_r=0.

Harlow, Summer. "Journalism's Change Agents: Black Lives Matter, #BlackoutTuesday, and a Shift Toward Activist Doxa." *Journalism & Mass*

Communication Quarterly 99, no. 3 (July 19, 2022): 742–62. https://doi.org /10.1177/10776990221108648.

Haynes, Suyin. "Several Antiracist Books Are Selling Out. Here's What Else Black Booksellers and Publishers Say You Should Read." *Time*, June 2, 2020. https:// time.com/5846732/books-to-read-about-anti-racism/.

Helin, Kurt. "LeBron James, Others around NBA Speak out after Death of George Floyd." NBCSports.com, May 27, 2020. https://nba.nbcsports.com/2020/05/27 /lebron-james-others-around-nba-speak-out-after-death-of-george-floyd/.

Hern, Alex. "Twitter Hides Donald Trump Tweet for 'Glorifying Violence.'" *The Guardian*, May 30, 2020. https://www.theguardian.com/technology/2020 /may/29/twitter-hides-donald-trump-tweet-glorifying-violence.

Hernandez, Daniela, Sarah Krouse, Brianna Abbott, and Charity Scott. "Early Data Show No Uptick in Covid-19 Transmission from Protests." *Wall Street Journal*, June 18, 2020. https://www.wsj.com/articles/recent-protests-may-not -be-covid-19-transmission-hotspots-11592498020.

Holland, Jesse J. "Black Lives Matter Movement Won't Endorse a Presidential Candidate." *PBS NewsHour*, September 19, 2015. https://www.pbs.org/news hour/politics/black-lives-matter-movement-wont-endorse-presidential -candidate.

Holloway, Kali. "Our 'Racial Reckoning' Is Turning Out to Be a White Lie." *The Nation*, July 19, 2021. https://www.thenation.com/article/society/black-lives -matter-backlash-2/.

Holloway, Kali. "The Whitelash Next Time." *The Nation*, September 8, 2020. https://www.thenation.com/article/society/black-lives-matter-backlash/.

Holt, Lanier Frush, and Dustin Carnahan. "Which Bad News to Choose? The Influence of Race and Social Identity on Story Selections Within Negative News Contexts." *Journalism & Mass Communication Quarterly* 97, no. 3 (December 19, 2019): 644–62. https://doi.org/10.1177/1077699019892632.

"Home—Black Lives Matter," n.d. https://blacklivesmatter.com/.

Horowitz, Juliana Menasce. "Support for Black Lives Matter Declined after George Floyd Protests, but Has Remained Unchanged Since." Pew Research Center, June 16, 2022. https://www.pewresearch.org/fact-tank/2021/09/27 /support-for-black-lives-matter-declined-after-george-floyd-protests-but -has-remained-unchanged-since/.

House, Christopher A. "Crying for Justice: The #BLACKLIVESMATTER Religious Rhetoric of Bishop T.D. Jakes." *Southern Communication Journal* 83, no. 1 (2018): 13–27. https://doi.org/10.1080/1041794x.2017.1387600.

Intelligencer. "Black Lives Matter Secretly Bought a $6 Million House," April 4, 2022. https://nymag.com/intelligencer/2022/04/black-lives-matter-6-million -dollar-house.html.

Jackson, David, Michael Collins, and Nicholas Wu. "Washington Archbishop Denounces Trump Visit to Catholic Shrine as 'baffling' and 'Reprehensible.'" *USA Today*, June 3, 2020. https://eu.usatoday.com/story/news/politics/2020 /06/02/george-floyd-trump-visit-catholic-shrine-amid-photo-op-criticism /3122549001/.

Jackson, Kellie Carter. *Force and Freedom: Black Abolitionists and the Politics of Violence*. University of Pennsylvania Press, 2019.

Jackson, Reggie. "The Inevitability of a White Backlash to the George Floyd Protests." *Milwaukee Independent*, June 12, 2020. http://www.milwaukeein dependent.com/featured/inevitability-white-backlash-george-floyd-protests/.

Jackson, Sarah, Moya Bailey, Brooke Foucault Welles, and Genie Lauren. *#HashtagActivism: Networks of Race and Gender Justice*. MIT Press, 2020.

Jennings, Carly. "The Love Note That Launched a Movement." *Footnotes* 48, no. 4 (July/August 2020): https://www.asanet.org/news-events/footnotes/jul-aug -2020/features/love-note-launched-movement.

Johnson, Amber. "Gender Futurity at the Intersection of Black Lives Matter and Afrofuturism." In *The Routledge Handbook of Gender and Communication*, edited by Marnel Niles Goins, Joan Faber McAlister, and Bryant Keith Alexander, 616–17. Routledge, 2020.

Johnson, Andre. "Andre E. Johnson on Self-Love." *Feminist Wire*, September 8, 2013. https://thefeministwire.com/2013/09/self-love/.

Johnson, Andre. "Confrontational and Intersectional Rhetoric: Black Lives Matter and the Shutdown of the Hernando De Soto (I-40) Bridge." In *The Rhetoric of Social Movements: Networks, Power, and New Media*, edited by Nathan Crick, 1st ed., 98–115. Routledge, n.d.

Johnson, Andre, and Anthony Stone. "'The Most Dangerous Negro in America': Rhetoric, Race, and the Prophetic Pessimism of Martin Luther King Jr." *Journal of Communication and Religion* 41, no. 1 (2018): 8–22.

Johnson, Greg. "Police Killings and Black Mental Health." *Penn Today*, June 23, 2020. https://penntoday.upenn.edu/news/police-killings-and-black-mental -health.

Johnson, Theodore. "We Are Not Our Vote." *New America*, September 15, 2016. https://www.newamerica.org/weekly/we-are-not-our-vote/.

Kaur, Harmeet. "Videos Often Contradict What Police Say in Reports. Here's Why Some Officers Continue to Lie." CNN, June 6, 2020. https://edition.cnn .com/2020/06/06/us/police-reports-lying-videos-misconduct-trnd/index .html.

Kearney, Mary Celeste, and Michael Kackman. *The Craft of Media Criticism: Critical Media Studies in Practice*. Routledge, 2018.

Kendi, Ibram X. *How to Be an Antiracist*. Random House Large Print, 2020.

Khan-Cullors, Patrisse, and Asha Bandele. *When They Call You a Terrorist: A Black Lives Matter Memoir.* St. Martin's Press, 2018.

King, Maya. "Black Lives Matter Launches a Political Action Committee." *Politico,* October 9, 2020. https://www.politico.com/news/2020/10/09/black-lives -matter-pac-428403.

Kishi, Roudabeh, and Sam Jones. "Demonstrations and Political Violence in America: New Data for Summer 2020." ACLED, September 7, 2022. https:// acleddata.com/2020/09/03/demonstrations-political-violence-in-america -new-data-for-summer-2020/.

Knowles, Hannah. "Judge Approves Derek Chauvin Plea Deal for Violating George Floyd's Rights." *Washington Post,* May 4, 2022. https://www.washington post.com/nation/2022/05/04/chauvin-federal-plea-deal/.

Langer, Gary. "63% Support Black Lives Matter as Recognition of Discrimination Jumps: POLL." ABC News, July 21, 2020. https://abcnews.go.com/Politics /63-support-black-lives-matter-recognition-discrimination-jumps/story?id =71779435.

LeBlanc, Paul. "Bishop at DC Church Outraged by Trump Visit: 'I Just Can't Believe What My Eyes Have Seen.'" CNN, June 2, 2020. https://edition.cnn .com/2020/06/01/politics/cnntv-bishop-trump-photo-op/index.html.

Levenson, Eric, and Bill Kirkos. "Two Ex-Officers Who Restrained George Floyd Sentenced to 3 Years and 3.5 Years in Federal Prison." CNN, July 27, 2022. https://edition.cnn.com/2022/07/27/us/tou-thao-kueng-george-floyd -sentence/index.html.

Levin, Dan. "Generation Z: Who They Are, in Their Own Words." *New York Times,* March 30, 2019. https://www.nytimes.com/2019/03/28/us/gen-z-in -their-words.html.

Lotz, Amanda D. "Assessing Qualitative Television Audience Research: Incorporating Feminist and Anthropological Theoretical Innovation." *Communication Theory* 10, no. 4 (November 2000): 447–67. https://doi.org /10.1111/j.1468-2885.2000.tb00202.x.

Luttrell, Johanna. *White People and Black Lives Matter: Ignorance, Empathy, and Justice.* 1st ed. Palgrave Macmillan, 2019.

Major Cities Chiefs Association. "Major Cities Chiefs Association (MCCA) Statement Regarding the Death of George Floyd." Press release, May 27, 2020. https://majorcitieschiefs.com/wp-content/uploads/2021/01/NEWS-RELEASE -Statement-regarding-Death-of-George-Floyd.pdf.

Mann, Brian, and Elizabeth Baker. "Black Protest Leaders to White Allies: 'It's Our Turn to Lead Our Own Fight.'" NPR, September 22, 2020. https://www. npr.org/2020/09/22/913094440/black-protest-leaders-to-white-allies-it-s-our -turn-to-lead-our-own-fight.

Mannix, Andy. "Minneapolis Police Cite 'Fluid' Situation for Troubling
    Misinformation Released after George Floyd Death." *Star Tribune*, June 3,
    2020. https://www.startribune.com/mpls-police-still-haven-t-explained
    -misinformation-after-floyd-s-death/570970152/.
Martin, Alfred L. "For Scholars . . . When Studying the Queer of Color Image
    Alone Isn't Enough." *Communication and Critical/Cultural Studies* 17, no. 1
    (January 2, 2020): 69–74. https://doi.org/10.1080/14791420.2020.1723797.
May, Vivian. *Pursuing Intersectionality, Unsettling Dominant Imaginaries.* 1st ed.
    Routledge, 2015.
McEvoy, Jemima. "Sales of 'White Fragility'—And Other Anti-Racism Books—
    Jumped Over 2000% After Protests Began." *Forbes*, July 22, 2020. https://www.
    forbes.com/sites/jemimamcevoy/2020/07/22/sales-of-white-fragility-and-other-
    anti-racism-books-jumped-over-2000-after-protests-began/?sh=46af336b303d.
Mehlek-Dawveed, Daniella. "Black Lives Matter Is Not Just Some Trendy Post to
    Add to Your Timeline." *The Tide*, n.d. https://thermtide.com/12691/popular/
    black-lives-matter-is-not-just-some-trendy-post-to-add-to-your-timeline/.
Mehta, Dhrumil. "National Media Coverage of Black Lives Matter Had Fallen
    During The Trump Era—Until Now." *FiveThirtyEight*, June 11, 2020. https://
    fivethirtyeight.com/features/national-media-coverage-of-black-lives-matter
    -had-fallen-during-the-trump-era-until-now/.
Merica, Dan. "Black Lives Matter Protesters Shut Down Sanders Event in Seattle."
    CNN, August 10, 2015. https://edition.cnn.com/2015/08/08/politics/bernie
    -sanders-black-lives-matter-protesters/index.html.
Mez, Kristin Kobes du. *Jesus and John Wayne: How White Evangelicals Corrupted
    a Faith and Fractured a Nation.* Liveright, 3.
Moniuszko, Sara M., and Anika Reed. "100 Resources to Take Action against
    Racism, Help Black Organizations and Learn to Be Anti-Racist." *USA Today*,
    May 29, 2020. https://eu.usatoday.com/story/life/2020/05/29/george-floyd
    -death-donations-resources-justice-petitions/5282539002/.
Monmouth University Polling Institute. "Protestors' Anger Justified Even If
    Actions May Not Be," June 2, 2020. https://www.monmouth.edu/polling
    -institute/reports/monmouthpoll_us_060220/.
Morrison, Aaron. "AP Exclusive: Black Lives Matter Opens Up about Its
    Finances." *AP News*, February 23, 2021. https://apnews.com/article/black
    -lives-matter-90-million-finances-8a80cad199f54c0c4b9e74283d27366f.
Morrison, Aaron. "Exclusive: Black Lives Matter Issues a Statement on Trump's
    Election." *Mic*, November 15, 2016. https://www.mic.com/articles/159496/
    exclusive-black-lives-matter-issues-a-statement-on-trump-s-election.
Morrison, Carlos, and Jacqueline Trimble. "Still Work to Be Done: The
    Million Man March and the 50th Anniversary Commemoration Selma to
    Montgomery March as Mythoform and Visual Rhetoric." *Howard Journal of*

Communications 28, no. 2 (March 10, 2017): 132–43. https://doi.org/10.1080/10
646175.2017.1287609.

Morrison, Sara. "Questions to Ask Yourself before Sharing Images of Police
Brutality." *Vox*, June 11, 2020. https://www.vox.com/recode/2020/6/11/21281028
/before-sharing-images-police-brutality-protest-george-floyd-ahmaud-arbery
-facebook-instagram-twitter.

Mosley, Tonya, and Allison Hagan. "Violence as A Form of Protest." WBUR, *Here
and Now*, June 11, 2020. https://www.wbur.org/hereandnow/2020/06/11
/voilence-protests-racial-justice.

Mundt, Marcia, Karen Ross, and Charla M Burnett. "Scaling Social Movements
Through Social Media: The Case of Black Lives Matter." *Social Media +
Society* 4, no. 4 (October 2018): 205630511880791. https://doi.org/10.1177
/2056305118807911.

Nakamura, Lisa. *Digitizing Race: Visual Cultures of the Internet*. 1st ed. University
of Minnesota Press, 2007.

Nash, Jennifer C. "Intersectionality and Its Discontents." *American Quarterly* 69,
no. 1 (2017): 117–29. https://doi.org/10.1353/aq.2017.0006.

Nielson, Rasmus Kleis, and Simge Andi. "Race and Leadership in the News
Media 2020: Evidence from Five Markets." *Reuters Institute for the Study of
Journalism*, July 16, 2020. https://reutersinstitute.politics.ox.ac.uk/race-and
-leadership-news-media-2020-evidence-five-markets.

O'Neil, Julie, Ashley E. English, and Jacqueline Lambiase. "After the Killing
of Atatiana Jefferson: Black Stakeholder Experiences Within a Municipal
Listening Structure." *Journalism & Mass Communication Quarterly* 99, no. 3
(July 4, 2022): 802–25. https://doi.org/10.1177/10776990221105588.

Oluo, Ijeoma. *So You Want to Talk About Race*. Seal Press, 2018.

Osnos, Evan. "'An Abuse of Sacred Symbols': Trump, a Bible, and a Sanctuary."
New Yorker, June 2, 2020. https://www.newyorker.com/news/daily-comment
/an-abuse-of-sacred-symbols-trump-a-bible-and-a-sanctuary.

Pande, Rukmini. *Squee from the Margins: Fandom and Race (Fandom & Culture)*.
1st ed. University of Iowa Press, 2018.

Parker-Pope, Tara. "How Safe Are Outdoor Gatherings?" *New York Times*, July 3,
2020. https://www.nytimes.com/2020/07/03/well/live/coronavirus-spread
-outdoors-party.html.

Perrin, Andrew. "23% of Users in U.S. Say Social Media Led Them to Change
Views on an Issue; Some Cite Black Lives Matter." Pew Research Center,
October 15, 2020. https://www.pewresearch.org/fact-tank/2020/10/15/23-of
-users-in-us-say-social-media-led-them-to-change-views-on-issue-some
-cite-black-lives-matter/.

Pinn, Anthony. "How Black Lives Matter Challenges Twentieth Century Models
of Protest." Berkley Center for Religion, Peace and World Affairs, October 24,

2016. https://berkleycenter.georgetown.edu/responses/how-black-lives-matter
-challenges-twentieth-century-models-of-protest.

Politico. "Obama's Full Remarks at Howard University Commencement
Ceremony," May 7, 2016. https://www.politico.com/story/2016/05/obamas
-howard-commencement-transcript-222931.

Poor People's Campaign: A National Call for Moral Revival. "Forward Together,
Not One Step Back Collection," n.d. https://poor-peoples-campaign-a-national
-call-for-moral-revival.myshopify.com/collections/forward-together-not
-one-step-back-collection.

Preston, Ashlee Marie. "Sorry, Consuming Trauma Porn Is Not Allyship." *Marie
Claire*, September 29, 2021. https://www.marieclaire.com/politics/a32802688
/stop-sharing-trauma-porn-black-deaths/.

Price, Melanye. "Opinion | Please Stop Showing the Video of George Floyd's
Death." *New York Times*, June 3, 2020. https://www.nytimes.com/2020/06/03
/opinion/george-floyd-video-social-media.html.

Roberts, Sarah. *Behind the Screen: Content Moderation in the Shadows of Social
Media*. Yale University Press, 2019.

Robinson, Lisa. "Some Honest Thoughts on #BlackLivesMatter, the Church and
Real Reconciliation." *Thinking and Living Theological Thoughts Out Loud*
(blog), May 13, 2016. https://theothoughts.com/2016/05/13/some-honest
-thoughts-on-Blacklivesmatter-thechurch-and-real-reconciliation/.

Romo, Vanessa. "U.S. Soccer Lifts Ban on Kneeling during National Anthem."
NPR, June 10, 2020. https://www.npr.org/sections/live-updates-protests-for-
racial-justice/2020/06/10/874531497/u-s-soccer-lifts-ban-on-kneeling-during
-national-anthem.

Ruiz, Pollyanna. "Covid Publics and Black Lives Matter: Posts, Placards and
Posters." *Javnost—The Public* 29, no. 2 (April 3, 2022): 165–78. https://doi.org
/10.1080/13183222.2022.2042787.

Rupar, Aaron. "What the New IG Report about Lafayette Square and the Gassing
of Protesters Actually Says." *Vox*, June 11, 2021. https://www.vox.com/2021
/6/11/22527796/ig-report-trump-bible-lafayette-square-protest.

Saad, By Lydia. "Black Americans Want Police to Retain Local Presence." Gallup,
July 21, 2022. https://news.gallup.com/poll/316571/black-americans-police
-retain-local-presence.aspx.

Salem, Sara. "Intersectionality and Its Discontents: Intersectionality as Traveling
Theory." *European Journal of Women's Studies* 25, no. 4 (April 22, 2016):
403–18. https://doi.org/10.1177/1350506816643999.

Sands, Darren. "DNC to Vote on Resolution Supporting Black Lives Matter."
BuzzFeed News, August 27, 2015. https://www.buzzfeednews.com/article
/darrensands/dnc-to-vote-on-resolution-supporting-black-lives-matter.

Sargent, Greg. "Trump and Tom Cotton Are Losing the Argument. New Polls
    Confirm It." *Washington Post*, June 5, 2020. https://www.washingtonpost.com
    /opinions/2020/06/05/trump-tom-cotton-are-losing-argument-new-polls
    -confirm-it/?utm_campaign=wp_main.
Scott, Robert A., and Donald L. Smith. "The Rhetoric of Confrontation." *Quarterly
    Journal of Speech* 55, no. 1 (January 31, 1969): 1–8. https://doi.org/10.1080
    /00335636909382922.
Segers, Grace. "Senate Republicans Block Jan. 6 Commission Bill That Would
    Have Investigated Capitol Riot." CBS News, May 29, 2021. https://www.cbs
    news.com/news/january-6-commission-bill-capitol-riot-senate-republicans
    -block/.
Silver, Eric, Kerby Goff, and John Iceland. "Social Order and Social Justice: Moral
    Intuitions, Systemic Racism Beliefs, and Americans' Divergent Attitudes
    toward Black Lives Matter and Police." *Criminology* 60, no. 2 (February 15,
    2022): 342–69. https://doi.org/10.1111/1745-9125.12303.
Singal, Jesse. "Does Asking White People for Moral Self-Reflection About Race
    Actually Work?" *The Cut*, August 18, 2015. https://www.thecut.com/2015/08
    /does-asking-whites-to-morally-self-reflect-work.html.
Staff. "Texas Police Chiefs Speak Out About Death of George Floyd." Reform
    Austin, August 18, 2020. https://www.reformaustin.org/public-safety/texas
    -police-chiefs-speak-out-on-death-of-george-floyd/.
Stewart, Emily. "How to Be a Good White Ally during the George Floyd Protests
    and Always." *Vox*, June 2, 2020. https://www.vox.com/2020/6/2/21278123
    /being-an-ally-racism-george-floyd-protests-white-people.
Taylor, Keeanga-Yamahtta. *From #BlackLivesMatter to Black Liberation*. 1st ed.
    Haymarket Books, 2016.
Taylor, Ryan. "Donald Trump Speech Transcript June 1: Trump May Deploy US
    Military to Cities." *Rev*, June 2, 2020. https://www.rev.com/blog/transcripts
    /donald-trump-speech-transcript-june-1-trump-may-deploy-us-military-to
    -cities.
Tensley, Brandon. "The 2016 Election Exposed Deep-Seated Racism. Where Do
    We Go from Here?" *Talk Poverty*, November 17, 2016. https://talkpoverty.org
    /2016/11/17/2016-election-exposed-deep-seated-racism-go/.
Thiede, Dana, and Heidi Wigdahl. "Reactions to the Death of George Floyd."
    kare11.com, May 26, 2020. https://www.kare11.com/article/news/local/
    reactions-to-death-of-george-floyd-restrained-by-minneapolis-police/89
    -baecfa83-0729-4182-a371-86d40ab5f0f0.
Thomas, Deja, and Juliana Menasce Horowitz. "Support for Black Lives Matter
    Has Decreased since June but Remains Strong among Black Americans." Pew
    Research Center, June 16, 2022. https://www.pewresearch.org/fact-tank/2020

/09/16/support-for-black-lives-matter-has-decreased-since-june-but-remains
-strong-among-black-americans/.

Torres, Andrea. "Miami Police Chief: No Training Teaches 'Deeply Disturbing'
Action in George Floyd's Death." WPLG, May 28, 2020. https://www.local10
.com/news/local/2020/05/27/miami-chief-to-officers-no-training-teaches
-deeply-disturbing-action-killing-george-floyd/.

Towns, Armond R. "Black 'Matter' Lives." *Women's Studies in Communication* 41,
no. 4 (October 2, 2018): 349–58. https://doi.org/10.1080/07491409.2018.1551985.

Umamaheswar, Janani. "Policing and Racial (In)Justice in the Media: Newspaper
Portrayals of the 'Black Lives Matter' Movement." *University of California
Press* 1, no. 1 (2020). https://doi.org/10.1525/001c.12143.

UNWomen Headquarters. "Intersectional Feminism: What It Means and Why
It Matters Right Now," July 1, 2020. https://www.unwomen.org/en/news/
stories/2020/6/explainer-intersectional-feminism-what-it-means-and-why
-it-matters.

Updegrove, Alexander H., Maisha N. Cooper, Erin A. Orrick, and Alex R.
Piquero. "Red States and Black Lives: Applying the Racial Threat Hypothesis
to the Black Lives Matter Movement." *Justice Quarterly* 37, no. 1 (October 24,
2018): 85–108. https://doi.org/10.1080/07418825.2018.1516797.

Vandenboom, Liza. "The Faith of the Black Lives Matter Movement." *Religion
Unplugged*, July 10, 2020. https://religionunplugged.com/news/2020/7/10/the
-faith-of-the-black-lives-matter-movement.

Walsh, Bryan, and Alison Snyder. "Scientists Caught between Pandemic and
Protests." *Axios*, June 11, 2020. https://www.axios.com/2020/06/10/black-lives
-matter-protests-coronavirus-science.

Wamsley, Laurel. "Derek Chauvin Found Guilty of George Floyd's Murder." NPR,
April 20, 2021. https://www.npr.org/sections/trial-over-killing-of-george-floyd
/2021/04/20/987777911/court-says-jury-has-reached-verdict-in-derek
-chauvins-murder-trial.

Waxman, Olivia. "What Martin Luther King Jr. Said at the March on Washington
About Police Brutality." *Time*, August 27, 2020. https://time.com/5882308
/march-on-washington-police-brutality/.

WCCO Staff. "State Trial Delayed for Tou Thao, J Alexander Kueng until January
2023." CBS News, October 13, 2022. https://www.cbsnews.com/minnesota
/news/state-trial-delayed-for-tou-thao-j-alexander-kueng-until-january-2023/.

"We Are Pushing Real Revolution": Black Lives Matter on Why They Don't Have
Faith in Any Candidate." *Democracy Now!*, March 9, 2016. https://www
.democracynow.org/2016/3/9/we_are_pushing_real_revolution_black.

"What Is Health Equity? | Health Equity | CDC," n.d. https://www.cdc.gov
/coronavirus/2019-ncov/community/health-equity/race-ethnicity.html.

Williams, Vanessa, and Scott Clement. "Despite Black Lives Matter, Young Black Americans Aren't Voting in Higher Numbers." *Washington Post*, May 14, 2016. https://www.washingtonpost.com/politics/despite-black-lives-matter-young -black-americans-arent-voting-in-higher-numbers/2016/05/14/e1780b3a-1176 -11e6-93ae-50921721165d_story.html.

Williamson, Vanessa, Kris-Stella Trump, and Katherine Levine Einstein. "Black Lives Matter: Evidence That Police-Caused Deaths Predict Protest Activity." *Perspectives on Politics* 16, no. 2 (May 16, 2018): 400–415. https://doi.org/10.1017 /s1537592717004273.

Wing, Nick. "When The Media Treats White Suspects and Killers Better Than Black Victims." *HuffPost*, August 14, 2014. https://www.huffpost.com/entry /media-black-victims_n_5673291.

Wright, Chrysalis, Kwame Gatlin, Damaris Acosta, and Christopher Taylor. "Portrayals of the Black Lives Matter Movement in Hard and Fake News and Consumer Attitudes Toward African Americans." *Howard Journal of Communications*, April 21, 2022, 1–23. https://doi.org/10.1080/10646175.2022 .2065458.

Zuckerman, Ethan, J. Nathan Matias, Rahul Bhargava, Fernando Bermejo, and Allan Ko. "Whose Death Matters? A Quantitative Analysis of Media Attention to Deaths of Black Americans in Police Confrontations, 2013–2016." *International Journal of Communication*, no. 13 (September 21, 2019): 27. http://ijoc.org/index.php/ijoc/article/view/8782.

INDEX

Abdullah, Melina, 24, 97, 120

Activists, 22–23, 54–55, 58–60, 80, 82–83, 109–10, 120–22, 127–28, 130, 144–45, 149–51, 155, 158

African Americans, 18, 23, 30, 41, 118, 122, 124, 128–29. *See also* Black Americans

Afro-Latina, 19

Akira, 31, 36, 40, 103, 128, 156–57

Alan, 60, 112

Allen, Reniqua, 120

Amnesty International, 50

Amy, 35, 42, 87–88, 129

Ancestors, 53, 55, 65

Anti-Blackness, 11, 20, 32, 38–39, 126, 145, 154, 158; national, 30; police racism, 40; violence, 49, 52, 66, 146, 155, 158, 166

Antifaith and antireligious narrative, 96

Arbery, Ahmaud, 4–5, 33

Arradondo, Medaria, 27

Ashley, 77–78, 132, 152–53, 161

Asian Americans for Black Lives Matter, 37

Attiah, Karen, 169–70

Autumn, 40, 78, 108, 137, 153

Bailey, Julius, 12

Bailey, Moya, 146–47, 150–51

Balquiss, 56, 158, 160, 162

Baltimore, Maryland, 127–28

bandele, asha, 50

Baptiste, Nathalie, 167

Battle, Michael, 97

Bilge, Sirma, 67, 71

Black activists, 56, 86, 88, 141, 163; young, 83, 119

Black Americans, 12, 16, 38, 147, 166, 167; communities, 123, 169; death, 22, 27, 143, 147, 158, 160, 162–63; elected officials, 124; folk religion, 97; organizers, 83, 86, 147; people of faith, 108; protesters, 10, 51, 53, 56; resilience, 108; social media users, 152; transwomen, 72, 75; voters, 119, 136, 140; women, 25, 72–73, 76, 78–79, 87, 96, 102; women victims of violence, 71. *See also* African Americans

Black church(es), 96, 105–6, 109, 115; in racial justice, 98; and religious leaders, 96; and social justice movements, 98

Black freedom movement, larger, 12

Black Liberation, 81, 82, 97–98, 106, 124

Black Lives Matter. *See* BLM

Black Lives Matter Global Network Foundation. *See* BLMGNF

ABOUT THE AUTHORS

Andre E. Johnson is associate professor of rhetoric and media studies at the University of Memphis. His research focuses on the intersection of rhetoric, race, and religion. He is the award-winning author of *No Future in This Country: The Prophetic Pessimism of Bishop Henry McNeal Turner* (2020) and editor of *The Speeches of Bishop Henry McNeal Turner: The Press, the Platform, and the Pulpit* (2023), both with University Press of Mississippi.

Amanda Nell Edgar studies issues of race and racism as they intersect with other identities, particularly gender and class. In 2021, she received the prestigious Karl R. Wallace Memorial Award from the National Communication Association, three years after receiving the Janice Hocker Rushing Early Career Research Award from the Southern States Communication Association. Her work has been published in most of the field's top journals, and her two previous books both received awards from the National Communication Association.

Printed in the USA
CPSIA information can be obtained
at www.ICGtesting.com
JSHW021550030224
56306JS00005B/11